Distinguishing Disabi

Distinguishing Disability

Parents, Privilege, and Special Education

COLIN ONG-DEAN

The University of Chicago Press

CHICAGO AND LONDON

COLIN ONG-DEAN is an education researcher in the Department of Education Studies at the University of California, San Diego.

The University of Chicago Press, Chicago 60637
The University of Chicago Press, Ltd., London
© 2009 by The University of Chicago
All rights reserved. Published 2009
Printed in the United States of America

18 17 16 15 14 13 12 11 10 09   1 2 3 4 5

ISBN-13: 978-0-226-63000-7 (cloth)
ISBN-13: 978-0-226-63001-4 (paper)
ISBN-10: 0-226-63000-5 (cloth)
ISBN-10: 0-226-63001-3 (paper)

Library of Congress Cataloging-in-Publication Data
Ong-Dean, Colin.
Distinguishing disability : parents, privilege, and special education / Colin Ong-Dean.
p.   cm.
Includes bibliographical references and index.
ISBN-13: 978-0-226-63000-7 (cloth : alk. paper)
ISBN-13: 978-0-226-63001-4 (pbk. : alk. paper)
ISBN-10: 0-226-63000-5 (cloth : alk. paper)
ISBN-10: 0-226-63001-3 (pbk. : alk. paper)
1. Children with disabilities—Education—United States.   2. Special education—Parent participation—United States.   I. Title.
LC4031.O54   2009
371.9—dc22   2008026881

To my mother and father, Patricia and William Dean

Contents

Acknowledgments

THE RESEARCH and writing of this book benefited in countless ways from others' help.

The book would never have been completed without the moral and intellectual support of my family. My wife, Mary Ong-Dean, has lent me her ears and her insights since this project was barely an idea, and whenever another deadline was coming around the bend, she graciously cared for our son while I holed up in the study. My mother, Patricia Dean, has given countless hours to editing nearly every version of every chapter here. Her patience, skill, and understanding in that work cannot be overstated. My father, William Dean, also commented on early chapter drafts and helped keep me from sliding into social scientific irrelevance.

I also owe a large debt of gratitude to current and former members of the faculty at the University of California–San Diego. Steven Epstein, who chaired my dissertation committee from the beginning, has repeatedly helped me to see the greatest potential of this research and pushed me to make the arguments as clear, relevant, and thorough as possible. Hugh Mehan, who later became my committee cochair, provided constant encouragement and many patient discussions about research strategy. I am also grateful to the other members of my dissertation committee: Maria Charles, who provided much advice on the quantitative analysis used in this research, John Skrentny, who provided strategic advice on framing the project, Michael Schudson, and Tom Humphries. At crucial stages along the way, I also benefited from the advice of Andy Scull, Harvey Goldman, Akos Rona-Tas, Paul Frymer, John Evans, Andrew Lakoff, and Leigh Star.

Many other colleagues and friends helped me by reading and commenting on drafts of my work, discussing my arguments, and providing advice on research issues. For their time in reading drafts of my work, I am grateful to Robert Bogdan, Martha Stoddard Holmes, Josh Dunsby, Bryan Archibald, Rachel Barley, and the anonymous reviewers of the book manuscript and of articles that stemmed from the same research. I benefited from numerous discussions related to the substance of my work with people from all types of backgrounds—in particular, Shannon McMullen, Dean Rivkin, Brenda McGee, Betty Schiemenz, Joan Landguth, Deborah Odam, Judith Preissle, Kit Tisdale, Anne Goldberg, Michael Matthews, Kathleen Anderson, and Sieglinde Lim de Sánchez. I am also grateful to Annette Lareau for excellent advice on conducting interviews.

Organizational support was also an important condition of my research. Early portions of the research were supported by an AERA/Spencer Foundation Pre-dissertation Fellowship. Later portions were supported by a grant from the American Educational Research Association, which receives funds for its AERA Grants Program from the National Center for Education Statistics and the Office of Educational Research and Improvement (U.S. Department of Education) and the National Science Foundation under NSF Grant REC-9980573. Opinions expressed in this book are, of course, my own and do not necessarily reflect those of the granting agencies.

Chapter 4 of this book appears, in somewhat different form, as "Reconsidering the Social Location of the Medical Model: An Examination of Disability in Parenting Literature," *Journal of Medical Humanities* 26 (2005): 2–3, 141–58. Chapter 3 draws substantially from analyses and arguments first presented in "High Roads and Low Roads: Learning Disability in California, 1976–1998," *Sociological Perspectives* 49 (2006): 1, 91–113.

Finally, I must thank the parents, mostly anonymous, who responded to surveys, submitted to interviews, and generously shared their time and experiences to participate in this research. I hope this book does justice to their perspectives and to their aspirations for their children and other people's children.

—— ✳ ——

Distinguishing Disability

MORE THAN thirty years ago, parents in the United States began to pressure schools to change the ways children with disabilities were diagnosed and accommodated. They gave voice to a variety of concerns: that their children's needs were not being recognized; that disabled children were needlessly segregated from other children; that children were mistreated and punished for behaviors resulting from disability; and that parents were not informed and seldom consulted about decisions affecting the education of their disabled (or putatively disabled) children. In the following decades, some of these concerns have begun to be addressed, and there has been a steady rise in the prominence of special education within the educational system.

Over these same years, there was a growing belief that parents had a responsibility to be actively involved in their children's education—to attend parent-teacher conferences, to help their children with homework, and to monitor their children's academic progress and social development. Accordingly, when the U.S. Congress established disabled children's educational rights in the Education for All Handicapped Children Act of 1975, it made parents responsible for defending those rights. To that end, parents were given rights to grant or deny permission for their children to be evaluated for disabilities, to attend meetings where their disabled children's educational placements would be determined, and to challenge those placements in the federal courts. They were also given the right to be informed about their rights as parents and about their children's rights, needs, and current performance. Later, in its 1982 decision in *Hendrick Hudson School District v. Rowley*,[1] the U.S. Supreme Court went so far as to assert that the law's

1

guarantee of parents' rights was more important than disabled children's substantive rights to an education. The Court gave the following reassurance about grounding children's rights in parents' rights: "As this very case demonstrates, parents and guardians will not lack ardor in seeking to assure that handicapped children receive all of the benefits to which they are entitled" (209). The Court did not consider what resources, besides ardor, Amy Rowley's parents and other parents needed to make an effective challenge to their children's schools.

While the creation of educational rights for disabled children follows in the footsteps of social reforms of the 1960s and 1970s, through which previously marginalized social groups gained access to new opportunities, this latest reform, unlike many of its predecessors, did not emphasize collective action or the goal of social justice. Instead, individual families were to advocate for individual children's rights toward the goal of meeting their "individualized" needs. This way of defining children's rights placed a heavy burden on parents—to inform themselves about their children's needs, to try to understand the complexities of special education, and, where necessary, to challenge the school's diagnosis and accommodation of their children's individual disabilities.

The title of this book is a double entendre meant to reflect the duality and the ambiguity of parents' efforts to advocate for their children with disabilities. In a first sense, "distinguishing disability" refers to the act of distinguishing disability within a particular child—that is, discerning traits that constitute evidence of a particular disability and determining the educational needs associated with disability. In the most basic sense, this book is concerned with how parents engage in this act. In a second sense, "distinguishing disability" refers to the way disability entails certain explanations for behavior and sets up particular expectations—that is, that certain children have the potential to succeed if their difficulties are seen in the right light and are met with the appropriate services and accommodations—which may be the very reason parents seek a particular disability diagnosis.

There is a crucial difference between "distinguishing disability" as revealing the objective truth ("distinguishing" as a verb) and "distinguishing disability" as a label ("distinguishing" as an adjective) that produces a desired result for a child. There is a constant tension and interplay between these two senses, i.e., between parents' claims to help establish the objective truth and the fact that parents' claims about their children are shaped by their desire to give their children whatever advantages a disability label may provide.

In order to be involved in the decisions that affect their children's education, parents must negotiate this tension. On the one hand, they are supposed to help educators distinguish, or identify, their children's disabilities and related needs, and all parties involved in that act are supposed to be discovering an objective truth. On the other hand, the disability diagnosis is not completely inert—that is, the diagnosis itself *distinguishes*. What might otherwise be seen as problems outside the school's purview are seen, given a particular diagnosis, as amenable to educational intervention. What was once seen as willful misbehavior, for instance, is now seen as the consequence of disability that can be corrected with a behavior. What was once seen as stupidity is now seen as the consequence of a disability that can be corrected through specific training.

In practice, there is a danger that parents' claims will be dismissed if they cannot keep this second sense of distinguishing disability at bay. If they cannot, they will appear to be seeking whatever services and accommodations will help their children regardless of the severity of the need or whether the need is even disability related. It is those parents who are most privileged—who have the most cultural and economic resources at their disposal—who can make the strongest claim to distinguish their children's particular disabilities and needs in an objective, scientifically and legally justified way. In so doing, privileged parents of disabled children, like privileged parents of nondisabled children, provide distinctive educational opportunities to their children and thereby perpetuate the hierarchies from which their own privileges come—not by helping their children to stay on top (as privileged parents of nondisabled children often do), but by keeping them from falling through the cracks.[2]

Ideally, parents and schools share a common interest in educating children according to their individual needs and abilities. Yet while we could assume that all parents have a primary interest in their own children's individual needs, we know that schools must consider all the realities that impinge on meeting those needs—that is, they must consider what it will mean for their budgets, the work that must be done at the individual and classroom level to accommodate a student's needs in a particular way, and the educational and behavioral outcomes for all students that may result from these accommodations. As such, schools usually believe their judgments about children's needs should prevail, and they do not appreciate being challenged by parents. When parents choose to exercise their rights by questioning whether their children's disability-related needs are being properly diagnosed and accommodated, they often must be prepared for confrontation. Some parents of children with disabilities therefore find themselves in frequent conflict with their children's schools, conflict that takes place against the backdrop of legal rights and responsibilities imposed on individual parents and schools. Each party to this conflict struggles to present its position as being the objective, disinterested position on the child's legitimate needs.

This conflict takes a variety of forms. In some cases it centers on the very identification of disability and disability-related behaviors. When parents attribute their children's behavior to conditions like attention deficit/hyperactivity disorder (ADHD) or Tourette syndrome (a neurological condition characterized by involuntary tics and, sometimes, uncontrollable outbursts of profanity), they may struggle with teachers who punish their children for what the teachers see as willful misbehavior. Other parents struggle with the schools over which disability diagnoses should apply, claiming, for instance, that their children are not mentally retarded but instead are learning disabled or autistic. Other conflicts center on the appropriate accommodation for a given disability. For instance, parents of children diagnosed with autism often find that schools resist implementing intensive intervention programs, which are now widely believed to make it possible for many autistic children to have average success in school and to become independent adults. To gain the services they believe their children need, some parents of autistic children spend large amounts of time and money fighting schools.

It is precisely because schools often try to manage students with disabilities in the easiest, cheapest ways that parents' advocacy is so important. In general, this advocacy—designed, after all, not so much to put their children on the top of the heap as to keep them from failing—deserves praise. However, recognizing the burden of advocacy that the law imposes on parents of disabled children, we also need to acknowledge that parents differ in how far they can shoulder this burden. Some parents successfully advocate for their children's educational rights and may even take some satisfaction in having been directly involved in shaping their education. Other parents are frustrated in their efforts. Still others, believing it is not possible or appropriate for them to intervene in complex decisions involved in identifying and accommodating children's disabilities, do not shoulder the burden at all.

The primary aim of this book is not so much to document the struggles parents face when advocating for their disabled children's rights as to show how parents are differently equipped for that struggle. As such, the focus here is on how parents' resources affect their involvement in identifying and accommodating their children's disabilities. These resources are understood broadly to include economic capital and cultural capital,[3] both of which are unequally available to different groups of parents and both of which affect the ways parents can act as advocates. In short, in the current cultural, legal, and institutional environment, parents with more economic and cultural resources—those I will call "privileged parents"—are much more likely to be involved in the diagnosis and accommodation of their children's disabilities. A secondary aim is to show that this relation between privilege and advocacy is often obscured by the very thinking and practices that make advocacy effective.

What it will mean to focus on privileged parents and the effects of privilege on advocacy in special education calls for some further explanation. In the rest of this introduction I will describe what I mean by "privileged parents" and try to give a sense of the ways we can observe their effects on the diagnosis and accommodation of children's disabilities.

"PRIVILEGED PARENTS"

The focus of this book is primarily on those I refer to as "privileged parents." As I have said, I am especially interested in the privileges that stem from economic and cultural capital. In practice, talking about privilege in these terms is not very different from talking about it in a generic, everyday way. When I refer to "privileged parents," I am referring to some combination of the traits that we normally associate with privilege in the United States, which generally imply or entail the possession of relatively exclusive economic and cultural capital. As such, "privileged parents" are those who are some combination of white, middle- to high-income, English-speaking, professional, and college educated. By the same token, when I refer to "disadvantaged parents," I have in mind some combination of the less advantageous counterparts to each of the categories of privilege; that is, African American or Latino, low-income, not English-speaking, working-class, and not college educated.

Whether a parent is "privileged" or "disadvantaged" is not absolute but a question of degree and of context. As such, when I say, for instance, that some parents are privileged, this may be only with respect to certain traits and the relevance of these traits in certain contexts. Although some parents are privileged most of the time and in most respects and others are disadvantaged most of the time and in most respects, many present a complex mix of privilege and disadvantage.

Consider Sharon Faber.[4] Sharon's son Dylan is autistic. At age fourteen, he cannot communicate verbally. He is currently educated at what is widely seen as an excellent private school for autistic children, and he lives in a residential facility run by the same school. These services are now provided almost entirely at public expense, but they came after years of tenacious advocacy on Sharon's part. Twice she brought Dylan's school to due process hearings in disputes over the services he should receive, and in both cases she and the district reached settlements that provided her with what she had originally sought.

It is apparent that Sharon's strong commitment to her son has been an important factor in what she has been able to accomplish as an advocate for him, despite considerable disadvantages. Shortly after Dylan entered preschool, her husband was diagnosed with a brain tumor, and two subsequent surgeries left him unable to perform his job. Sharon, who had not had paid employment in years, got a job working with developmentally disabled children, based mainly on the knowledge she had acquired helping her own son on his intensive behavioral intervention program. Although this job provided medical benefits for her family, the pay was low. Soon afterward she and her husband divorced, leaving her a low-income single mother with two sons, one severely autistic.

Yet while Sharon has clearly overcome some disadvantages through sheer tenacity, other aspects of her story suggest the importance of the relative advantages she had while married. As a computer programmer/systems analyst, her husband was in a field with a relatively high average annual income (about $70,000 in 2007, according to the Bureau of Labor Statistics). The extra income and family connections she had at that time made it possible, though not easy, to hire a lawyer, outside specialists, and two aides to provide Dylan's in-home training. These initial expenditures clearly helped lay the groundwork for Dylan's future accommodations. Reflecting on what would have happened to Dylan had she started to advocate in her current situation, Sharon puts it fairly simply: "I'm sure I wouldn't have gotten what I have now." Although Sharon's level of formal education is not high—she spent some time in college but did not graduate—she possesses cultural capital that is often associated with a college education: she is articulate and self-confident, and she clearly has great sophistication about her son's needs—acquired in part through her own reading—and understanding of her legal rights. Finally, Sharon has been able to obtain support for her advocacy from other parents. In this sense, living in an area with a relatively high median income and a high average level of education, she is likely to have benefited from social connections to more privileged parents. At her son's elementary and middle schools, average student scores on tests of academic performance are near the top of the statewide distribution, and over half of the parents have at least a college degree.

Because Sharon has clearly been an exceptionally effective advocate for Dylan throughout his academic career, she serves as a reminder of what parents with socioeconomic disadvantages can do for their disabled children. At the same time, because the privilege she has enjoyed is apparently critical to what she has accomplished, her case also supports the central argument of this book that parents' advocacy depends in important respects on their relatively exclusive resources. Finally, her case supports the further point that our current expectations for parental advocacy may make it difficult for parents and others to see the role privilege plays. When I ask Sharon how she thinks she compares with other parents, she acknowledges that "a lot of parents don't do anything" but does not consider that the absence of economic and cultural resources like those that helped her might hinder other parents' involvement. "I just don't understand how anybody wouldn't do that," she says, "because it's your child's future and his life. You've got to figure out what best you can do for them and do it." When pressed, she speculates that age is a factor—that older parents are better advocates—without recognizing the strong tendency for people with higher socioeconomic status to have children when they are older, as she herself did.[5]

THE ELUSIVE EFFECTS OF PRIVILEGE

That parents who are successful advocates for their children often do not see their advocacy as being undergirded by privilege is not surprising. Some parents, like Sharon, are grappling with substantial disadvantages, which surely loom larger than the privileges they may enjoy. Furthermore, children's disability-related needs have often exposed their parents to difficulties and anxieties they never anticipated. As such, they may implicitly compare themselves with parents who have more typical children and similar social backgrounds rather than with parents having similar children and different social backgrounds.

Perhaps more important, while it is difficult to diagnose children's disabilities and identify the related needs, it is perhaps even more difficult to diagnose the relation of parents' resources and perspectives to that process. It is in the nature of these needs that they are often difficult to identify. What seems obvious to a parent may seem debatable to the school, and vice versa. However, parents who wish to participate in determining their disabled children's educational accommodations must make their own advocacy seem incidental to the facts of the child's particular rights and needs. Parents must act like lawyers (sometimes quite literally), showing that their version of the facts is not a particular interpretation of the truth but the only version grounded in reality.

All of this makes it very difficult to say how, in any given instance, the pathway from children's objective needs to their eventual diagnoses and accommodations was affected by the parents' advocacy and the privileges undergirding it. Would the children, placed in different families, have been identified with the same needs? Would a given middle-class child with learning disabled traits be more or less likely to be diagnosed as disabled than a lower-class child with the same traits? We could know this only if we could somehow identify other children with the essentially the same needs and observe what happens to them in different kinds of families. Such an examination, however, presupposes the existence of simple answers to questions whose very ambiguity makes them a site for social struggle.

Thus, although effective participation in special education often requires parents to draw on their personal resources to make complex and rigorous legal and scientific arguments, the very complexity and rigor of these arguments obscures the ways they depend on the parents' social advantages. The contribution of parents' resources and dispositions to such arguments is masked precisely when that contribution is most effective. When listening to the stories parents tell of their often poignant struggles to have their children's needs met, it may seem perverse to suggest that recognition of these needs depended on the parents' privileges. The problem is that, by the very nature of the situation, we are unlikely to know about similar children whose needs go unidentified because no one can make effective claims on their behalf.

How, then, do we observe the effect of parents' resources and dispositions on the disability claims they make on their children's behalf? Not, it seems, directly. Rather, we observe the effect indirectly by analyzing the means of making disability claims and to whom these means, in general, are more available. On the one hand, this means considering the historical, legal, and cultural contexts that enable privileged parents to take an active role in the identification and accommodation of children's disabilities. On the other hand, it means examining parents' attitudes and practices—not to claim that in any individual case they have decisively made the difference between recognition and nonrecognition of a child's needs, but to document particular configurations of parents' attitudes and practices; to consider how these attitudes and practices are supported by parents' economic and cultural capital; and to show which practices seem to be effective in resolving parents' disagreements with their children's schools.

IN SHORT, this book takes a broad look at the historical, cultural, and institutional conditions under which parents have advocated for their disabled children in the United States for the past thirty to forty years and the relation of these conditions to parents' differing resources and dispositions. In telling this story, I draw on a wide range of evidence: the legal history of disabled children's educational rights; broad shifts in patterns of disability diagnosis; parents' personal attitudes, resources, and experiences as reported on surveys and in interviews; the popular literature for parents of disabled children; and parents' individual challenges in the special education administrative hearing system.

If one accepts the argument of the book, one may conclude that the existing special education system is fundamentally inequitable and that privileged parents implicitly contribute to that inequity when they draw on their resources to advocate for their children. I want to be clear, however, that I do not intend to criticize parents' impulse to advocate for their children or to deny that some parents, by sharing knowledge, giving support, and lobbying and organizing for change, manage to help not only their own children but also other people's. Privileged parents' actions must be considered against a background of laws, institutional practices, and their own children's difficulties. Against this background, one cannot reasonably expect privileged parents not to draw on their advantages in advocating for their children. For the privileged parents of disabled children who read the book, I only hope it might provoke some critical thoughts about the influence of their privileges and about what they might do to promote a more equitable system of special education.

OVERVIEW

Chapter 1 sets the institutional background for parents' advocacy in special education by considering the evolution of disabled children's educational rights, which provide legal grounds for parents to make disability claims. I argue that the educational rights of disabled children, established in the 1975 Education for All Handicapped Children Act (EAHCA), arose within a broad context of social reform. In this context, extending educational rights to disabled children was conceived as part of a democratic and egalitarian project for furthering the social equality and integration of disabled people, for remedying social inequalities within special education, and for allowing parents to be active participants in institutional decision making. However, owing in part to inherent limitations of the EAHCA's provisions and in part to evolving interpretations of those provisions, the EAHCA has not realized the potential for broad social reform; instead, it has mainly enabled parents to raise individualized, technical disputes over their children's disability diagnoses and needs.

In chapter 2 I give an overview of research on cultural capital and parenting and how it might relate to special education, followed by an examination of disabled children's parents—their perspectives and practices—based on interviews and survey responses. My findings suggest that many privileged parents consider themselves to be at least as well informed as their children's schools about their children's disabilities and related needs. These parents describe conflicts with their children's schools, which gives some indication of how they may use their cultural capital to challenge the school's authority. Responses from disadvantaged parents suggest that these parents are often unable or reluctant to be advocates for their disabled children. Although the evidence in this chapter does not constitute proof that privileged parents use cultural capital to intervene in their children's education, it is consistent with earlier arguments claiming such a link, and it helps to flesh out this relationship in the context of special education.

Having described the legal framework for parents' action and the resources parents can bring to their advocacy, I move in chapter 3 to consider how disability diagnoses and parental practices are distributed across different groups of parents and what kinds of arguments about parents' involvement can initially be made based on this distribution. By analyzing data on school district demographics and learning disability (LD) diagnoses, I show that in the 1970s the LD diagnosis seems to have been more prevalent among relatively privileged children, but that over time it has become more prevalent among less privileged children. I argue that this shift reflects a process in which relatively privileged parents were the initial advocates for recognition of LD, but as LD diagnosis became more frequent it came to serve institutional needs, leading to higher rates of LD diagnosis among disadvantaged students. I then consider other disability conditions—mental retardation, ADHD, autistic spectrum disorders—and the ways the practice of diagnosing these conditions might be compared or contrasted with the practice of diagnosing LD.

In chapter 4, I delve into the literature for parents of disabled children to consider how the cultural construction of disabilities speaks to a particular audience. This analysis generally suggests relations among disability, parenting, social class, and race similar to those hypothesized in chapter 2. Here I argue that the assumptions this literature makes about parents' practices and the ways disability can and should be identified imply an audience of white, middle- to upper-class parents. In this sense the literature for parents of disabled children, like the law defining disabled children's educational rights, constitutes a resource for specific groups of parents and their children and reinforces their advantages at a moment when they are most vulnerable.

Chapter 5, the final substantive chapter of the book, examines administrative hearings in which parents challenge their disabled children's educational evaluation and placement. In making disability claims at the individual level, these parents bring all their resources to bear. After a theoretical discussion of the relation between economic capital and cultural capital, I examine the distribution of administrative hearings ("due process" hearings) across different demographic types of school districts and briefly consider the unusual but important case of the Los Angeles Unified School District. The rest of the chapter analyzes cases at the individual level, considering the interrelated contributions of parents' economic and cultural capital that can be inferred from due process hearing decisions and due process hearing orders. In particular, I consider three opportunities available to parents in the administrative hearing process: the opportunity to obtain professional services (e.g., attorneys or evaluating psychologists) to support their claims at a hearing; the opportunity to obtain services and private placements for their children and to claim the right to reimbursement at a hearing; and the opportunity to make personal testimony at a hearing.

In the final chapter of the book, I step back to consider the relevance of the foregoing chapters to the study of disability and the study of social reproduction, suggesting not only that the intersection between them should be further explored, but also that the present examination of this intersection points to deeper limitations of each field of study.

Throughout the book I refer to parents, like Sharon Faber, with whom I conducted one-on-one interviews. While these interviews, thirteen in all, are not the primary basis for the arguments here, they help to flesh out those arguments and to put a human face on the parents who are at their center. In their complexity, their stories may also suggest other arguments and other directions for future research. Ultimately, this book should be regarded neither as a definitive statement of the connections of privilege to special education nor as a call for specific reforms in special education, but as a thumbnail sketch of a largely unexplored territory.

———— ✳ ————

CHAPTER ONE

From Social Reform to Technical Management

The Legal Evolution of the Education for All Handicapped Children Act of 1975

THE EDUCATION for All Handicapped Children Act of 1975 (EAHCA)[1] was the product of egalitarian and democratic impulses. It targeted multiple forms of exclusion and inequality at once. First and foremost, it addressed the exclusion of a large proportion of disabled[2] children from the nation's public schools and called on the schools to seek out those who had been excluded in the past. Its supporters forcefully rejected the idea that disabled children could not benefit from an education, arguing that public education must adapt to meet their needs and help them realize their full potential. Furthermore, these same supporters hoped that, by integrating disabled children into the public education system, the EAHCA would make nondisabled schoolchildren more aware of disabled people and more accepting of their differences. Thus the act emphasized the importance of "mainstreaming" disabled students—providing their special education services in a regular education classroom—not just to provide a better education to disabled students, but also as a way of promoting the acceptance and social integration of disabled people in the broader society. By enlisting parents to help in this integration—by giving them rights to participate in diagnostic and placement decisions that could profoundly affect their children's lives—the EAHCA also challenged the lay-professional hierarchy that had excluded parents from decision making in the quasi-medical field of special education. Finally, aware of the tendency for minority students to be disproportionately assigned stigmatizing disability labels that limited their educational opportunities, some supporters saw the EAHCA's strong provisions for parents' right to participate in decision making as one means of addressing this inequity.

This chapter explains how and why the EAHCA and its successor, the Individuals with Disabilities Education Act (IDEA), have fallen short of these ambitious promises for social reform. Evidence of the EAHCA's original social agenda is gleaned from its legislative history and from the legal initiatives in which it is rooted, as well as from the bill's own content. The decline of this agenda is traced in the evolving legal interpretation of the EAHCA, in the pattern of actions brought under it, and in the pattern of practices within special education since its passage. Although this decline can be attributed to various causes, I argue here that it was integrally related to the original provision of parents' right to be involved in the identification and accommodation of their children's disabilities. The promise of this decision was that, by giving all parents that right, the EAHCA would create democratic solutions to the problems of special education. In reality, however, that right seems to have reduced the problems in special education to isolated cases, emphasizing the improved technical management of individual disabled children's education while muting broader social concerns about special education. Thus, rather than providing a democratic solution, the EAHCA appears to have provided an individualized and competitive environment in which the parents with the most resources to advocate for their children can, at least in some cases, obtain better educational accommodations. This claim, in turn, provides the backdrop for the following chapters, which consider the individualized circumstances of parents' involvement and the ways parental privilege is an important part of these circumstances.

THE CREATION OF DISABLED CHILDREN'S EDUCATIONAL RIGHTS

Before 1973, there was no federal law in the United States that protected the specific educational rights of children with disabilities. Indeed, in many cases disability was taken as a legitimate reason for excluding a child from public education. Congress asserted in 1975 that there were one million disabled children of school age in the United States who were not receiving any educational services.[3] While some were excluded from public education altogether, many others were placed in highly segregated environments within public education, where their cognitive and social abilities actually regressed. Furthermore, disability diagnosis frequently occurred with little public oversight, and public school children were allegedly given many erroneous diagnoses, which led to inadequate and inappropriate education and to lifelong stigmatization.[4]

The first federal law defining the civil rights of disabled people in the United States (including the specific right to a public education) was nothing more than a paragraph appended to a bill funding vocational rehabilitation for people with disabilities. This paragraph, Section 504 of the Rehabilitation Act of 1973, reads as follows: "No otherwise qualified handicapped individual in the United States . . . shall, solely by reason of his handicap, be excluded from the participation in, be denied the benefits of, or be subjected to discrimination under any program or activity receiving federal financial assistance."[5]

The language was largely borrowed from the Civil Rights Act of 1964, which addressed racial and gender discrimination. There seemed to be no lobbying for the bill and no conflict or controversy surrounding its passage. Indeed, although the claim is disputed by at least one activist,[6] it is often said that Section 504 was drafted entirely without input from activists or advocates for disabled people.[7] Yet at some point *after* the bill was signed, disability activists realized the tremendous potential of what had been passed into law and mobilized to pressure the Department of Health, Education, and Welfare (HEW) to write and sign implementing regulations. The HEW secretaries under Presidents Ford and Carter were reluctant to sign these regulations, fearing enormous costs and political backlash. Ultimately Joseph Califano, the Carter-appointed secretary of HEW, signed regulations in 1977 after activists protested outside his home and staged sit-in demonstrations in HEW's Washington offices and in eight regional HEW offices.

The next bill to deal with disability legislation, the EAHCA, was in many ways more significant than the Rehabilitation Act. Owing to its origins in prior legal decisions, the EAHCA had very specific and exacting provisions, which the Rehabilitation Act lacked.[8] Two prior legal decisions particularly influenced the EAHCA: *Pennsylvania Association for Retarded Children v. Commonwealth of Pennsylvania (PARC)*[9] and *Mills v. Board of Education of the District of Columbia (Mills)*.[10]

The initial federal court claim in *PARC* was brought by the parents of thirteen mentally retarded persons between the ages of six and twenty-one who lived Pennsylvania but had been excluded from the Pennsylvania public schools. Laws in the state of Pennsylvania had relieved the public schools of any duty to educate or train retarded children whom a school psychologist had deemed "uneducable and untrainable."[11] The parents in *PARC* claimed that these laws were unconstitutional for at least two reasons. First, because of the way they were applied, the parents alleged that their children were being denied due process rights under the Fourteenth Amendment to the

U.S. Constitution, which guarantees an individual the right to notice and a hearing before being deprived by state law of a right, privilege, or immunity. Second, the parents alleged that these laws violated the equal protection clause of the Fourteenth Amendment because they treated retarded children differently than other children without a rational basis for doing so.

Before a hearing was completed, the parties in *PARC* reached an agreement in October 1971, which the court then ordered them to follow. The first part of the agreement called for the state attorney general to issue a series of opinions precluding any interpretation of existing state laws that would allow the exclusion of mentally retarded children from a public education. Where the public schools were previously allowed to put the responsibility for mentally retarded children solely on the state Department of Welfare, now the schools were forced to share that responsibility. Where the public schools were previously allowed to entirely exclude mentally retarded children with a mental age of less than five years, now they were required at the very least to place such children in special classrooms. It was also agreed that the state of Pennsylvania would, in the future, provide access to a free public education for every mentally retarded person aged four to twenty-one and would undertake to locate such individuals who had been excluded in the past based on mental retardation.

A second part of the settlement provided that, before a child could be put in an educational placement based on being identified as mentally retarded, the child's parents or guardians must be notified of the intended change of placement and given the opportunity for a due process hearing. At such a hearing, parents could present evidence to an impartial hearing officer to challenge the appropriateness of the proposed placement.

Because these provisions were contained in a consent agreement and were not devised by the court, they did not in themselves establish a legal precedent. However, because of the presence of one dissenter in the defendant class—the Lancaster-Lebanon Intermediate Unit, which alleged that the court lacked jurisdiction over the consent—the court was required to justify its decision to impose the terms of the agreement on all parties. This justification required the court to find that the plaintiffs' claims were not "wholly insubstantial and frivolous" and that they had a "colorable claim"—a legal term for a claim that is legally sound and that, if supported with facts in a trial, could allow the plaintiff to win an action under the law.

The court therefore summarized statements and testimony that had been presented at the unconcluded hearing to demonstrate the importance of the plaintiffs' claims. The substance of the court's argument, based on the plaintiffs' testimony, was that mentally retarded people had experienced a long history of stigmatizing in the United States—which had made possible such mistreatment as compulsory sterilization and forced segregation—and that the public schools were often guilty of perpetuating that stigma. The court wrote, "Experts agree that it is primarily the school which imposes the mentally-retarded label and concomitant stigmatization upon children, either initially or later on through a change in educational assignment. This follows from the fact that the school constitutes the first social institution with which the child comes into contact" (295).

Because of the social discrimination mentally retarded people had been subjected to and the schools' role in producing and perpetuating that discrimination, the court found that the plaintiffs' claim was in fact colorable.

The *PARC* court not only claimed that schools were responsible for remedying the historical discrimination against mentally retarded children; in considering the equal protection claims raised by the plaintiffs, it also supported a broader understanding of the social function of education. In finding that the Pennsylvania public schools could not justify excluding mentally retarded students, the court relied on the plaintiffs' expert witnesses, who claimed that *all* mentally retarded persons were capable of benefiting from an education and that most could become self-sufficient if they were provided an adequate education. The plaintiffs acknowledged that the kinds of educational benefits they sought went beyond the dominant institutional understanding of what schools were supposed to teach, but they alleged that this dominant understanding was too narrow. In effect, the plaintiffs staked their claim of mentally retarded children's right to education on an expanded notion of education's purpose. Alan Abeson summarizes the relevant testimony of the *PARC* plaintiffs in the following way: "Education cannot be defined solely as the provision of academic experiences to children. Rather, education must be seen as a continuous process by which individuals learn to cope and function within their environment. Thus, for children to learn to clothe and feed themselves is a legitimate outcome achievable through an educational program."[12]

Because there was no rational basis for denying retarded children the right to an education (granting this expanded notion of "education"), the court granted them equal protection and equal rights to public education. In the process, it depicted the standard view of education, based exclusively on traditional academic skills and knowledge, as arbitrary and elitist.

The plaintiffs in *Mills*, not unlike the *PARC* plaintiffs, were children of school age who had been excluded from public education based on being identified with disabilities. The original plaintiffs were seven black children living in the District of Columbia, who had been "labeled as behavioral problems, mentally retarded, emotionally disturbed or hyperactive, and denied admission to the public schools or excluded therefrom after admission, with no provision for alternative educational placement or periodic review" (868). The main defendant in the case was the Board of Education of the District of Columbia.

Even though the plaintiffs were all black and allegedly disabled, the case addressed neither racial discrimination nor discrimination based on disability. Rather, the case was certified as a class action representing "all . . . District of Columbia residents of school age who are eligible for a free public education and who have been, or may be, excluded from such education or otherwise deprived by defendants of access to publicly supported education" (870). This characterization of the plaintiff class without reference to actual disability status was significant. It meant that, from the beginning, the schools' right to characterize certain students as disabled and to justify differential treatment on that basis was viewed with a skeptical eye.

Before the case reached a hearing, the board made a number of agreements and resolutions to satisfy the plaintiffs' demands. In addition to meeting specific demands of the original seven plaintiffs, the board agreed, through an interim agreement, to undertake a search for all children who were currently being excluded from the District of Columbia public schools and to submit the results to the plaintiffs' counsel. The board also passed a resolution declaring that *all* children could benefit from a public education and, when necessary, should be evaluated to determine what special services might be needed due to disability. Finally, the board resolved that "no change in the kind of education provided for a child will be made against his wishes or the wishes of his parent or guardian unless he has been accorded a full hearing on the matter consistent with due process" (872).

Although *PARC* and *Mills* produced similar results for the plaintiffs, their reasoning was different. Most important, whereas the *PARC* court addressed the claims of a plaintiff class of "mentally retarded children," the *Mills* court addressed the claims of children regardless of their disability status. As such, the *PARC* plaintiffs' right to a public education was protected by the Fourteenth Amendment equal protection clause only if there was no rational basis for excluding mentally retarded children from public education. Thus the *PARC* court sought to prove that there was, in fact, no rational basis for exclusion by citing expert testimony on the ability of mentally retarded children to benefit from an education.

The *Mills* plaintiffs, by contrast, encompassed all school-age children without regard to disability status. Exclusion, not actual disability, was the basis of their class, and there could be no question of a rational basis for excluding a class that was defined simply by being excluded. Nor was the court interested in hearing arguments for excluding children from the educational system after the schools had properly identified their disabilities. Rather, the *Mills* court ordered the defendants to provide a public education to all school-age children *"regardless* of the degree of the child's mental, physical, or emotional disability or impairment" (878, emphasis mine).[13]

Furthermore, the *Mills* court was clearly skeptical that the children currently being excluded based on disability had been properly identified as disabled in the first place. The decision refers to five of the seven original plaintiffs as "allegedly" having particular disabilities—for example, "Steven allegedly was slightly brain-damaged and hyperactive."[14] Elsewhere, the plaintiffs are referred to as having been "labeled"—language borrowed directly from the plaintiffs' complaint—with specific disabilities. In keeping with this skeptical attitude, the court ordered the defendants to provide to the court a list of children, currently excluded from the public schools based on disability, giving

> the name of the child's parent or guardian, the child's name, age, address and telephone number, the date of his suspension, expulsion, exclusion or denial of placement and, *without attributing a particular characteristic to any specific child,* a breakdown of such list, showing the *alleged* causal characteristics for such nonattendance (e.g., educable mentally retarded, trainable mentally retarded, emotionally disturbed, specific learning disability, crippled/other health impaired, hearing impaired, visually impaired, multiple handicapped) and the number of children possessing each such *alleged* characteristic (879, emphases mine).

The purpose of this list was apparently not to help each child find a placement suited to his or her disability, inasmuch as the district was specifically barred from "attributing a particular characteristic to any specific child," but to critically examine the *patterns* in the defendants' overall practices of labeling students as handicapped and excluding them from an education on that basis (i.e., by giving a breakdown of cases of nonattendance by "alleged" disabilities).

Yet while the *Mills* decision perhaps went further than *PARC* in its critical attitude toward school authority and the schools' attempts to distinguish children according to their educationally relevant disabilities (an attitude that would recede in later legal decisions and legislation), both *PARC* and *Mills* shared a fundamentally social orientation—that is, both were class-action suits that defined the problems of disabled children not in terms of disability, but as the consequence of cultural prejudices and institutional deficiencies. The EAHCA, built on the foundation of these cases, held the promise to bring about the kind of social reform that the *PARC* and *Mills* cases sought on a smaller scale.

Though more detailed in its provisions than the *PARC* and *Mills* agreements, the EAHCA contained many of the same provisions as these early cases.[15] Specifically, the EAHCA required public schools to provide a "free, appropriate public education for all handicapped children between the ages of three and eighteen," with the upper age limit rising to twenty-one in 1980. Furthermore, it required that parents' consent to their children's evaluation and placement in special education be sought, a requirement that could be overridden only if an impartial administrative ("due process") hearing led to a decision in favor of the school's proposed evaluation or placement. Similarly, before a child's special education placement could be changed, the parents' consent had to be obtained by the school or overridden in a due process hearing. And finally, parents had the right to pursue new placements denied by the school district through a due process hearing. If the parents were not satisfied with the results, they had the right to appeal in the state or federal courts.

The EAHCA went beyond *PARC* and *Mills* by stipulating that special education placements must be based on an "individualized education program" (IEP) specially designed to meet the child's unique disability-related needs. The IEP existed as a written document, produced annually, that specified the services to be provided to the child, the child's current level of performance, short-term and long-term goals, and criteria for determining whether goals were being met. Perhaps most important, the IEP needed to be approved by parents and presented at an IEP meeting, to which the parents were invited and where they could discuss the IEP with a special education supervisor, the child's teacher, and, where appropriate, the student.

THE PROMISE OF THE EAHCA

Like Section 504 of the Rehabilitation Act of 1973, the EAHCA was not controversial before it was passed. Congressional debate on the bill focused mainly on the need to minimize its costs, with no serious challenges to its overall desirability. R. Shep Melnick observes, "Not one interest group

opposed the bill. Only the White House and HEW Secretary Caspar Wein-
berger spoke against it. The bill passed both houses by margins so lopsided
that President Ford decided not to veto it."[16] The Senate voted 83-10 in favor
of it, and the House voted 375-44 in favor.

However, unlike Section 504, the EAHCA was not written and passed as
an afterthought. It was a highly detailed bill with an exceedingly large number of congressional cosponsors—with 29 in the Senate, the bill had more
Senate cosponsors than all but 4 of the 588 bills passed by the Ninety-fourth
Congress. Before it was passed, proponents also had ample opportunity to
explain what they saw as the bill's importance and its potential. Senate
hearings were held in Washington, DC; Newark, New Jersey; Boston, Massachusetts; Columbia, South Carolina; St. Paul, Minnesota; and Harrisburg,
Pennsylvania. The hearings' transcripts totaled 3,550 pages and included
testimony from panels of parents of disabled children, special educators,
disability activists, local politicians, and others.[17]

Proponents of the bill argued that broad social goals could be achieved
by provisions that sought to bring all disabled children into the public education system; to integrate disabled children into regular classrooms as much
as possible; to improve the quality of education for disabled children; to
eliminate racial bias in evaluation for disabilities; and in support of all these
things, to include parents in special education decision making. Although
the courts would later interpret these provisions in ways that had little to do
with social reform, proponents were hopeful that the law would not be a
narrow one.

The Promise of the EAHCA: Into the Schools and into the Mainstream

Including disabled children in public education and improving the quality
of their education were the most basic goals of the EAHCA. In the Senate
hearings on the EAHCA, representatives from the American Coalition of
Citizens with Disabilities repeatedly mentioned that the federal Office for
the Education of the Handicapped had found that 45 percent of handicapped
children were being excluded from all access to public education. As other
participants in the hearings frequently pointed out, the special education
that was provided to some disabled students was often little more than warehousing. At the very least, the new law needed to overcome this exclusion
and warehousing.

The case for providing an education to disabled children was made on
both humanitarian grounds—the claim that they have a fundamental right

to the benefits of a public education—and economic grounds. The economic arguments were straightforward. For instance, a mother testified in the EAHCA hearings that her son, diagnosed as mentally retarded, had made tremendous gains when a local public school began a program for mentally retarded students. It was his experience in this program, she felt, that had made it possible for him later to get a job. As a result, she said, "he has paid back $3,400 in income taxes, so he now has benefited the people."[18] Senator Harrison Williams, the bill's main sponsor, made a similar point at the opening of the hearings by noting that it cost roughly $200,000 to institutionalize a handicapped person for life, whereas an investment of $20,000 in the education of each handicapped child could "insure productive lives" for 90 percent of them. Turning to the humanitarian argument for educational rights, Williams went on to note,

> But perhaps the most important is that these children have a right to appropriate educational services. They have the right to believe and to dream about this country in the same way that any other children do. They have the right to know that this Nation will provide them equal protection of the law and equal rights under the Constitution, and their parents have the right to know that their attempt to press local educational agencies for appropriate services is not something for which they must plead.[19]

Another apparent goal of the EAHCA was to bring disabled children into the social mainstream and thereby to change their image and status in the broader society. As a condition of receiving federal funding, the EAHCA required that a state's schools establish

> procedures to assure that, to the maximum extent appropriate, handicapped children . . . are educated with children who are not handicapped, and that special classes, separate schooling, or other removal of handicapped children from the regular educational environment occurs only when the nature or severity of the handicap is such that education in regular classes with the use of supplementary aids and services cannot be achieved satisfactorily.[20]

The same goal is reasserted later in the EAHCA through the requirement that schools demonstrate their efforts to "assure that handicapped children receive special education and related services in the *least restrictive environment* consistent with their needs,"[21] a requirement that is generally understood to favor placing disabled students in classrooms with nondisabled students ("mainstreaming").

The mainstreaming preference posed a challenge to an entire way of thinking about disabled people and their relation to society. In the EAHCA hearings, Charles Barnett, the commissioner of the South Carolina Department of Mental Retardation, praised the "revolution that is taking place in services to the handicapped" and described a "normalization" philosophy as perhaps the "most powerful concept to come on the scene in over a decade." He described normalization as applying to any category of disability the "concept... that the handicapped should be as much a part of the mainstream of society as their particular abilities and disabilities would permit."[22]

Mainstreaming was embraced as a means of improving the general population's understanding of people with disabilities and as an affirmation of the benefits of a more diverse, tolerant society. The first parent who testified before the Senate in support of the EAHCA struck this note when she said, "If the normal child grows up seeing these problems, I think they'll understand a lot more.... I think in the long run everyone will benefit from [programs for handicapped children]."[23] This social reform aspect of mainstreaming could itself be seen as having indirect economic benefits, inasmuch as social acceptance of disabled people should lead to economic integration. Irvin Schloss, a representative of the American Foundation for the Blind, observed that a broader societal understanding of handicaps "would greatly help in adult life when it comes time to get employment. There is no mystery about the handicapped."[24]

The Promise of the EAHCA: Racial Equality

The EAHCA addressed the problem of racial and cultural discrimination in special education by requiring states to establish "procedures to assure that testing and evaluation materials and procedures utilized for the purposes of evaluation and placement of handicapped children will be selected and administered *so as not to be racially or culturally discriminatory.* Such materials or procedures shall be provided and administered in the child's native language or mode of communication, unless it is clearly not feasible to do so."[25]

Dr. Oliver Hurley, a black professor of special education and one of the EAHCA hearing witnesses, observed that it was hardly news that black schoolchildren were more likely to be diagnosed as mentally retarded than were white schoolchildren. "It is fairly common knowledge and belief in the black community," he testified, "that many of our children are being labeled mentally retarded and emotionally disturbed who are neither, that this is the school's way of avoiding accountability."[26] Nor was this knowledge confined to the black community. Four years before the first EAHCA hearings, the

President's Committee on Mental Retardation had held a conference, and a report from that conference, titled "The Six-Hour Retarded Child," was included in the hearing records. As its title suggested, this report focused on the problem of children being diagnosed as mentally retarded who, outside school, were indistinguishable from "normal" children. The report informs readers that in California "the rate of placement of Spanish surname children in special education is about three times higher than Anglo children; the Negro rate is close to four times higher than the Anglo rate.... The question must be raised: To what extent are children classified as mentally retarded when the true nature of their learning disabilities stems from environmental factors?"[27]

Interestingly, although Hurley was concerned with racial discrimination in special education, he made no comment at the hearings on the EAHCA's specific provisions for culturally and racially nondiscriminatory testing. It seems that he regarded the EAHCA's IEP and due process requirements as more important means for addressing racial inequality in special education. He claimed, in fact, that the EAHCA's requirement for a written IEP and due process rights allowing parents' involvement in developing and approving an IEP would "substantially help" to alleviate the problem of minority overrepresentation in classes for the mentally retarded, presumably because minority parents would be enabled to challenge the means by which their children were being diagnosed as retarded.

The Promise of the EAHCA: Due Process Rights and the Democratization of Decision Making

The EAHCA's provision of due process rights satisfied a basic belief among some parents that special education decision making should be more democratic and that their interests and knowledge as parents belonged in the special education process every bit as much as the interests and knowledge of institutional actors. In the words of one witness at the EAHCA hearings, the mother of a child diagnosed with learning disabilities and hyperactivity, "Who knows the child better than those who live with him?... Parents, as consumers of education, should have more say in the quality of the product their school systems produce."[28] Similarly, an attorney who worked with the Association for Retarded Children and the Council for Exceptional Children testified, "I like the idea of guaranteeing the due process with regard to the classification of these children. In my experience as a lawyer, this has been one of the biggest problems that parents of these children face that have come to me. . . . The administrators will say, 'Well this is our determination. If you don't like it, go someplace else, or get your own education.' These parents become really distraught because they obviously know, to a large extent, what their children can or cannot do."[29]

Like Hurley, others held that giving due process rights to parents might be one effective means of addressing the systemic problems of special education. Clune and Van Pelt point out that Congress assumed that the EAHCA's due process provisions would be "relatively informal, inexpensive, quick, and substantively oriented" and would therefore "lead to more systematic pressure on school systems, put handicapped children on an educational par with nonhandicapped children, and lead to uniformity of treatment among handicapped children."[30] Similarly, disability advocates "hoped that results in individual cases would be followed across the board, producing a general pattern of compliance" (14). In a *California Law Review* article reprinted in the hearings record, David Kirp, William Buss, and Peter Kuriloff argued that it was possible that creating a due process hearing system in special education might "contribute to improving the content of special education because the reasons for each classification would be out in the open. If the reasons were invalid, they would be exposed, and the resulting public disapproval would force adjustments in a salutary direction" (121 [1729]).[31]

Yet the system that Kirp, Buss, and Kuriloff envisioned was different from the one that the hearing witnesses were discussing and that the EAHCA ultimately created. Whereas Kirp, Buss, and Kuriloff imagined the system as one that was open to the public, allowing for a steady improvement of special education practices through the expansion of common norms, actual due process hearings were private. And whereas they imagined hearings where nonprofit organizations could advocate for children collectively, actual hearings are centered on the student's "individualized" educational plan, making joint action impossible in due process hearings. These actual conditions were perhaps one reason that the due process system was not, as some hoped, the basis for systemic reform of special education.

THE LIMITS OF REFORM

While the bill's proponents understandably presented an optimistic view of the EAHCA's potential impact, and of the due process hearing system in particular, Kirp, Buss, and Kuriloff were much more cautious. Indeed, they warned that a system that put too much faith in procedure would fail to produce change: "There is a risk that over-emphasis on procedure will divert frontal attacks on the deficiencies of special education itself" (122 [1730]). Their warning now seems prescient.

Perhaps as a result of the emphasis on parents' due process rights—an emphasis furthered, in part, by the *Rowley* decision discussed below—evidence of the systemwide changes early reformers sought is often lacking. For instance, although the "mainstreaming"[32] of students with disabilities continues to be a popular cause among special education reformers, their constant calls for more inclusive education seem to indicate lack of real progress in mainstreaming disabled students.[33] As Danielson and Bellamy note, apparent increases in the percentage of disabled students who are mainstreamed often depend on the overall expansion of disability categories like learning disability, for which rates of mainstreaming have always been relatively high. Their analysis of the first twelve years of the EAHCA suggests very little change in the rate at which *students* (all students, not just disabled students) were placed in separate educational facilities. Singer et al.'s findings are even more discouraging. From 1976 to 1986, a time during which the *total* special education population rose from 8.33 percent to 10.97 percent of the total school population, they find little change even in the percentage of special education students who were segregated (in special classes or in special schools), indicating an actual growth in the overall proportion of students who were segregated based on disability. Similarly, McLeskey and Pacchiano find that over the course of the 1980s there was a rapid increase in the proportion of learning disabled students put in restrictive settings, at the same time as the proportion of students diagnosed as learning disabled steadily increased.

At best, the level of segregation in the U.S special education system got no worse during the 1990s. Although some researchers found that restrictive placements for mentally retarded and learning disabled students declined in the 1990s,[34] these gains were apparently offset by increases of restrictive placements in other disability categories. A 2005 report to Congress submitted by the Office of Special Education and Rehabilitative Services found that from 1993 to 2003 the proportion of special education students who were outside the regular classroom for at least 21 percent of the day declined from 56.6 percent to 50.1 percent. However, since the special education population had increased over the same period from 8.1 percent of the student population to 9.1 percent, the overall proportion of students in such placements remained essentially unchanged at 4.6 percent of the total student population.[35]

The track record on achieving racial equality in special education has not been much better. The segregation of students based on disability has a disproportionate impact on disadvantaged minority students, who are more likely than other students to be placed in restrictive placements.[36] This is due in part to an ongoing tendency for them to be diagnosed with disabilities such as mental retardation and emotional disturbance at a higher rate than white students, which lead to the most restrictive placements. Meier, Stewart, and England examined black representation in classes for educable mentally retarded (EMR) students from 1973 to 1984, including the beginning years of the EAHCA, and found only a modest decline in the average black overrepresentation in EMR classes—from a high in 1973 of 2.25 times their representation in the districtwide population to a low in 1984 of 1.95 times their districtwide representation.[37] More recent evidence continues to show marked overrepresentation of African American students with EMR. Fierros and Conroy also find that even *within* disability categories, minority students are more likely than white students to be placed in restrictive placements.[38]

The evidence on parent participation in the IEP process is more complex. Early studies suggested that a large proportion of parents with children in special education did not attend annual IEP meetings. In 1987 Singer and Butler reported on five metropolitan school systems, finding that parents' attendance at IEP meetings was below 50 percent in four of the five systems.[39] By the late 1990s, data on nationwide random samples of students were available that suggested much higher rates of participation. The Special Education Elementary Longitudinal Study (SEELS), featuring waves of interviews with randomly selected parents of disabled children in 2000 and 2002, found that 93 percent of parents interviewed in the summer of 2000 said they had attended an IEP meeting in the current or preceding school year, and 86 percent of parents in the second wave reported they had.[40]

These rates of attendance varied across demographic groups, though not drastically. Across years, white parents reported attendance at rates ranging from 7.4 percent to 13.1 percent higher than African American and Hispanic parents. Similarly, families with household incomes of $25,000 and below reported attendance rates ranging from 6.5 percent to 8.6 percent below higher-income groups.

One possibly significant omission from this report was the number and sex of parents attending meetings. Since the parents interviewed were overwhelming mothers—almost 90 percent in both years—the high level of attendance is likely to reflect the average level of *mothers'* attendance at IEP meetings. Fathers' levels of attendance are likely to be lower and may well vary by social class. In *Home Advantage*, Annette Lareau finds that while fathers generally have a low level of involvement in their children's education, upper-middle-class fathers often maintain an important symbolic role and, when they choose to become involved, bring greater weight to family involvement than mothers. By profession, many upper-middle-class men are accustomed to speaking with authority, which is likely to extend to contexts like the IEP meeting. Janet Davis, a sociology professor at a community college, reports that when she really needed to get something accomplished at an IEP meeting, she would just bring her husband: "I hate that we are still at that point, but I can bring my husband, and he can know absolutely nothing about what the IEP meeting is about . . . and I sit him down with a legal pad, and every once in a while, he'll repeat something they say, and it's like, [gasps] the dad's there. 'It must be important. Dad took off work. We must pay attention.'"

Perhaps more important, however, parents in different groups reported substantially different feelings about their involvement in decision making. In wave one of the SEELS study, for instance, 43.6 percent of parents with household incomes of $25,000 or below said they would like to be more involved with decision making, whereas only 21.0 percent of parents with household incomes above $50,000 said the same. Similarly, African American parents were almost twice as likely to say they wanted to be more involved (46.6 percent) as white parents (26.3 percent); 39.3 percent of Hispanic parents reported the same.

Early on, qualitative studies have revealed parents' widespread disenchantment with IEP meetings and their disenfranchisement from meaningful decision making. For instance, in his ethnographic research on parents of disabled children, David Engel finds that parents with children in special education are frequently intimidated and discouraged by the proceedings in IEP meetings. Thus they are typically reluctant to bring a strong challenge to the school's special education decisions, even when convinced that their children have been incorrectly diagnosed or that they are receiving the wrong treatment. When parents attend IEP meetings, interaction is often structured to make them token participants. Mehan, Hertweck, and Meihls studied the process by which students are evaluated for disabilities and placed in special education and found that, despite parents' formal inclusion in the IEP process, institutional interests and professional perspectives dominate. Parents have the opportunity to talk but are often made to feel that their opinions are irrelevant next to the opaque technical reports of school professionals.[41]

Although feeling marginalized from special education decision making may be common to all groups of parents, poor and minority parents might be especially vulnerable, owing to the lack of congruence between their own assumptions, beliefs, desires, and styles of interaction and those of professionals. Summarizing a body of research on the relation of "culturally diverse" families to the special education system, Beth Harry writes, "Assumptions concerning the importance of objectivity, as well as the need for legal accountability, have led to a form of home-school discourse that is impersonal and decontextualized in nature. This has resulted in the exclusion... of many parents, in particular, parents from diverse cultural backgrounds whose styles of interaction are often distinctly personalistic and reliant on highly contextualized communication."[42]

Some studies, Harry observes elsewhere, suggest that minority families may have a higher threshold than other families for what qualifies as a sign of disability, so that the school is more likely to initiate a search for disability than the parents are. She cites other studies indicating that certain minority groups place less value than white middle-class families do on the goals of independence and economic productivity, which United States special education often gives priority. As such, minority families may see the reigning definition of "appropriate education," focusing on providing skills that will allow the disabled child to be an independent adult, as describing an *inappropriate* education. Finally, Harry's own research on Puerto Rican families' interaction with the special education system suggests that, owing to a cultural habit of showing respect for authority, these parents defer to school professionals despite having little trust in their decisions. In general, she finds, these parents expressed dissent only by not participating in decision making.[43]

This is not to say that reluctance to challenge the school system is confined to poor and minority parents. For instance, David and Wendy Holden, two high school teachers, were initially reluctant to demand that the school assess their son for possible Asperger syndrome (AS). Their reluctance, according to Wendy, was not due to intimidation by the school but was because they were "afraid of alienating his teachers" and because, as educators themselves, they had believed the school would share their sense of the primacy of the student's needs. With this attitude, they were patient for three years while the school declined their requests that Joseph be assessed for AS.

At the end of Joseph's fifth-grade year, however, there was an incident in which a teacher wrongly accused him of writing on the bathroom walls. Joseph had a "meltdown," which led to a two-day suspension from school. Wendy, convinced that this incident could have been avoided if the school had simply recognized Joseph's needs, demanded an assessment for AS. Her demand resulted in an AS diagnosis that was recognized by the school. At the end of Joseph's sixth-grade year, Wendy and David came to an IEP meeting with a long list of accommodations that Wendy had chosen based on her online research, and the parents were granted exactly what they wanted. They had brought with them an advocate who had helped them see that instead of trying not to upset the school, they should have, in Wendy's words, "gone in there loaded for bear and shot their legs out from under them."

Ultimately, it was critical that Wendy and David knew they had rights and knew how to assert them. Wendy attributes this awareness to their education, which was notably above the local average. In their town, a small, rural community in the South, Wendy observes, "it is more common to drop out of high school than stay." Its 2000 census figures suggest this is only a slight exaggeration, with slightly over 50 percent of persons over twenty-five having graduated from high school and fewer than 4 percent holding a bachelor's degree. As teachers with college educations—David has a bachelor's degree, Wendy plans to return to college to earn hers—Wendy and David are highly educated for this community. In Wendy's view, this education gives her and David a greater understanding of institutional practice and legal responsibility than most local parents have. "I think the level of education makes a huge difference," she says, "I think it helped us realize that [the school] could not possibly be as free of responsibility as they were letting on."

Many parents, she claims, do not understand that schools cannot just make decisions as they please but must go through a particular process and that, as parents, they can hold schools to that obligation. Wendy offered an anecdote that, for her, epitomized the problem. In her substitute teaching in special education classrooms, Wendy observed a disabled girl whose health problems had caused her to go completely blind over the summer. When this girl returned to her special education classroom the following year, no attempt was made to teach her skills that would help her adjust to her blindness. "If she was my daughter," Wendy says, "I would have sued the school system by now." Yet, according to Wendy, these parents and most other local parents with children in special education have no idea what happens in the classroom and have no notion of the school's legal responsibility to educate their children.

Despite their difficulties, the Holdens were perhaps fortunate inasmuch as, understanding their rights, they were able to assert them and obtain what they wanted for Joseph in IEP meetings. Perhaps because the services she sought were more costly, Sharon Faber, whose autistic son lacked and continues to lack all ability to communicate verbally, has had to go further into the IEP process. She has twice requested due process hearings to challenge the school's refusal to provide specific services to her son. Sharon sees these challenges as having resulted not only in the specific services she requested at the time, but also in the school district's ongoing willingness to comply with her requests in order to avoid more hearings.

What it takes to make these claims work is not just the threat of a hearing, although even that first step is something many parents find daunting. When Sharon made her hearing requests, the school refused, both times, to enter mediation and pursued its case all the way to the scheduled day of the hearing. Both times, the hearing officer ordered them to meet briefly one more time to try to reach an agreement, which resulted in agreements favorable to Sharon. "I came with guns loaded," Sharon explains. She had an attorney and expert witnesses lined up to support her claims. Only then, after Sharon had spent many hours and thousands of dollars preparing her case, did the school meet her demands, understanding that she would be a formidable opponent at a hearing.

In short, while the due process rights parents are given through the IEP process may allow some to obtain what their children need, for many parents the prospect remains daunting. In the following chapters I will consider in more detail the conditions, individual, social, and cultural, that make privileged parents' advocacy more likely. The rest of this chapter considers how and why due process rights remain at the center of educational rights for disabled children and how this has turned disputes in special education into individualized, technical affairs.

THE CHANGING INTERPRETATION OF THE EAHCA

The EAHCA has surely produced some gains in the education of disabled children, especially at the extremes: few are now totally excluded from public education, and some have access to very costly accommodations at public expense. In other areas where the EAHCA sought to make social reforms, progress has been more limited. This is true of many laws seeking important social reforms, which often face an uphill battle. Their fate often rests on their interpretation in the courts.

As with any law, the meaning of the EAHCA is subject to interpretation, and because of its construal in the courts the EAHCA has become, over time, less a basis for social reform and more a call for improved technical management of individual cases. This tendency was furthered particularly by the U.S. Supreme Court's 1982 decision in *Hendrick Hudson School District v. Rowley*,[44] which put strict limits on the federal courts' ability to make judgments about the substantive rights of disabled students to an appropriate education.

The plaintiff in *Rowley* was Amy Rowley, a girl in the first grade with "minimal residual hearing," who relied on lipreading to understand what was said in her classes. Amy's parents requested that the school provide her with a sign-language interpreter, a request that the school denied and that was also denied in a due process hearing. When Amy's parents appealed this decision to the district court for the Southern District of New York, the court found in their favor,[45] holding that a free, appropriate education, as defined by the EAHCA, required "an opportunity to achieve [her] full potential commensurate with the opportunity provided to other children" (534) and that Amy Rowley was not being provided this opportunity. The district court based this decision on its belief that, although Amy was performing above average academically, she was a very intelligent and energetic child and could do substantially better if provided with a sign-language interpreter. The Second Circuit Court of Appeals affirmed this decision.

The Supreme Court reversed and remanded the district court decision, finding that the EAHCA's substantive definition of a "free, appropriate public education" was minimal and should be understood only as providing a "basic floor of opportunity" consisting of "personalized instruction" and "supportive services" that "permit the child to benefit from the instruction" and comport with the child's IEP. The court held that the EAHCA's procedural protections were much more important than its minimal substantive definition of an appropriate education. Indeed, the *Rowley* court claimed that the law's emphasis on procedural requirements reflected a "legislative conviction" that the *substance* of an appropriate education would usually be realized simply by meeting the law's *procedural* requirements—in particular, the requirements for including parents in the formulation of the IEP. With these procedural rights in place, the Court argued, "parents and guardians will not lack ardor in seeking to assure that handicapped children receive all of the benefits to which they are entitled" (209).

Unlike the *PARC* and *Mills* courts, which were willing to challenge educational practice by bringing to bear a historical perspective on the treatment of disabled children and a critical and questioning attitude toward educational practice, the *Rowley* court objected to the courts' trying to determine the substance of an appropriate education after state and local agencies had already reached a determination. The *Rowley* court deferred to the authority of the schools and generally called on the lower courts to do the same. As the majority opinion remarked, "We previously have cautioned that courts lack the 'specialized knowledge and experience' necessary to resolve 'persistent and difficult questions of educational policy'" (208). Interpreting the law's requirement that the federal courts judge special education disputes based on the "preponderance of the evidence," the *Rowley* court claimed that the federal courts were not thereby invited "to substitute their own notions of sound educational policy for those of the school authorities which they review" (206).

Of course, perhaps as a consequence of changes wrought by the EAHCA itself, the problem that presented itself in *Rowley* was surely less severe than the problems in *PARC* and *Mills*, and it is perhaps not surprising, therefore, that the *PARC* and *Mills* courts were more inclined to challenge the authority of the schools than the *Rowley* court was. Yet the EAHCA itself had been ambitiously framed, and it was clearly not the case that it was meant to address only the most severe problems involved with the education of children with disabilities. Nor was it meant only to give disabled children access to public education. It was also intended to ensure that, where possible, they would be in the same classrooms with nondisabled children; that they would not be assigned disability labels in a racially discriminatory fashion; and that their education would be tailored to reflect their own needs, not the schools' convenience. One reason parents were given rights to participate in decision making was that schools' own tendencies were often at odds with these goals. Parents' involvement was intended, in the eyes of some, at least, to bring about systemic change. In this sense, the Court's caution against legal interpretations that challenged schools on "persistent and difficult questions of educational policy" seemed to undermine some of the deepest aims and underlying beliefs of the law.

Since the *Rowley* decision, the federal courts have been less likely to entertain the same kinds of challenges to the authority of the schools that had made the *PARC* and *Mills* decisions possible. Because of this, such challenges are largely confined to due process hearings. At this level, disputes are individualized and highly technical (perhaps because the presiding officer is required to have specialized knowledge of special education). Unlike the lawsuits that preceded them, they are often limited in the impact they can have on other cases. In California, for instance, due process hearing decisions do not set precedents—they are not binding on subsequent decisions. Thus parents must fight their battles on their own, without benefiting from the achievements of others.

Perhaps as a result of the standards established by *Rowley*, legal decisions in claims brought under the EAHCA seem to favor schools more over time. The ratio of circuit court cases in which *schools* appeal district court decisions to cases in which *parents* do so reverses over time. As table 1.1 shows,

TABLE 1.1 Before and after *Rowley*: EAHCA/IDEA Appeals to Circuit Courts
Arising from Placement, Accommodation, and Evaluation Disputes

Years	School/Parent Appeals Ratio
1978–81	12/5
1983–86*	15/25

Note: I have examined appeals arising from judgments on placement, accommodation, and
evaluation because only these cases would be affected by *Rowley*. Other types of appeals from
district court decisions, such as those concerned with the applicable statute of limitations would
not necessarily be affected by *Rowley*.
* The 1986 cutoff avoids any increase in parents' appeals that might have been produced by the
creation of a new right, by amendments to the EAHCA passed in August 1986 (PL 99-372), for
parents to seek reimbursement for attorney's fees in the federal courts. Some cases in this
period had to be eliminated because the district court decisions being appealed were made
before *Rowley*.

school appeals were more frequent than parent appeals before *Rowley* and
less frequent than parent appeals after *Rowley*. Insofar as the likelihood of
appeals reflects the unfavorable nature of decisions for the appealing party,
it seems that *Rowley* may have contributed to a growing number of decisions
unfavorable to parents.

Another effect of *Rowley* seems to be discouraging class-action lawsuits
brought by parents with children in special education. Although class-action
lawsuits in general have declined as a result of various trends in the federal
courts, the *Rowley* decision has the potential to further discourage class actions.[46] This can be seen by comparing class-action cases before and after
Rowley.

In 1979 *Armstrong v. Kline*, a class-action lawsuit brought under the
EAHCA, was decided.[47] The plaintiffs in *Armstrong* were a group of parents
of disabled children in Pennsylvania who alleged that a Pennsylvania law
limiting to 180 the number of days children were eligible for instruction
violated the rights of their children, who regressed in skills and behavior
when not receiving instruction over the summer.[48] Turning to the legislative
history of the EAHCA, the district court found that a primary intent of that
law was to make disabled children as independent as possible. The court
also accepted the plaintiffs' contention that the interruption in educational
programming over the summer months was causing the disabled students
to regress, making them unlikely to attain the independence that was the
EAHCA's goal.

Thirteen years later, after the *Rowley* decision, a class-action lawsuit originally brought by the parents of four disabled children in Arizona was settled in *Hoeft v. Tucson Unified School District*.[49] The plaintiffs' claim, which again concerned provision of instructional services over the summer (or "extended school year" [ESY] services), alleged that the district had overly narrow eligibility criteria for ESY services and that, in violation of the requirement to individualize educational programs, the district followed an implicit policy of offering the same amount of ESY services to every student. Finding in favor of the defendants, the court noted that the eligibility criteria for ESY services, which the parents questioned, involved precisely the types of "technical questions" that are "best resolved with the benefit of agency expertise and a fully developed administrative record" (1305) and invoked the *Rowley* decision as the basis for deferring to the school's expertise. The effect of the *Hoeft* decision was to require each of the plaintiffs to make individual challenges to the school's denial of ESY services, on the apparent assumption that if the school was systematically violating students' rights to an individualized education, this would have to be proved by considering the technical merits of individual decisions.

At the same time that the *Hoeft* decision illustrates the impact of *Rowley* on the courts' deference to school authority, the underlying facts in the case might also reveal how schools have adjusted their practices so that they at least appear to provide individualized, technically appropriate accommodations. In *Armstrong*, the defendant was vulnerable because of a rule that explicitly imposed a common standard (180-day limit on instruction) on all students, which clearly showed that placements were not being decided through a technical determination of students' individual needs. In the later *Hoeft* case, however, the defendants did not have explicit rules, although the plaintiffs alleged that they did have tacit rules. The *Hoeft* plaintiffs could only hang this claim on the evidence of collective experience, which allegedly *showed* that the district offered only one amount of ESY services. Since in theory the district could have made appropriate, individualized determinations of each student's individual needs and arrived at the same amount for each student, the court determined that the plaintiffs' claims also needed to be pursued individually, not through a class action.

The *Hoeft* decision, then, illustrates how class-action lawsuits brought under the EAHCA may now be more difficult, inasmuch as it assumes that special education challenges should be concerned with the technically defined needs of one child, an area where the school will normally start with some advantage. Parents may be able to challenge that advantage by bringing their own knowledge of technical issues or by hiring professionals

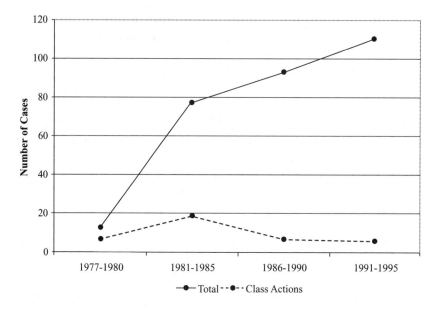

FIGURE 1.1 Circuit court decisions and circuit court class-action decisions in claims brought under the EAHCA/IDEA, 1977 to 1995. In 1990, amendments to the EAHCA changed its name to the Individuals with Disabilities Education Act (IDEA).

with that knowledge, but they will find it difficult to challenge it by bringing together other parents in a class action. As figure 1.1 clearly shows, while the total number of claims brought under the EAHCA has increased steadily since its passage, class actions have continuously declined as a proportion of all cases. Following *Rowley* (i.e., beginning in 1981-85), class actions also decline in absolute numbers. Thus, while 54 percent of cases (7 of 13) in 1977-80 were class actions, in 1991-95 only 5 percent (6 of 110) were.

The weakening of the EAHCA's substantive goals is also apparent in the courts' interpretation of its mainstreaming or "least restrictive environment" (LRE) requirement. As I argued above, the mainstreaming preference was originally seen not just as benefiting the individual disabled child, but also as promoting the social integration of disabled people. In keeping with this understanding, the federal regulations implementing the EAHCA's LRE requirement do not allow schools to segregate disabled students simply on the grounds that it is more efficient or that it produces a technically superior education. Rather, segregation is allowed only when "the nature or severity of the disability is such that education in regular classes with the use of supplementary aids and services cannot be achieved satisfactorily."[50] Yet the courts have interpreted LRE in ways that seem to violate these regulations.

Thomas and Rapport suggest four main ways the courts have come to interpret the LRE requirement. First, there is what they term a "qualified deference" standard, which tends to follow *Rowley* by deferring to the judgment about LRE made by a state's due process system (i.e., what is determined in an individual student's due process hearing to be the "least restrictive environment" appropriate to that child's needs). Second, there is a "portability" standard, which permits a more restrictive placement where such a placement offers services superior to those that can be offered in a less restrictive placement. Third, there is an "inclusion" standard, which essentially follows a strict interpretation of the EAHCA by requiring that restrictive placements be used only where a satisfactory placement cannot be made in a less restrictive placement. Finally, Thomas and Rapport describe a fourth, "balancing" standard in which the costs and benefits for the child and for the district of different placements are analyzed and the placement that seems to maximize benefits relative to costs is chosen.[51]

These interpretations have various implications with respect to the preference for mainstreaming and to when the school should prevail in LRE disputes. However, three of the four interpretations share a common tendency to treat the mainstreaming requirement as more technical and complex than the actual language of the EAHCA and its implementing regulations seems to suggest. Only the inclusion standard seems to take seriously the idea that disabled children should be placed in regular classrooms *whenever* their education can be achieved "satisfactorily" there—a standard that is more social and political in its orientation than it is technical. Yet even the inclusion standard determines what a "satisfactory" placement is by balancing benefits to disabled students against costs to nondisabled classmates, thereby ignoring, in Thomas and Rapport's view, the original law's belief that mainstreaming had benefits that went beyond the disabled student's education. In short, none of the current legal interpretations of the mainstreaming requirement is interested in the social integration of people with disabilities in the way that early advocates for the EAHCA might have hoped.

PARENTS' RIGHTS, CHILDREN'S NEEDS, AND SOCIAL DIFFERENCE

In all fairness, the EAHCA was largely successful in its goal of providing all disabled children with a public education.[52] Further, it has allowed at least some parents to become more actively involved in special education decisions and thereby to improve the lives of their disabled children. With respect to other goals that proponents seemed to have had in mind, however, its achievements are questionable. A sizable percentage of the ever-growing special education population spends most or all of the time in school in "segregated" placements, apart from nondisabled peers. Racial inequities in special education placements also remain a significant problem. Finally, the due process rights parents are given, which were supposed to address these issues alongside individual students' needs, seem to be out of the reach of many. While parents' attendance at IEP meetings may be high, many do not feel adequately involved in decision making, and this seems to be a particular problem for poor and minority parents. And whereas the collective actions that gave rise to the EAHCA once gave voice to concerns about social justice, the EAHCA no longer seems to have these same concerns.

However, while the EAHCA has closed some doors, it has opened others. In this chapter I have discussed the reasons that disadvantaged parents are unlikely to advocate successfully for their disabled children's educational rights, but I have only touched on the reasons that privileged parents might manage to advocate successfully for their children. This is the primary task of the chapters that follow.

CHAPTER TWO

———— ✳ ————

Disabled Children's Parents

CHAPTER 1 discussed the federal legislation that created educational rights for disabled children and its effects on children and their parents. I argued that the legislation, while giving parents the right to advocate for their disabled children, ultimately supported a particular interpretation of the parents' role, a role individualized in form and technical in content. That interpretation, I argued, has likely discouraged the involvement of most parents with relatively low incomes and little formal education. This chapter and the rest of the book will focus primarily on how and why parents who are more privileged are better able to advocate successfully for their children. In general I argue that, within existing cultural and institutional frameworks, privileged parents' cultural and economic capital helps them to make disability claims for their children and to negotiate accommodations in the special education system. In this chapter I use parents' responses to a written survey and in interviews to draw general portraits of privileged parents and consider how their privileges shape the ways they perceive, respond to, and advocate for their children's needs.

As I have suggested above, the privilege I am examining is not absolute or all-encompassing. A given parent might be privileged compared with some parents and disadvantaged compared with others, privileged with respect to some life circumstances and disadvantaged with respect to others. Nor does the fact that some parents can draw on privileges that others lack make them reprehensible. On the contrary, the sacrifices such parents make are hardly necessary and are often extraordinary. Having children who struggle in school and in life leads some to give up on their children and distance themselves from them. Those parents who choose instead to use their resources to advocate for their children—though they may see it not as a choice, but as an inescapable part of being a parent—may do so at great personal cost.

It is possible to recognize both the privilege and the caring involved, for instance, in Angela Nelson's advocacy for her son Aaron. Angela put her rising career as a nurse manager on hold in order to stay home and assist in her son's intensive therapy, which involved a commitment that is, as she puts it, "not for every family." Financially, this decision was presumably enabled by the income of her husband, who, as a firefighter, would bring home a salary well above the national median, but it also entailed a career sacrifice for Angela. "I was young and just going up the ladder," she says, "but family was more important, and I had to step back, which was really a hard thing for me, but I did." Simply put, not all mothers could afford to make this decision, but not all mothers who could afford to make it would make it. (That is not to say that all mothers should make this decision, or that the mother should be burdened, though she often is, with deciding between child and career instead of sharing responsibility with others, including the child's father.)

In addition to having the financial freedom to work with her child full time, Angela has a background in nursing that has been useful when she has tried to advocate for her son's needs. Her level of education is not exceptionally high—she has a degree in nursing from a two-year college—but it is exceptionally relevant to her son's needs, and she has put it to good use. From the time Aaron was one year old, Angela suspected he had a hearing problem. He was given multiple hearing tests, but Angela was never told he had a hearing deficit. Instead, he was given an autism diagnosis. Angela began reading, turning both to the professional literature on autism and to literature addressed to a lay audience. When I ask her about the influence her nursing background had on her ability to research her son's needs, she says it was probably very important: "When you're in nursing school," she says, "you're researching everything, and you figure out how to gain access to research papers.... People who never even learned that, I mean, they have no access to anything."

Over the years, Angela remained unconvinced that Aaron's difficulties were not due to a hearing problem, despite being told by clinicians that only autism could explain his behavior. Although it took years, Angela pushed for further testing until, when Aaron was twelve years old, it was recognized that he could not, in fact, hear at all. After the audiologist suggested Aaron might have "auditory neuropathy," Angela again put her research skills to work: she tracked down the author of an article claiming that auditory neuropathy was sometimes the cause of false autism diagnoses. The author put her in touch with a specialist who, in turn, gave Aaron a positive diagnosis of auditory neuropathy and helped put him on a fast track for a cochlear implant. With the implant, Aaron is learning to hear and making "good progress," although the future is uncertain and, at thirteen, he still has no formal means of communicating.

While Angela is understandably upset over the educational opportunities Aaron lost while being incorrectly identified as autistic, she also understands that, based on her education and her understanding of her rights, she has enjoyed certain advantages in advocating for her son, and she has tried to help parents who lack those advantages. The educational system, she says, "is only fair for the people who are educated or who educate themselves, and the other kids just suffer." When her son first entered school, the local school district typically refused to provide services to autistic children; so, along with Sharon Faber (discussed in the introduction) and another mother, Angela founded an organization to teach other parents about their children's needs and help them advocate for them. She used to attend IEP meetings with other parents and work long hours counseling parents on how to get what their children needed. She now wonders if she might have identified her own son's needs sooner had she spent less time helping other parents.

Yet my interest is not in how much concern privileged parents show toward other people's children or even how much they have for their own children. I assume that privileged parents are no more or less virtuous than other parents. Angela's altruism is probably above average among parents in a similar social class position, as it would be among parents in different positions. Disadvantaged parents and privileged parents alike are probably most concerned with their own children's well-being, which is understandable. What distinguishes privileged parents, then, is not their desire to see their children succeed, but their belief that they can and should help them succeed in school and their possessing the economic and cultural resources to do so. In short, parents' social class *does* affect their *ability* to advocate for their children.

In the end, whether or not they want to be, parents who want their disabled children to receive educational services that may allow them to succeed in school and prosper in life are involved in an implicitly competitive struggle for scarce resources. In such competitive fields, it helps to have resources that distinguish you from others and that let you accumulate and use the rewards won through competition. In short, it helps to have what sociologists, loosely borrowing from the field of economics, call "capital." Two types of capital are of particular interest: economic capital and cultural capital. While in its ordinary sociological usage economic capital seems to refer, without much controversy, to money and the ways ordinary people (not just "capitalists") can use it to get or stay ahead, cultural capital and its effects form a much more difficult and debated topic. Accordingly, before turning to a discussion of the parents who participated in my interview and survey research, I first give a brief background on cultural capital and the particular way I use it to understand how parents differ in their ability to advocate for their disabled children.

CULTURAL CAPITAL AND PARENTING

The concept of cultural capital was first introduced to sociology by Pierre Bourdieu and Jean-Claude Passeron, who conceived of it as "instruments for the appropriation of symbolic wealth socially designated as being worthy of being sought and possessed."[1] Much subsequent interpretation of this concept—and in particular Bourdieu's use of it—has focused on the ability to acquire and express knowledge of "high" cultural forms such as abstract painting or classical music. Following this understanding of cultural capital, some researchers have argued that essentially arbitrary forms of knowledge form the basis of class privileges that are transmitted across generations. Through the different educational opportunities they are given and through their distinctive home and family environments, children of upper-class (and to some extent middle-class) backgrounds develop elite cultural capital (e.g., artistic tastes or manners of speaking) as a natural part of growing up that disadvantaged children can acquire only with difficulty.

Based on this original conception of cultural capital, it was argued that children of privileged social class backgrounds do better in school not simply because they are better students or because their objective academic skills are stronger, but because they display elite cultural traits that other children cannot acquire through school, since the most elite forms of cultural capital are *not* part of the school curriculum, although they are a basis for perceiving privileged children's performance as superior.

Crucially, though, while the academic criteria that value these elite traits are clearly class-biased, their application, it was argued, is not. In other words, working-class, middle-class, and upper-class students are all judged by the same criteria—and to some extent given access to the same curriculum in school. In this way the school system not only helps to reproduce the advantages of privileged students, but also legitimates them by seeming to rank students objectively, according to their natural traits. Therefore, while educators and others may recognize the greater achievements of privileged students, they will often ascribe those achievements to the greater discipline or superior natural intelligence ostensibly associated with higher social class position. This tendency to recognize arbitrary social hierarchies as natural and necessary, Bourdieu terms "misrecognition," and the educational system clearly plays a pivotal role in sustaining this misrecognition.

Recent research has taken exception to this understanding of cultural capital. In particular, Annette Lareau (with others) has argued that cultural capital is perhaps better understood not only as the appreciation of "high" cultural forms but, more generically, as "institutionalized, i.e., widely shared, high status cultural signals (attitudes, preferences, formal knowledge, behaviors, goods and credentials) used for social and cultural exclusion."[2] Following this broader definition, cultural capital may include more practical, less grandiose forms of knowledge—for instance, depending on the context, strong academic and communicative skills or knowledge of educational jargon and institutional practices. In this sense cultural capital may reflect, as Bourdieu intended it, a social relationship in which some individuals benefit from relatively exclusive access to cultural knowledge and dispositions, but these forms may also have value besides revealing the status of their owners. They may include, for instance, the ability to navigate complex bureaucracies and to negotiate with technically trained professionals.

Furthermore, Lareau argues against the notion that the influence of cultural capital stops at the doors of the school. Indeed, a central focus of her work has been the various ways upper-middle-class parents contribute to their children's future success by intervening on their behalf in various institutional contexts—particularly in schools, where upper-middle-class children are able to receive "customized educational experiences" because of their parents' advocacy. That is, upper-middle-class parents regularly volunteer in their children's classrooms, request specific teachers, offer them criticisms and suggestions, and call for them to make special considerations in teaching their individual children and evaluating their performance.

For Lareau, these interventions crucially depend on privileged parents' own cultural capital. High parental involvement requires that parents have the academic skills to help their children with homework; the disposition to critically assess the pedagogical style of their children's teachers; the disposition to monitor their children's academic development; and a familiarity with technical and scientific discourse that allows them to fully understand their children's teachers and to be persuasive with them. Upper-middle-class parents can more easily meet these requirements owing to the cultural capital implicit in their educational backgrounds and occupations—that is, they are more likely than other parents to have strong academic skills, to see themselves as socially equal (or superior) to their children's teachers, and to feel comfortable using technical legal and scientific language.

Lareau and Shumar find that, in addition to lacking the requisite cultural capital for effective involvement, disadvantaged parents face other conditions that discourage their involvement in their children's education: logistical difficulties, such as rigid work schedules and limited access to transportation, make it difficult for low-income parents to attend parent-teacher meetings and school events; low-income parents socialize with relatives more than with the parents of their children's classmates, making it less likely that they will acquire indirect knowledge about their children's schools; and finally, poor, working-class, and minority parents minimize interaction with schools because they expect that schools will discriminate against them or find fault with their styles of parenting, which historically differ from the styles of white, middle-class parents.[3] At the same time as these circumstances block disadvantaged parents' involvement with their children's education, however, they presumably also further limit their accumulation of the specific forms of cultural capital that help more privileged parents to be involved—for example, by limiting their awareness and understanding of educational discourse and practice.

The current emphasis on parents' involvement in education is relatively new. Writing in 1989, Lareau observed, "Until two decades ago, there were few indications that teachers expected or asked parents to take on an aggressive educational role at home or that parents acted in this fashion. Today, however, teachers across the nation want parents to provide an advantageous educational environment for children at home, to participate in school events, and generally to support teachers' efforts" (Lareau 2000, 175). In Peter Brown's view, this shift toward what he calls a "parentocracy" gives parents the right and responsibility to determine how their children are educated and requires that the state assume less responsibility for education, with the result that parents with the most resources are able to shape the educational system to favor their children.[4]

This is not to say that, by opening the doors to parents' involvement, public school systems now openly sanction class bias in educational opportunity. If this were true, it would clearly undermine the legitimacy accorded public education—precisely the reason Bourdieu expected that public schools necessarily *prevented* parents' direct involvement in schooling. The sense of legitimacy—the belief that public schools are essentially democratic, egalitarian institutions—is preserved by the official belief that high involvement is something parents of all backgrounds can and should aspire to. To the extent that certain groups of parents (in particular, low-income parents and parents from disadvantaged minority groups) show low levels of school involvement, it is often attributed to the low value they place on education—by researchers and, as Lareau shows, by teachers. Privileged parents' involvement, by contrast, is perceived as nothing more than good parenting, perhaps because the very definition of the proper home-school relationship has been shaped by privileged groups. As Lareau puts it, "social class shapes the alignment of social groups with the standards of institutions."[5] Privileged parents thus do not have to demand that schools accept their approach to advocacy for their children; it is already assumed that their approach is the most legitimate.

These observations have rarely been applied specifically to understanding parents' involvement in special education. It is clear, however, that many of the same barriers to their involvement exist in special education and, if anything, are higher there. Despite the legal mandate for parents' involvement in special education, decision making is often dominated by school administrators, special education teachers, and school psychologists, who cast themselves as having essential scientific (and legal) knowledge that parents lack. Kimberly Reid and Jan Weatherly Valle summarize the situation in the following way:

> School professionals, speaking from an authority based on the Western conception of science as an objective, indisputable truth, position themselves (intentionally or unintentionally) in a dominant rather than a collaborative role with parents. It is paradoxical, indeed, that the discourse of special education—a system of practices in which parent-professional collaboration is legally mandated—operates simultaneously out of a scientific framework that by its very nature gives authority to professionals.[6]

I argue here that, to the extent that parents can overcome these obstacles, it is through the same privileges that middle-class and upper-middle-class parents have in the general education system—that is, their cultural capital. The difference is perhaps not simply the added difficulty of surmounting the obstacles in special education—owing both to the technical nature of special education decisions and, implicitly, the potential costs of making special education accommodations. Rather, it is also the fact that, in overcoming these higher obstacles—that is, in living up to the high expectation for rigor and technical sophistication embodied in scientific and legal discourse of special education—parents' advocacy may seem to transcend subjectivity and self-interest. In this sense, I argue that parents' involvement in special education, though powerfully affected by their social class, can easily be misrecognized as solely the consequence of natural concern and accurate perception of their children's rights and needs. Parents who do not participate are easily seen, then, as not caring or as being "in denial."

The rest of this chapter focuses on how parents' cultural capital (and to some extent their economic capital) shapes their experiences in special education and the attitudes and practices that underlie those experiences, concluding with an observation about the ways parents may misrecognize the meaning of their own involvement.

The following sections present parents' responses to a paper survey in 2003 and a series of interviews conducted in 2007 and 2008 (see appendix). The parents represented in these responses—157 survey respondents and 16 interviewees (including two interviews in which a mother and father were simultaneously interviewed, and one that included their son)—come from varied backgrounds and have children with a range of disabilities, including learning disabilities, Asperger syndrome, autism, ADHD, mental retardation, and speech and language impairments. Neither survey respondents nor interviewees, however, can be considered representative of the broader population of parents of children with disabilities in the United States. On the contrary, they clearly have more education and income than the average parent and, in all likelihood, more than the average parent in special education, where low-income students and minority students are generally overrepresented (with the important exception of Hispanic students).

PARENTS EDUCATING THEMSELVES

Parents of students in general education can become involved in their children's education based on their own academic strengths and their ability to speak articulately and with confidence to teachers. But parents of children with disabilities, if they wish to have an impact on their education, may also need to know something about disabilities—in particular, how they are diagnosed and what kinds of educational approaches might be called for in working with disabled students. There are various ways parents can educate themselves. They can read books, attend lectures, read magazines, journals, or online articles, or speak to people in the field. (In chapter 4, I examine the literature for parents of children with disabilities in some detail.)

TABLE 2.1 Time Spent Learning about Child's Disability

	No time at all	1–2 hours	3–10 hours	More than 10 hours
Before child's diagnosis	46.8%	13.5%	9.6%	30.1%
First month after child's diagnosis	3.9%	14.9%	22.7%	58.4%

	No time at all/ less than once a month	At least once a month	At least once a week
Currently	26.3%	46.1%	27.6%

Because I was interested in how such self-education might lead parents to advocate for disability diagnoses or reflect the initiative they generally take in identifying their children's needs, the survey I distributed asked parents how much time they had spent teaching themselves about their children's disabilities *before* their children were diagnosed with a disability, as well as in the first month after the diagnosis and at present. They were instructed to include in this time reading, attending conferences and lectures, or speaking with professionals, but *not* direct experience with their children. The figures in table 2.1 summarize their responses.

Accepting parents' self-reports at face value, it appears that almost all respondents had spent at least some time educating themselves about their children's disability at some time before or after a diagnosis was given. Self-educating in the first month *after* diagnosis is not a particularly distinguishing trait; the overwhelming majority of parents do so, and most are clustered in the two highest amounts of self-education (three to ten hours and more than ten hours). Self-educating *before* a diagnosis appears to be a more distinguishing trait, with 46.8 percent reporting that they spent "no time at all" teaching themselves about their children's conditions before a diagnosis was given. Parents were also asked to estimate their use of specific sources of knowledge about disability. These estimates also suggest that most respondents made a considerable investment in self-education. Over half of the respondents said they had attended two or more support group meetings related to their children's disabilities. About half said they had read twenty or more articles, and about one-fourth reported more than fifty articles.[7] Finally, more than half of the parents said they had read two or more books about their children's disabilities, and about a quarter reported ten or more books.

Some variation in responses to this question is doubtless related to the age at which it is generally believed possible to identify a given disability—for instance, mental retardation is essentially predicted at birth when a child has Down syndrome. Depending on the disability, then, some parents will have little or no opportunity to research a diagnosis before it is given. However, there are some interesting variations within categories that begin to give a picture of the differences among parents.

For instance, one mother of a learning disabled child reports that her child was diagnosed at age three. This same mother, a sonographer with a household income above $100,000, reports relatively high levels of self-education. She spent only one to two hours before the diagnosis was given but more than ten hours in the first month after diagnosis, and at present she spends time learning at least once a month. She estimates that she has read fifty articles and five books about learning disabilities. Most notably, despite having spent only one to two hours teaching herself about learning disabilities before her daughter was diagnosed, she claims she was the first person to recognize that her daughter had a learning disability.

In contrast, an African American mother with a high school education and an annual household income less than $17,499 says she was not aware of her son's learning disability until a diagnosis was given at age six, and she reports having spent no time at all teaching herself about her son's disability before that, although she reports a moderate amount of self-education afterward—three to ten hours in the first month after diagnosis, and once a week in the present—and says she has read six articles and three books about her son's disability. She is unsure how she can help her son, however, explaining that he is behind academically and needs services immediately, but is on a waiting list and "may not be helped for another year . . . and that's not acceptable." Yet she seems an unlikely candidate to push for services from her son's school, writing on the survey that the school has been "very helpful." Instead, she hopes the survey itself will be a source of assistance. She provides her name and phone number (not requested on the survey) and writes, "He needs the help now. Please."

Interviews provided more details about parents' efforts at self-education and a clearer sense of the possible links between self-education and social class. Paula Harris, an English professor at a small liberal arts college with a five-year-old son diagnosed with Asperger syndrome (AS) at age four, suggests a fairly impressive effort at self-education. Before her son's diagnosis, she had begun reading *Raising Your Spirited Child*, a popular book that helps parents to see their "intense, sensitive, perceptive, persistent, and energetic" children as something other than disabled. Yet when she spoke to her son's teacher about this book, the teacher suggested that her son might be "mildly autistic." This suggestion came as a shock to Paula, but she went online and began to research the issue, beginning with Internet searches on the term "mild autism." She found many descriptions of AS, which finally resonated with her perceptions when she read about the need to teach AS children how to hug, a persistent problem with her own son. Before her son was diagnosed, she began getting books on AS from the library, and after diagnosis she began buying "lots of different books." She favorably compares a book by Tony Attwood, a leading author on AS, with another popular book on AS because the former provides a chapter-by-chapter discussion of specific aspects of autism, a "very thorough, well-researched, comprehensive, exhaustive discussion of what you're likely to see." In addition to more technical books like these, she got first-person accounts about AS and books to give to her son when the time came to tell him about his diagnosis. In all, she estimates having read twenty articles and more than ten books on AS. Susan Moore, the mother of a fifteen-year-old autistic boy, claims to have read "hundreds" of articles and thirty to forty books about autism. In addition, she has attended numerous seminars, including seminars led by O. Ivar Lovaas, a leading autism researcher.

DIAGNOSES

In keeping with the interest here in parents' participation in identifying disabilities, the surveys and interviews targeted parents of children with disabilities that are potentially subjective in nature. As such, it is not surprising that respondents who report that a disability was diagnosed at birth are relatively rare. The median age of diagnosis is five years. Average age of diagnosis for each disability category predictably follows from the characteristic presentation of the condition. Thus mental retardation, which can often be identified through marked delays in a child's early intellectual development or from well-defined genetic conditions such as Down syndrome, has the lowest median age of diagnosis (one and a half years).[8] Specific learning disabilities, where diagnosis often depends on an unexpected failure to perform academically, has the highest median age of diagnosis (seven and a half years). In the prolonged period between birth and diagnosis, parents have frequent opportunities to analyze their children's behavior, teach themselves about possible disabilities, and arrive at conclusions about what their children "have."

Parents often claim to have had a hand in producing a diagnosis. In response to the question, "Who first said that your child had this disability?" many parents did not choose either of the standard institutional routes of "school evaluation team" or "a personal physician or psychiatrist" but instead chose "other." Although "self" was not one of the options, twenty-one respondents (13.5 percent of all respondents) used this opportunity to indicate in some way that they had been the first (or among the first) to identify the disability or to direct others to evaluate for disability. In answering the question, a white mother (with some college education, but income and occupation not reported) of a child identified as having learning disabilities at age eight, writes, "myself, I had to convince schools." A white-Asian mother (a self-described "family CEO," household income in the $55,000 to $75,000 range, education not reported) explains her son's diagnoses with LD and ADD at age eight: "I recognized by self-educating, Dr (psychiatrist) confirmed."[9]

As in these examples, many of the parents who claim they were the first to identify their children's disabilities claim their awareness came very early, but the subjectivity of the signs delayed clinical recognition. A white mother (a teacher with a master's degree in cross-cultural education and household income in the $55,000 to $75,000 range) whose son was diagnosed at age five with pervasive developmental disorder (a condition on the autistic spectrum) claims she recognized the disability "on day born until someone (doctor) finally listened and tested him at age $4\frac{1}{2}$." Similarly, a white mother (a criminal defense lawyer with a household income in the $75,000 to $100,000 range) whose son has learning disabilities, OCD, and ADD writes, "I always knew. Psych @ Developmental Clinic @ [name of regional mental health center] agreed when son was 2.5 years old."

Karen Talbert, a white woman with a bachelor's degree in comparative literature and a household income above $100,000, described, in an interview and a survey, a prolonged struggle to have her son's multiple diagnoses recognized. After she "became an expert" on her son Sam—she estimates having read fifty books and (presumably joking) ten thousand articles on her son's disabilities—she became a "fearless advocate," which resulted in services and opportunities for her son that, she says, similar children were denied. (She was not always fearless, however. Before her first IEP meeting, she was extremely nervous and had to take antianxiety medication.) She estimates that she brought Sam to the Child Find program[10] in her area three times between ages three and five, but to no avail. In preschool, Sam was given the assignment of learning the names of all the children in his class, but Karen found he was unable to learn to match children's names to their pictures. Recalling that Sam had also confused his half-sister with a cousin, she went to the Internet and searched on "child cannot recognize faces" and found the term "face-blindness," which then led her to descriptions of Asperger syndrome. "I made the connection," she says. "And I went into school, and I said, 'This is what we see,' and they had no idea. They still didn't. They didn't quite get it." Ultimately, however, the school did recognize Sam as having AS.

In addition to claiming they had identified their children's disabilities, parents often express doubts about given diagnoses. One white mother with a master's degree in physical therapy and a household income in the $75,000 to $100,000 range says she doubted her son's diagnosis of ADD at age eight. "I knew there was something else going on," she writes. "Went to talking therapy. Got accommodations in classroom that never worked. Age 15 bought my own private psych test for son—found Asperger's and ADD and specific learning disabilities."

A white father, a medical school professor with a household income greater than $100,000, whose son was diagnosed with LD and ADD, also doubts his son's diagnosis. He explains, "brother's Asperger's Syndrome has some features of brother's ADD,"[11] apparently indicating that he believes his son diagnosed with ADD may actually have Asperger syndrome, like his brother. The original diagnoses of LD and ADD were made by a "private physician or psychiatrist" when the boy was eight, because the father doubted the school's judgment: the "school just said he was 'immature.'" At the end of the survey, the father issues this indictment of the school system: "Public schools *woefully* inadequate in addressing my ADD son's issues. Teachers often unfamiliar with his IEP and unwilling to accommodate; unwilling to expend resources to keep him at the district level, would not provide him with ed resources. I have extremely poor feeling about the expertise of the school . . . in addressing learning disabled children's needs."

Similarly, a white father (a social worker with a master's degree in social work and a household income in the $55,000 to $75,000 range) gives a good indication of some parents' skepticism about the schools' competence in diagnosing and dealing with disabilities. Explaining who first identified his son's disabilities (LD and speech and language impairments, with diagnosis at age fifteen), he writes, "I noticed it." He claims to have spent ten or more hours learning about his son's disabilities before diagnosis. Describing his conflicts with his son's school, he writes, "I believe the school's response has been superficial—the people working with my son are poorly trained and lack specific knowledge."

PARENTS' RELATIONSHIP WITH THE SCHOOL

As these latter examples suggest, parents' claim to knowledge about their children's disabilities often coexists with a skeptical attitude about the school's expertise. While schools may seek to dominate decision making in special education, existing law implicitly sanctions an assertive role for parents, and many clearly believe they are, or ought to be, in a leading role.

In general, survey respondents seem more likely to believe they teach the school about their children's disabilities than to believe the school teaches them. As table 2.2 shows, the overwhelming majority of parents, about 87 percent, agree or strongly agree that they "help the school" to understand their child's disability. While most parents also believe that the school helps them, to some degree, to understand their children, the corresponding figure is smaller, about 62 percent. When responses to these two questions are combined, as they are in the table, slightly over half of parents rate their own contribution to the school's understanding about equally with the school's contribution to theirs (their responses fall along the diagonal running from the top left corner to the lower right corner of the table), but while 38 percent rate their own contribution higher than the school's (their responses are above and to the right of the diagonal), almost none rate the school's contribution higher than their own.

That parents often see themselves as making greater contributions to knowledge about their children's disability than the school does is one sign of how they view their relationship to their children's school, but it is an ambiguous sign. Do they find this relationship appropriate or frustrating? Do they want to be in the position of teaching their children's teachers, or do they feel that the school should know more than they do, so that parents would not have to teach them? While one should remember that it is not possible to determine from this survey the overall tendencies of the population from which these parents are sampled, individual parents' responses give a sense of what at least some mean when they say they contribute more to understanding than the child's school does—a group that, for convenience, I will refer to as "dominant contributors."

TABLE 2.2 Who Helps Whom? Parents' Beliefs about Parent-School Knowledge-Sharing (% of Total Responses)

Statement 2: I have been able		Statement 1: The school has been able to help me understand my child's disability.			
		Strongly agree	Agree	Disagree	Strongly disagree
to help the school	Strongly agree	21%	7%	7%	3%
understand	Agree	3%	28%	12%	6%
my child's	Disagree	1%	2%	5%	3%
disability.	Strongly disagree	—	—	—	2%

Note: Half-point scores were assigned where respondents checked two adjacent categories for the same question (e.g., "strongly agree" and "agree").

Dominant contributors display a wide range of feelings about their relationship with the school. Some view their role in informing schools about disability as a positive form of cooperation. Others see that role as a sign of the school's inadequacies and misplaced priorities, which are a source of conflict between schools and dissatisfied parents. Often, however, individual respondents combine these perspectives, reflecting an ambivalent relationship in which they sometimes are able to contribute and experience cooperation with the school and sometimes meet resistance and experience conflict.

From one perspective, dominant contributors appear to be content with their roles. Of the fifty-nine dominant contributors, fifty agreed or strongly agreed with the statement, "In matters involving my child's disability, I have a positive relationship with my child's school." One parent who fits this description, a white nurse (household income above $100,000) with an ADD son, writes, "school has been very supportive and helpful. Teachers and support staff willing to read info and books I have given to them." Other dominant contributors who felt they had a positive relationship with the school left blank the end of the survey, where they were asked to describe any conflicts with their children's schools.

Others described conflicts but still felt they had a positive relationship, perhaps because they believed they were ultimately helping the schools to recognize and properly accommodate their children's disabilities. One dominant contributor, whose daughter was diagnosed as autistic at age three and a half, identified herself as a homemaker with a bachelor's degree in biol-ogy and an annual household income higher than $100,000. She reports that she spent more than ten hours learning about her daughter's disabil-ity *before* she was diagnosed and estimates that she has read one hundred articles and one hundred books on autism (perhaps an overestimate, but certainly not a number typical of all respondents). Despite reporting serious conflicts with the schools, she recognizes the advantages that income and education have given her in advocating for her daughter. She writes, "We had to go to mediation and fight the school district very hard to get the right placement and services for our daughter. If we had not been so educated and had the money to fight, our daughter would have lost out. (Presently, we are *very* happy with her services.)" Another dominant contributor (a nurse-practitioner with a household income above $100,000) writes that her conflicts with her child's school were "too many to list! They range from outright violation of his civil rights to failing to comply with his IEP." Nonetheless, she concludes by saying, "Despite the many conflicts over the years, we have maintained a positive relationship with the school."

Interviews often yielded evidence of a pattern in which parents had initially been discontented with the school's approach but were now com-fortable with their children's accommodations insofar as they had been able to demonstrate that the school needed to accept their input. Carla Patter-son, a white woman with a bachelor's degree in biology and psychology who owns a small business with her husband, seems to be content with the current accommodations for her son Silas, which include a one-on-one aide in a mainstream classroom, but she has had to coerce and persuade to get what she felt her son needed. For instance, at the end of Silas's fourth-grade year, Carla wanted him to attend a weeklong summer camp for children with autistic spectrum disorders. The school district resisted, arguing that the special camp was too short and that Silas would have a comparable experience at a five-week district-run camp, for a general population of stu-dents, if he were provided extra services to help him with his social skills needs. Carla, who thought Silas could not make the gains she sought in a camp where he would "once again be an 'other'" and that was not designed specifically for children on the autistic spectrum, countered by presenting a list of out-of-state programs for autistic children that were six to eight weeks long and cost $3,000 to $5,000. "*These* are comparable," she told the school. In response, the school agreed to provide for the original camp that Carla requested.

Carla speculates that the school may have been persuaded by the validity of her claim but may also have recognized that she could pose an effective legal challenge—in conflicts like these, she explains, she would never directly threaten to take the school to a due process hearing but would simply say, "It doesn't serve any of our purposes to have to take this into litigation." She goes on to explain, "They know that I know people who have gone through due process. . . . They know that I've educated myself about this stuff. They know that I know who to talk to and what . . . resources are available to me to make this happen." While she believes the school staff members are reasonably knowledgeable about AS students' needs, she has nevertheless brought "numerous" books, Web sites, and other sources of information to their attention, and they seem to incorporate this information into their practice.

Perhaps the most frustrated parents, then, are those who feel they are not allowed to contribute their own knowledge, regardless of the school's contribution. A white homemaker with a bachelor's degree in biology and a household income above $100,000 (not the same one mentioned above) "disagrees" that she helps the school to understand her child's disability and "strongly disagrees" that the school helps her to understand it. Although not a contributor to the school's understanding, she clearly feels she *should* be playing a stronger role in relation to school professionals, who themselves lack expertise:

> School personnel have the attitude that they know everything (even though they don't) and parents know very little. Parents are not treated as valuable members of the IEP team—our observations and comments matter very little. School personnel feel they need to "get to know your child first" even if this means delaying services. "Free and appropriate" education to my child's school personnel means "free and cheapest." My child is not receiving an appropriate education because school personnel refuse to acknowledge their lack of expertise in servicing high-functioning autistic children.

As this last example shows, some parents may not believe they contribute to the school's understanding but still think they ought to. One parent, the white mother of an autistic boy (graduate degree in curriculum and instruction, household income above $100,000) serves as a reminder that even relatively privileged children and their parents can be seriously mistreated (while one might question her belief that her education makes her a special target for mistreatment). She "strongly disagrees" that she has a positive relationship with the school and that knowledge is shared in either direction. The following excerpt is from a long statement detailing her struggles to get an appropriate placement for her child in the special education system:

Several complaints were made to the state concerning the appalling way our child was treated while in the district's care. He was removed from his classroom and placed in a $9' \times 7'$ space. . . . where he only occasionally saw his teacher. This was all done without our knowledge or consent. He would be man-handled by staff who had never been appropriately trained. Parents are not treated like valued members of the I.E.P. team. In fact, it's been our experience that the more educated you are on the law, your child's disability, and district policy, the greater the likelihood that you will be treated with contempt and arrogance. . . . The standard policy appears to be—dupe parents into agreeing to the I.E.P. using whatever means possible including using fraud and deception.

PARENTS WHO DO NOT FIGHT

Not all parents of disabled children battle their children's schools. There are at least three possible reasons for this. First, some parents may be fortunate enough to have their children enrolled in schools that willingly provide everything they require. Second, parents may see problems but find alternatives to fighting the school for changes. Still others might not recognize problems or not see it as worthwhile or appropriate for them to challenge the schools.

By her own account, Ann Willis seems to fit into the second category. "I just get so upset," she explains. When her daughter Rebecca, who had been identified as having a learning disability, was in the third grade, Ann did fight to have her removed from a segregated class, where little was being done to help her with her particular needs. However, she became so upset that she could not even understand what was happening in her interactions with the school, so she ultimately addressed the problems that concerned her by removing Rebecca from the public schools altogether and working one-on-one with her daughter. These adjustments were presumably facilitated by the family's income and occupational background. Ann is an English professor at a community college, and her husband, now retired, taught Spanish at a prep school and holds a PhD in philosophy. Just before their daughter reentered public school, briefly, in the eighth grade, she asked her mother, "What if it's really horrible?" Ann told Rebecca her backup plan, which included homeschooling, tutoring in French from a neighbor, and the opportunity to sit in on classes taught by her colleagues and her husband's colleagues. When Rebecca entered high school, she enrolled in a private prep school, and most of the tuition was paid through a tuition reimbursement plan included with her father's position. Ann says that they have also "done a lot of work" with Rebecca to help her overcome her reading difficulties. "I understand," Ann says, "that not everybody can just circumvent the school system."

Similarly, Michelle Hayes, a former schoolteacher who turned to computer programming when she was pregnant to increase her income, has largely avoided conflict with her daughter Bethany's school. While she has apparently invested considerable time researching Bethany's needs—concluding that her current AS diagnosis does not adequately acknowledge the severity of her language needs—she is cautious about asserting this knowledge at Bethany's school, and she suspects that her current teacher, as a new teacher, is defensive about getting advice from a former teacher. While she believes that Bethany is not receiving the services she needs at school, she has never threatened a due process hearing. "I don't like conflict," she says. "I want my daughter to think of school in a positive way." She did, however, make a sophisticated attempt to persuade the school to provide her daughter with a different reading curriculum than the one being used, which she did not like. Suspecting that Bethany had an auditory processing problem, Michelle found evidence that the reading curriculum called for strong auditory skills and had her tested for an auditory processing disorder. She gathered this information and presented it to the school, but when the school said it would not be possible to use a different curriculum, Michelle relented.

Instead of fighting the school, Michelle focuses on ways she can help Bethany directly and collaborate with the school. She works with her at home a great deal, which she believes is better than any instruction Bethany could be given by school staff, who do not know her as well. She has also developed special materials combining images and words to teach Bethany vocabulary. She brings these materials to Bethany's school, and the teachers use them not only with her daughter but, she is told, with other students as well—one teacher even suggested that Michelle "market them."

Michelle is very conscious of what it takes to be persuasive as a mother. When Bethany first came to school, Michelle was a single mother, and school staff focused on possible problems in the home environment to explain Bethany's behavioral issues. According to Michelle, everyone assumed that, being a single mother, she could not be smart or a good mother. Once she was married, however, everything changed. No one asked about the home environment anymore, and her opinions suddenly counted. In voicing these opinions, however, her background in education also mattered: "It helps if you can quote developmental psychologists' theories and names to teachers.

They'll stop and listen to you." If you mention names like Erikson and Piaget, she says, the teacher will think, "She might know something."

Other parents seem not to intervene because they simply lack the disposition to criticize their children's schools, perhaps because they lack the elite cultural capital of other parents. Belinda Stein, for instance, is the mother of an eleven-year-old boy who was diagnosed with ADHD at age three. She has some college education and is training to be a special education teacher, but she estimates that she has read only four articles and no books related to her son's disability. She has little to report in the way of conflict with her son's school, despite mentioning issues that lead other parents to serious conflicts with the school. For instance, her son has all of his academic classes in a separate special education classroom. Belinda notes that her son's classroom is filled with students with lower academic skills than his and many behavior problems. However, rather than pushing the school to mainstream her son, Belinda has accepted its judgment that her son belongs in a separate classroom. Much to her chagrin, he has become friends with the students in his segregated classroom and does not socialize well in the regular classroom. Similarly, Belinda apparently made little objection when the school announced the previous year that it was terminating his speech/language and occupational therapy services. Although she says she directly asked the school staff at the IEP meeting if they were terminating her son's services because he no longer needed them or because they wanted to save on costs, she apparently accepted at face value their explanation that his speech had improved and that he had learned to control his shaking hands on his own. She explains that it was hard to know whether they were correct. Notably, when asked to compare herself with other parents, Belinda says that she sees a lot of parents with children in special education who seem to complain about "every little thing."

Finally, while cultural capital may be important, economic capital and local opportunities are also crucial. Some parents seem to have the disposition to challenge the school but apparently lack other resources or opportunities. The mother of a girl with Rett syndrome (white, some college, household income in the $35,000 to $45,000 range), presumably unable to sue the district or to obtain service privately, writes,

> My major problem with my daughter's school is that they have *extremely* violent children in with children that are *quite* passive, therefore the passive kids are hit, scratched, bit, smacked, etc. and the school's administration director, when confronted by me, responded by saying, "If you have a problem or concern

about your child's safety, maybe you should find another program." I find this unacceptable, but my hands are tied, because there is no other program available in [city name] for my child in appropriateness.

MISRECOGNITION

From the descriptions above, it should be apparent that, among parents who advocate strongly for their children, some are conscious of the advantages their class backgrounds give them. For many, however, this consciousness often seems to be mixed with a lack of awareness. I would cautiously suggest that this lack of awareness is akin to the misrecognition that Lareau has identified with respect to social class and parenting in general education. That is, the tendency to perceive differences in parents' involvement in terms of moral and personal differences between them, rather than in terms of their class-based resources and the institutional conditions in which these resources can be used, seems to be a means by which some parents turn the issue of involvement in special education into an issue of parents' personal devotion to their children—and perhaps thereby reveal the broader culture's misrecognition of this same issue.

As I noted in the introduction, for instance, Sharon Faber was quite aware that in her own situation, paying for $200-an-hour advocates and in-home therapists for her son—which she could not have afforded after her divorce—was probably critical to what she was able to obtain for him later. Yet earlier in the interview she said she could not understand how everyone would not advocate for their children as she did: "You've got to figure out what you can do for [your children] and do it." When asked why some parents might not be as effective at advocating as she was (though she claims many *are* as effective or even more effective), she cites only age as a factor, speculating that younger parents might be more naive (not recognizing the class implications of the ages at which people have children). Similarly, Karen Talbert seems to recognize the class-specific details that undergird her successful advocacy for her son. She says, for instance, that she is effective in IEP meetings because she has "the ability to use a lot of twenty-dollar words." Yet when asked why some parents are not aggressive advocates for their children, she says, "Why am I not a rocket scientist? You know? It's just not in their personality." Paula Harris, who, like her husband, is an English professor at a small liberal arts college, understands that the school treats them differently based on their status, adding, "I don't think that's a good thing." Yet she clearly sees parents' involvement at least partly in moral terms: "I was surprised to hear that they call these IEP meetings, and nobody shows up. You know, the parents don't care."

While comments like these frequently came up in interviews, they do not tell everything about privileged parents' understanding of their own advocacy and other parents' lack of it. A few appear to place the influence of their privileges front and center. Carla Patterson, for instance, says that "plenty of kids are not getting services because their parents don't know how to advocate." She goes on to explain that her town has a high proportion of low-income, single-parent families with little exposure to the outside world. Speculating about the reasons some parents are not successful advocates, she says, "I don't think it's that they don't care, and I don't think it has anything to do with ignorance. I think it has to do with life circumstances. My husband and I are very fortunate. We own a small business. . . . he had some college, I have a college degree. We're both relatively educated. We've both had the opportunity to learn about stuff and be able to advocate."

This brings us back to an issue presented but deferred at the beginning of the chapter: the relation of parents' moral character to their advocacy. While it might not be appropriate here to make any judgments about that relation, we can see that parents make their own judgments. To say that some of these judgments are based on "misrecognition" may not be entirely fair. Parents were asked in a deliberately vague and open-ended way to compare themselves with other parents with similar children. Insofar as they were implicitly comparing themselves with disadvantaged parents primarily in moral terms, it might be correct to say they have misrecognized what advocacy is about. Furthermore, since statements like these, emphasizing parents' moral responsibility to act as advocates, tend to support a system that systematically ignores the inequities imposed by seemingly fair and egalitarian procedures (e.g., the due process rights created by the EAHCA), they may contribute to a broader misrecognition. But in answering the question, some parents may have had in mind parents like themselves, who have resources for advocacy as they have but who may not choose to advocate as strongly. Compared with these parents, the strong advocates may have some justification for feeling that their devotion to their children is stronger.

This is not to say, however, that advocacy must always be seen as virtuous. As we have seen, some parents want to avoid conflict and seek to meet their children's needs directly, by using their own time and resources. This may or may not be a superior approach. Other parents seem to see trusting the school as a better way to behave. Belinda Stein, for instance, has apparently accepted her son's placement in a separate special education classroom and the termination of his services with minimal explanation. As noted, she sees herself as different from other parents she sees, who seem to "complain about every little thing." From her perspective and that of others, strong advocacy is apparently not as virtuous as the advocates might believe it is.

CHAPTER THREE

———— ✳ ————

High Roads and Low Roads to Disability

When I was in school, kids were either bad or stupid. And then there was a ton of learning disabilities. Or everybody is ADHD—that was why they weren't learning. Now everybody who's not learning is autistic, or on the spectrum.
Laura Cray, mother of a child diagnosed with learning disabilities

The more labels you have, the more help you can get.
Michelle Hayes, mother of a child diagnosed with Asperger syndrome

AS WE SAW in chapter 1, existing law supports a certain kind of advocacy on behalf of disabled children, an advocacy that requires parents to make individualized and technical claims on their children's behalf. If the school does not already recognize that the child has a disability, then the claim of disability itself may be the first one parents make. This claim presupposes that they believe there is reason for it—that they can judge whether their child has a disability and that they have the right and responsibility to push the school to recognize and accommodate it. In chapter 2, I indicated that these beliefs may be a distinguishing trait of white, educated, middle- to upper-class families. Further, these same beliefs—as well as the education, income, social ties, and attitudes that undergird them—may be the key to gaining recognition of a disability despite the school's initial resistance, a resistance that is not uncommon. Schools may resist for a variety of reasons: a disability claim may challenge school authority; it may force the school to adopt new practices; or it may strain the school's budget.

As a result of these connections among parents' background, disability claims, and the process of gaining recognition, we can expect that some share of students would not be diagnosed with disabilities had their parents not made use of their social advantages. Yet proving that parents have produced such a diagnosis in any one instance is tricky. It presupposes that we know how the child would have appeared to others without privileged parents' advocacy and that the child's own performance and behaviors, by themselves, would not have led to a disability diagnosis. However, since these parents are in fact present, drawing attention to some children and not to others, to some facts about the child and not to others, and along the way shaping what others know and believe about the child and even what the child knows and believes about himself or herself, we can hardly begin to perceive the child as he or she is, or might have been, without their intervention. In short, our knowledge of the child is irrevocably altered by the parents' actions. Further complicating the picture, to be effective advocates parents must make the case that the child's problems are obvious and would eventually have been discovered by competent school personnel. Hence it is precisely when parents' advocacy has been effective that its influence may be hardest to detect.

Thus, as I explained in the introduction, it is difficult to directly observe how parental privilege influences the recognition of children's disabilities and related needs, because it is so hard to separate cause and effect at the individual level. Accordingly, in this book I search for indirect evidence of this influence by looking at the economic, cultural, and institutional resources generally available to privileged parents, at the attitudes and behaviors of parents in the special education system, and at the historical experiences of different groups of children in special education. In short, rather than looking for causes and effects at the individual level, I look for patterns that confirm the existence of the probable conditions and the probable outcomes of privileged parents' gaining disability diagnoses for their children. Thus, in chapter 2 I looked at how the attitudes and practices of parents with children in special education may be related to their cultural (and economic) capital. In chapter 4, I consider how the literature for parents of disabled children seems to assume a target audience composed primarily of privileged parents who are being encouraged and prepared by the literature to make disability claims. Finally, in chapter 5, I pull together various strands of the book's argument to explain how privileged parents challenge school authority through due process hearings.

In this chapter I consider whether and how privileged parents might have contributed to their children's diagnoses by examining the distribution of disability diagnoses and the factors that affect that distribution. To be properly understood, the distribution must be examined in multiple dimensions. One dimension is historical. In recent decades, the percentage of students with diagnosed disabilities has rapidly expanded. In 1976, just before the EAHCA was first implemented, the percentage of students receiving special education services was 7.99. By 1987 the figure was 9.35, and in 2002 it was 11.33—a relative increase of about 42 percent from 1976 to 2002.[1]

A second aspect of the distribution of disability diagnoses is the dimension within which disability varies by type. Historical trends are different for different disabilities, and the distribution of diagnoses across disability categories changes significantly across time. For instance, from 1976 to 2002, the number of students diagnosed with LD expanded from about 1.9 percent of the public school population to about 5.5 percent. During the same period, however, the percentage of students classified as mentally retarded rapidly declined, from about 2.7 in 1976 to 1.0 in 2002.[2] By viewing these different dimensions simultaneously—by looking at changes in rates of different diagnoses across time—we can begin to understand the complexity of each individual dimension.

A final aspect to consider is the distribution of disability diagnoses across social groups. Just as historical variation is different for different diagnoses, the joint distribution of disability in the historical and diagnosis-specific dimensions, in turn, depends on the social group being considered. That is, historical shifts in the rate of diagnosis across disability types are different for different social groups.

With these dimensions in mind, I argue that when a particular disability diagnosis is emerging (being newly identified or identified by new, broader criteria), privileged students are more likely to be overrepresented with that diagnosis. I ground this argument in the idea that privileged parents advocate for disability diagnoses precisely at the time when they are emerging. To the extent that they are successful this means, of course, that privileged parents are partly responsible for a rise in the prevalence of a diagnosis. This in turn can perhaps be linked, both as cause and as consequence, to the improving accommodations available for the particular diagnosis. As they become aware of the accommodations available to a child with a particular diagnosis, privileged parents may be motivated to use their resources to advocate for such a diagnosis. At the same time, they may have strong expectations about what will be provided to their children, so that their advocacy will, over time, tend to improve the accommodations available for the given diagnosis.

As a particular disability diagnosis ages, however, we might expect a shift in its social profile. As the diagnosis becomes institutionalized, it becomes easier for schools to recognize—more school professionals are equipped to identify and accommodate the disability, and federal or state funding for it expands. Thus schools' resistance to recognizing it will lower, making it easier for less privileged parents to persuade the school there is a disability. At the same time, when the diagnosis becomes institutionalized the school likely will find that assigning it sometimes meets school needs—for instance, that it can be used to increase funding or to segregate troublesome or slow students. We can thus expect that, as time passes, a diagnosis that was once a means for privileged students who struggle academically to obtain valued services and accommodations will become more prevalent among disadvantaged students.

As I discuss below, such a pattern can be seen most clearly for the LD diagnosis, which was most prevalent among relatively privileged children when it was first being recognized. The historical and social distribution of other diagnoses (mental retardation, ADHD, and autistic spectrum conditions) will also be discussed in this chapter, although in somewhat less detail.

To argue that rates of disability diagnosis are related to historical and social factors is not to say that disability diagnoses are simply fabricated, having no relation to a child's organic condition. Rather, before a disability can be claimed, problems must be perceived and interpreted as signs of disability. These observations and interpretations depend on a wide range of social and historical conditions.

A first condition for identifying children's disabilities is the historical establishment of disabled children's educational rights. Once their rights to special education were established, being recognized as disabled became a possible source of benefits. For parents whose children were struggling in school, including the many who struggled despite coming from relatively privileged backgrounds, a disability diagnosis could open new possibilities: individualized instruction in particular areas of need; special accommodations when taking tests and completing assignments; and, potentially, a renewed hope for academic success. Thus, unlike the past, when being identified as disabled often meant being excluded from an education, these children sought access to new benefits from within the educational system by being *identified* as disabled.

This transition, from using disability to deny educational services to using it to claim them, is followed by a period when the number of disability diagnoses steadily increases, an increase that, I argue, can be at least partially attributed to parents' own efforts to gain recognition of disability. Since a rise in the number of children in special education may entail extra effort and costs for the school—especially in the early years of special education—schools sometimes have an interest in limiting access by subjecting the claim of disability to rigorous standards of proof. This in turn implies another possible condition—not only that parents desire a particular disability diagnosis but that they can employ scientific data and reasoning to advocate for it.

Parents who use a scientific framework when making claims on their children's behalf represent a segment of a larger group of lay actors who claim expertise in medical-scientific fields. To understand the challenges parents face as lay actors claiming some scientific expertise, it is useful to consider previous research on the division between lay actors and medical professionals.

SCIENCE, MEDICINE, AND THE LAY ACTOR

In the mid-twentieth century, the American medical profession enjoyed unprecedented prestige and authority. In 1951 Talcott Parsons's description of the "sick role" in contemporary American society captured the sense of legitimacy accorded to doctors: in the sick role, Parsons claimed, individuals were not blamed for their sickness and were exempted from many ordinary social obligations, but only if they sought medical help and followed the doctor's orders. The doctor's authority over the patient was justified by the superiority of "his" scientific training and knowledge and the disinterested way "he" made decisions on the patient's behalf. At the same time, the doctor supposedly served a "gatekeeping" function in society, applying objective scientific knowledge to determine who had the right to be excused from social obligations on grounds of illness and who was "faking it." In this last regard, Parsons identified an even more crucial reason the decision-making authority of the doctor must be separated from that of the patient—the patient had too much of a stake in the doctor's decisions (to make a diagnosis or not, to medicate or not) to be trusted to contribute to them.[3]

In recent decades this view of the absolute divide between patient and physician has been eroded by sociological critiques and by the changing nature of the physician's role. Though physicians never did make decisions in an entirely autonomous fashion, they surely do so even less now. Most significant for our purposes here, there appears to be a growing tendency for patients (and would-be patients) to acquire knowledge about medical diagnoses and treatments, to arrive at their own views of their needs, and to press their views in their individual interactions with doctors and elsewhere. This has resulted in the emergence of what Steven Epstein calls "lay expertise."[4]

Yet that some lay experts successfully make claims does not mean there is no longer a barrier between lay actors and medical authority. Although lay experts have chipped away at it, the barrier is largely intact and is still high. The assumption is still strong that medicine, like science, should be left to professionals, whose detached stance conforms to the ostensible nature of science itself—impersonal, universal, and objective. Thus, surmounting the lay/professional (patient/doctor) barrier depends on lay actors becoming lay *experts*. This means acquiring and accepting much of the knowledge, language, and perspectives already recognized by the relevant professionals. Accordingly, Epstein observes that when AIDS activists succeeded in shaping AIDS researchers' beliefs about how research should be conducted, their success was "widely understood as a testament to the activists' forceful argumentation and successful mastery of the *arcana*."[5]

The research on lay interventions into science and medicine has had relatively little to say about the relation of such interventions to the lay expert's social background. One exception can be found in Epstein's research. Epstein considers it crucial that within the gay community that was the primary source of AIDS activism there were many highly educated middle-class white professional men who, as such, were more likely to have medical knowledge, to have the background and disposition favoring the acquisition of technical, scientific knowledge, and to have social ties to others with similar characteristics. Some activists had professional backgrounds in medicine but, Epstein claims, "More typically . . . the stars of the [AIDS] treatment activist movement were science novices, but ones who were unusually articulate, self-confident, and well educated" (229).

As I noted in chapter 2, there is some reason to believe that parents too may differ in their inclination to appropriate and use scientific knowledge in their parenting and, specifically, that privileged parents may see themselves as having, or being able to acquire, the knowledge of disabilities that entitles them to participate in special education decision making. This chapter, then, explores one possible outcome of this perspective by looking at disability diagnosis. In so doing, however, I go against the tendency of most previous research on the social factors underlying children's disability diagnosis. As I discuss in the following section, that research has been dominated by a concern with disadvantaged students' "overrepresentation" with particular disability diagnoses against an assumed background of a "true" (objective and unbiased) prevalence of disability.

DISPROPORTIONALITY IN SPECIAL EDUCATION

Extensive research has documented that different social groups are diagnosed with disabilities at differing rates. The bulk of this research is concerned with inequalities across racial-ethnic groups, typically claiming that children from disadvantaged minority groups are more likely to be diagnosed with disabilities than white and Asian American children. In 1968 Lloyd Dunn speculated in a groundbreaking article that many students were diagnosed as mentally retarded based on discriminatory perceptions of racial minorities, which caused inappropriate referrals and biased evaluations. In 1973 Jane Mercer affirmed that black and Mexican American students were being diagnosed as mentally retarded at disproportionately high rates owing to discriminatory testing practices. Almost thirty years later, African American students were still considerably more likely than white students to be diagnosed as mentally retarded. Similar claims have been made about African American, Hispanic, and American Indian students' greater vulnerability to the diagnoses of emotional disturbance, ADD/ADHD, and learning disability.[6]

The nearly exclusive focus on the overrepresentation of racial-ethnic minorities in special education seems to reflect a self-perpetuating cycle of research findings, data gathering, and further research on the same issues. On the one hand, this means that social class has been largely ignored as a variable. As MacMillan and Reschly notice, research after Dunn's article, which linked overrepresentation with mental retardation to a broad range of social disadvantages, has "focused on ethnic overrepresentation, largely ignoring the main effects of poverty and the interaction of poverty and ethnic group."[7] On the other hand, this means that instances where disadvantaged minority students are actually *less* likely than white students to be diagnosed with disabilities are downplayed among research findings and are seldom cited elsewhere.

To the extent that researchers do acknowledge white disability rates being higher than minority disability rates, this is generally referred to as minority "underrepresentation." One might legitimately ask why this is so, since in theory we could just as well speak of white "overrepresentation" in these cases. Since the question is never posed in the literature, its answer can only be inferred. Following one logic, we can see why, when minority disability rates are higher than majority students' rates, one might be more inclined to focus on the causes of their overrepresentation than on the causes of white underrepresentation: a long history of racial-ethnic discrimination in the United States and elsewhere shows that dominant majorities often represent disadvantaged minorities as physically inferior because of disease, deformity, or disability. By another logic, one might also explain minority *under*representation as another instance of how disadvantaged minorities are denied equal educational opportunities despite having an objective need for them.

However, such arguments must be made against the background of disability diagnoses of white students. That is, for minority students to be "over-represented" at one point and "underrepresented" at another, we must assume that white students are represented at the "right" rate. It follows from this assumption that, when minority students are diagnosed with a disability at higher rates, the difference between minority and white students corresponds to the percentage of minority students who have "false" diagnoses. Conversely, when minority students are diagnosed at lower rates, the difference corresponds to the percentage of minority students who are "true" cases but have not been diagnosed. In either case, white students' rates of diagnosis can be taken to represent the "true" rate.

The distinction between true and false diagnoses is surely useful, even if the ambiguity of diagnoses such as ADHD, LD, or Asperger syndrome should make us cautious about seeing the distinction as absolute. However, to speak of the ways minority students are given false diagnoses or denied true ones while ignoring the distinct social processes any diagnosis, true or false, must pass through is to subscribe to what David Bloor calls "the sociology of error." The sociology of error describes an outdated notion in which only scientific errors require a sociological explanation, while scientific truths are imagined to be self-sufficient, coming from nowhere. To criticize the sociology of error is not to say there is no such thing as error. I argue, in fact, that privileged students *are* more likely to be given accurate diagnoses—that is, diagnoses that distinguish particular needs based in some bona fide physiological or developmental difference from most students. Yet it is just as important to understand how this accurate identification of needs occurs as to understand what happens when it does not.

Contrary to the reigning assumptions, minority students have not always been diagnosed with disabilities at higher rates than white students. The clearest evidence of this comes from the early years of the learning disability (LD) diagnosis. In fact, it was often claimed in the 1970s and early 1980s that LD was a white, middle-class condition, a claim supported by research showing that white, middle-class children were, in fact, "overrepresented" with LD.[8] In recent years, however, the reverse pattern is generally claimed—

that is, that minority students are overrepresented with LD, as with other conditions.[9] This history, which I summarize below, leads me to argue that there are two "roads" to LD, which I shall call a "high road" and a "low road."

LEARNING DISABILITY: THE HIGH ROAD

At its inception, LD was arguably the creation of white, middle- to upper-class parents. The term "learning disabilities" was first coined by Samuel Kirk in 1963 at a conference held by the Fund for Perceptually Handicapped Children. The Fund was headquartered in the wealthy suburb of Evanston, Illinois, and was run by a group of "well-resourced" parents.[10] In the year following Kirk's presentation, some of the same parents formed a new organization, using Kirk's term in its name: the Association for Children with Learning Disabilities (ACLD), which later became the Learning Disabilities Association. This group became an important advocacy organization, and in 1985 it issued a definition of learning disabilities that became one of several influential definitions in circulation.[11]

After LD was broadly accepted as a real diagnosis, privileged parents were probably instrumental in its being applied at the individual level as well. James Carrier claims that the early construction of LD was particularly embraced by middle-class parents, who found it to be "the most desirable label for a failing child."[12] Citing studies from the late 1960s and early 1970s, Carrier notes that middle-class parents would have been in a particularly advantageous position to support LD diagnoses for their children because they had the wealth and disposition to participate in professional decision making. Furthermore, middle-class children were perhaps more likely to be diagnosed with LD because average to above-average IQs—one common criterion of LD diagnosis—are more likely among middle-class children than among disadvantaged children. LD, in other words, was (and often still is) defined in part as the cause of academic failure for students whose IQ would lead one to expect academic success. This also made the LD diagnosis more attractive than others, insofar as it suggested that LD was quite different from being "stupid"—something that parents' organizations such as the Association for Children with Learning Disabilities emphasized by pushing special education professionals to adopt definitions of LD that not only distinguished LD from mental retardation but made the two mutually exclusive.

The early road to LD, then, was a "high road" in three senses: first, it was created with the support of privileged parents; second, it afforded students certain advantages that otherwise might not have been available; and third, after the diagnosis itself was created, it was relatively privileged parents who could and did pursue it. The third point must also be considered in light of the fact that before LD was widely recognized, schools were apt to resist acknowledging its existence, and recognition often depended on the intervention of parents with relevant knowledge and an ability to advocate effectively.

At the individual level, parents presumably had to push to have the new disability label recognized. As I discussed in chapter 2, many privileged parents with children in special education regard themselves as knowledgeable actors with the right and responsibility to intervene in their children's education. Such an orientation is clearly relevant if schools are seen as lacking expertise on disabilities. In a letter printed in the October 24, 1982, issue of the *Los Angeles Times,* Frieda Gockel, the mother of a learning disabled child and president of the California chapter of the ACLD, wrote, "Because many teachers have little or no knowledge about learning disabilities, it is very important that parents gain as much knowledge as they can, follow up on their gut-level feelings and concerns and persist in getting proper diagnosis and help for their child." Needless to say, taking on this role normally requires substantial self-confidence and cultural capital.

LEARNING DISABILITY: THE LOW ROAD

We can also speak of a "low road" to LD, which emerges over time as the increasing institutionalization of LD has made LD diagnosis a relatively easy way for schools to remove disadvantaged students from the regular classroom. Thus LD diagnosis follows a low road as, increasingly, an important consideration in making the diagnosis is meeting the school's needs, not the possible benefit to the student from a diagnosis and related accommodations. Another characteristic of a "low road" is that diagnoses and accommodations are applied to disadvantaged children, whose parents, in turn, lack the necessary resources to participate in decision making. Hence LD increasingly becomes a road that disadvantaged students travel to further disadvantages.

There are a variety of reasons we might expect an increase over time in disadvantaged minority students' representation among all students diagnosed with LD. Once the LD diagnosis was institutionalized in the 1980s and beyond, little extra effort was required for schools to recognize a student as learning disabled. With increasing legal pressure to minimize the number of minority children diagnosed as mentally retarded,[13] the same effects of disadvantage and discrimination that had once produced high rates of mental retardation diagnosis among minority students were more likely to be expressed through an LD diagnosis.[14] Furthermore, the rise of the LD diagnosis coincides with growing pressure to place disadvantaged students in special education. Budget cutbacks and crises in large urban school districts, often with large proportions of minority students, create pressure to increase federal and state funding through special education placements. The emergence of high-stakes testing has also led schools needing to show improvement to place their low-scoring students (who are especially likely to be from disadvantaged minority groups) in special education classrooms where they have been, until recently, exempt from testing. Finally, the gradual implementation of racial desegregation in school districts has, according to Tamela McNulty Eitle, been met with a backlash among white parents, who pressure schools to place more minority students in special education, thereby "resegregating" their children's schools.[15]

There is also some reason to believe the road to LD is now a low road in that it is disadvantageous to those so diagnosed. For instance, studies on special education funding show that, within a variety of disability categories, including LD, less is spent per capita for minority students than for white students. Minority students diagnosed with LD are also more likely to be placed in a separate classroom or a separate institution than are white students with the same diagnosis. Segregating students with disabilities, of course, is not necessarily bad for them. However, since the current trend in advocacy for students with learning disabilities is toward including them in the regular classroom, the higher proportions of minority students in separate placements may very well reflect racial discrimination.[16]

LEARNING DISABILITY IN CALIFORNIA, 1976–2002

For reasons already discussed, it would be difficult to show parents' role (initially critical, then declining in importance) in directly producing disability diagnoses. Nevertheless, if the preceding argument is accurate, we might still hope for indirect evidence of this role from data on the students diagnosed with LD. Initially, LD students should be predominantly middle to upper class. Over time, they should be increasingly likely to be poor and minority students. Because data on students' social class and disability status are not available for the relevant time periods, I have instead conducted an analysis, using historical data from California school districts, that roughly estimates students' social class through the use of more readily available data on race, as I explain below.[17]

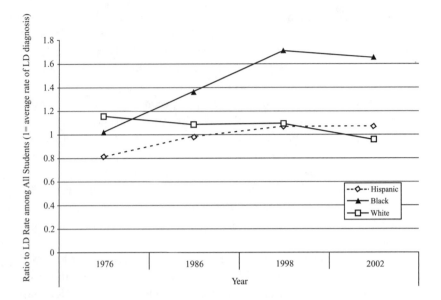

FIGURE 3.1 Historical patterns in relative rates of LD diagnosis by racial-ethnic group. Data source: Elementary and Secondary School Compliance Reports, Office for Civil Rights, U.S. Department of Education.

Figure 3.1 shows the ratio of different racial groups' rates of LD diagnosis to the average rate in specific years. These rates reveal in a fairly simple manner a shift in the representation of racial-ethnic groups with LD in the direction the "high road/low road" hypothesis would lead us to expect if we accept for the time being that white students are both privileged by race and more likely to be privileged by social class than black and Hispanic students. We can see, for instance, that in 1976 white students were diagnosed with LD at a rate higher than the average, while black students were diagnosed at close to the overall average LD rate and Hispanic students were diagnosed at well below the average rate. (That the white LD rate is not itself close to the overall average rate [1.0], even though whites are the majority, can be explained in terms of the very low rates for Hispanic students and for Asian students, who are not represented here, and the nonproportionality of ratios—distance below 1.0 being more significant than distance above.)

By 1986 the overall rate of LD diagnosis had increased by about 2.9 percent from the 1976 rate of 1.6 percent (a sign of its increasing institutionalization) at the same time as black and Hispanic students' LD rates rose relative to the white LD rate—again, as the high road/low road hypothesis leads us to expect. The black rate rose to a point well above the white LD rate, while the Hispanic rate came closer to the white rate but still remained slightly below it. The same trend occurs between 1986 and 1998, with the black LD rate now much higher than the overall rate (about 1.7 times the overall rate) and the Hispanic rate nearly the same as the white rate. By 2002 both black and Hispanic students were diagnosed with LD at rates higher than white students.

Lacking solid historical data linking students' social class to their diagnostic status, it is necessary to find other means of supporting the argument that middle- to upper-class children are initially more likely to be diagnosed with LD. It is possible, using these same data, to make some observations that may be more closely related to students' social class than to their race alone. Specifically, by adding a variable at the school-district level measuring the percentage of within-district students from disadvantaged minority groups, we can obtain a very rough proxy for the districts' social class profile, since the percentage of disadvantaged minority students in a district is negatively correlated with the social class position of its students, a correlation that may be especially salient in California.[18]

Figures 3.2 through 3.5 illustrate the historical change in the effect of this variable on relative rates of LD diagnosis. These figures graph the change in relative rates of LD diagnosis across districts with different racial compositions, running from the districts with the lowest proportions of minority students to those with the highest proportions. By grouping districts into five groups with roughly similar proportions of minority students and graphing the ratio of different groups' rates of LD diagnosis to the cross-district, cross-race average, we can see the effects of a district's racial composition (which, again, I take to be a proxy for social class) on LD rates, apart from individual students' race. While this method lends itself well to visual representation, it does not allow for variation within district "fifths" and does not tell us about the actual strength of the apparent associations. More rigorous statistical models have been estimated using these same data (although the results are not presented here), and statistically significant findings from these models support the claims below.[19]

Figure 3.2 shows a breakdown of LD rates across districts with differing proportions of minority students in 1976. As seen in figure 3.1, 1976 was a year in which white students were diagnosed with LD at higher rates than minority students.[20] However, in figure 3.2 black students are generally diagnosed with LD at a higher rate than white students, while Hispanic students' rate hovers around the white rate. This reveals that the overall tendency for minority students to be diagnosed at lower rates in 1976 is a

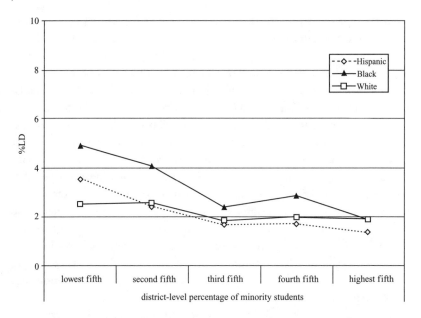

FIGURE 3.2 Average district-level LD rates by race-ethnicity and district minority percentage, 1976. Data source: Elementary and Secondary School Compliance Reports, Office for Civil Rights, U.S. Department of Education.

consequence of the lower rates of diagnosis in the *districts* minority students are enrolled in. That is, within districts with similar proportions of minority students, minority students are diagnosed with LD at rates close to or above the white rate, but because minority students are disproportionately enrolled in high-minority districts, where LD rates are low *for all groups,* the overall LD rate for minority students is lower than the rate for white students. Presumably this partially reflects students' social class, since students enrolled in high-minority districts should, on average, have a lower social class position than students in other districts. The pattern observed in figure 3.2, then, gives some support to the first part of the high road/low road hypothesis.

Corresponding to the second part of the hypothesis is the gradual shift across the years from the pattern observed in 1976 to something more closely resembling parallel, widely spaced horizontal lines. This later trend, where the LD rate remains relatively flat across districts, suggests that the LD diagnosis is now institutionalized, that is, recognized more or less uniformly across school districts. It also apparently reveals that, as the LD diagnosis becomes institutionalized, within-district discrimination rises, since the distance between lines increases, with black students being diagnosed at

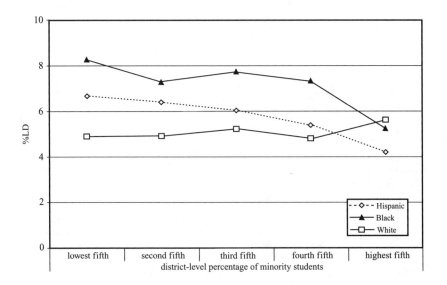

FIGURE 3.3 Average district-level LD rates by race-ethnicity and district minority percentage, 1986. *Data source*: Elementary and Secondary School Compliance Reports, Office for Civil Rights, U.S. Department of Education.

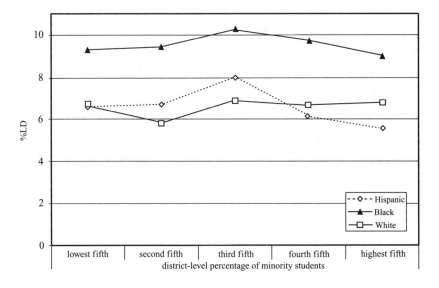

FIGURE 3.4 Average district-level LD rates by race-ethnicity and district minority percentage, 1998. Data source: Elementary and Secondary School Compliance Reports, Office for Civil Rights, U.S. Department of Education.

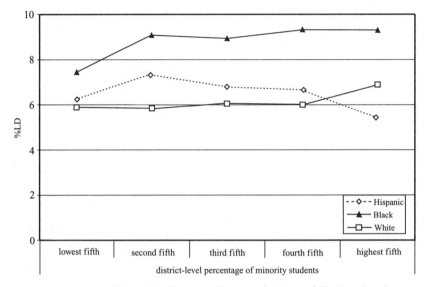

FIGURE 3.5 Average district-level LD rates by race-ethnicity and district minority percentage, 2002. Data source: Elementary and Secondary School Compliance Reports, Office for Civil Rights, U.S. Department of Education.

rates well above those of white students in every category of school district in both 1998 and 2002. While the pattern is less pronounced for Hispanic students, it is still true that by 2002 they are diagnosed with LD at higher rates than white students in four out of five school-district categories.

The thesis here should not apply only to learning disabilities. Children might be expected to travel high or low roads to other disability diagnoses for reasons similar to those I have proposed for LD. In the following, I will briefly discuss other disability diagnoses by considering their social meaning, their distribution, and the likelihood that parents are involved in advocating for them. Owing in part to a lack of comparable historical data, I do not present the same kinds of statistical analysis for these diagnoses.

HIGH ROADS AND LOW ROADS TO
OTHER DISABILITIES

Mental Retardation

If LD was the first disability parents sought out, this is perhaps because of the more stigmatizing nature of most disabilities that preceded it, the most notable being mental retardation.[21] As a consequence of its stigmatizing nature, there probably never has been and never is likely to be a "high road" to mental retardation. In other words, it is difficult to imagine that well-resourced parents would often seek out a diagnosis of mental retardation for their children. Indeed, mental retardation is in a sense the low road against which the high road to LD was initially defined, inasmuch as parents and researchers often described LD and its precursor, minimal brain damage, as difficulties with learning *not* caused by the cognitive deficits of mental retardation, which were generally understood as imposing intrinsic limits on learning. It is also indicative of the low status of mental retardation that disadvantaged minority students have often been diagnosed as mentally retarded at disproportionately high rates and that some early class-action lawsuits were attempts to *resist* a diagnosis of mental retardation. These attempts presumably explain some of the decline in minority mental retardation diagnosis over the past thirty years, which can be seen in figure 3.6. Notably, however, as recently as 2000, black students were still diagnosed as mentally retarded at considerably higher rates than white students.

That mental retardation diagnoses can fluctuate in this manner clearly indicates the somewhat subjective nature of the category, which may reside in the decision to refer a child for evaluation, in the testing methods used, or in the weight given to the child's "adaptive functioning" in nonacademic environments. Accordingly, a fairly high percentage of mental retardation diagnoses—recent estimates are in the 30–50 percent range—cannot be traced to a specific organic cause.[22] Of course, this also leaves a substantial proportion of mental retardation diagnoses thought to be traceable to a *known* organic cause. Some causes, such as Down syndrome, which is defined by readily identifiable chromosomal abnormalities, are seen as inevitably tied to mental retardation or, at least, to low-average cognitive ability.

In the past, when a given diagnosis of mental retardation seemed inevitable, many parents sought to disown the problem. In the 1950s and 1960s, psychologists and physicians commonly—though not universally—advised parents to have their mentally retarded children institutionalized in order to preserve the "togetherness" of the remaining family members.[23] Underlying such advice was perhaps the understanding that mental retardation could stigmatize whole families. Although the American eugenics movement declined after World War II, mental retardation was still, according to Katherine Castles, "often viewed as part of a more general, genetically based social deviance that might reveal the 'bad stock' of the entire family."[24] The pressure to dissociate oneself from the mentally retarded child could therefore be strong.

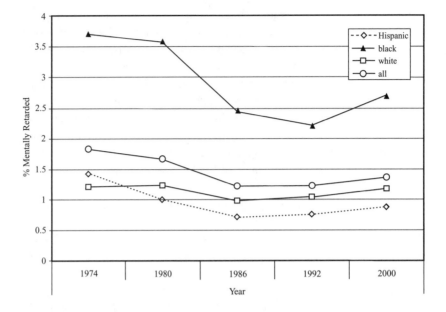

FIGURE 3.6 Mental retardation by racial-ethnic group, United States, 1974 to 2000. Data source: Elementary and Secondary School Compliance Reports, Office for Civil Rights, U.S. Department of Education.

For families who could afford private placements for their retarded children, this perhaps also seemed like an appealing way of avoiding the stigma and difficulty associated with keeping the child at home. For example, shortly after the birth of his son Neil, doctors informed the noted psychologist Erik Erikson that Neil had Down syndrome. Following the doctors' advice, Erikson decided to have Neil placed in an institution, where he spent the rest of his life, dying at age twenty-one. For years the Eriksons kept Neil's existence hidden from their other children, claiming he had died at birth.[25] While less well-off families might have been able to place their mentally retarded children in publicly funded institutions, space was limited. Thus some of the less privileged parents who wanted an institutional placement but could not afford a private one may have been obliged to care for their children themselves, while parents with more resources were able to hide the presence of mental retardation in their families.

Even fairly well-off parents could face enormous costs in placing their mentally retarded children in residential institutions. In the *PARC* case mentioned in chapter 1, for instance, one of the plaintiffs, a lawyer whose mentally retarded fifteen-year-old daughter was enrolled in a residential school, testified that his daughter's school cost him $12,000 annually—over half the median value of a house in the United States at that time.[26] He contends, "The moment a public facility is indicated, even just on the drawing board or on brochures, or papers of any kind which will look reasonably appropriate, I will assure Your Honors that ninety-five per cent or more of all parents will rush to get their children in there because every one of the parents is laboring under a backbreaking financial burden."[27]

In referring to "every one of the parents" as "laboring under a backbreaking financial burden," he presumably omits, in a fairly typical manner, the families who were simply unable to afford any type of private services for their children.

While some privileged parents, by using their resources to have their mentally retarded children placed in separate homes, may have been trying to distance themselves from the stigma of mental retardation or simply to make their lives easier, others led the way in demanding that their children have the right to public education and that families with mentally retarded children be accepted into the community of "normal" families. In much the same way that middle-class parents demanded the recognition and accommodation of learning disabilities, some middle-class parents of mentally retarded children demanded the schools recognize that, given the right educational accommodations, their children's failure was not inevitable. Although membership in organizations for parents of mentally retarded children could be diverse, historical accounts emphasize the role of those organizations in achieving the goals of middle-class parents and in representing mental retardation itself as a problem of "normal" white, middle-class families.[28]

Some interesting parallels can be drawn between parents' relationship with mentally retarded children and their relationship with LD children. Initially, the very presence of mentally retarded children in public schools (as opposed to their complete exclusion) was the result of middle-class parents' initiatives. In the 1950s, well before any federal law guaranteed such children's educational rights, it was well-resourced parents at the state and local levels who were gaining access to the public schools for their retarded children. As with LD in the early years, schools were not eager to accommodate large numbers of mentally retarded children in their programs. In this sense, for a retarded child simply to be enrolled in school was often a mark of the family's resources. However, once retarded children's right to an education was established—and there was funding to support it—schools were able to use the mental retardation diagnosis as a way of discriminating against their least advantaged students. Presumably this outcome was not intended by the parent groups that originally lobbied for public education for retarded children.

ATTENTION DEFICIT/HYPERACTIVITY DISORDER

In 1980 the American Psychiatric Association introduced a new term to the third edition of its *Diagnostic and Statistical Manual of Mental Disorders* (DSM-III): "attention deficit disorder" (ADD). This replaced and revised the previous category of "hyperkinesis"—roughly speaking, a more clinical term for "hyperactivity." In 1987 a revised version of DSM-III changed the term to "attention deficit/hyperactivity disorder" (ADHD), which it has remained to the present. In the 1990s, the number of American children and adults diagnosed with ADHD exploded. By one estimate, the number of ADHD diagnoses in the United States was about 900,000 in 1990 and reached almost 5 million in 1998.[29] At the same time, the terms "ADHD" and "ADD" entered the popular vocabulary. A search of the online LexisNexis database, for instance, locates 9 articles in the *New York Times* using the phrase "attention deficit disorder" between 1985 and 1989, 44 articles between 1990 and 1994, 147 articles between 1995 and 1999, and 227 articles between 2000 and 2005.[30]

While there is some evidence of high and low roads to ADHD, identifying those roads is difficult, especially owing to lack of data specifically identifying ADHD students. However, as I will indicate, a diagnosis of ADHD may encourage parental advocacy insofar as it is, like the LD diagnosis, a relatively nonstigmatizing way to obtain valued accommodations.

Data on ADHD diagnoses are scarce: estimates have sometimes been made based on the number of prescriptions for Ritalin, once the drug most commonly used for treating ADHD. (Currently, Adderall is said to be more popular.) Unlike LD and mental retardation, ADHD is not a condition that educational agencies are required to tabulate and report to the federal government. Indeed, until the U.S. Department of Education issued a memorandum on ADHD in September 1991, it was unclear whether it could even be a basis for special education accommodations.[31] After this memorandum, it was left to state and local education agencies to decide whether they would classify their ADHD students as having a "specific learning disability," "serious emotional disturbance," or "other health impairment." ADHD was thereby recognized as a condition that potentially qualified students for special education services, but it was not recognized as a specific category for reporting. A report released by the Centers for Disease Control and Prevention in 2005 (described below) provides perhaps the first reliable estimates of how ADHD diagnosis varies across social groups.

ADHD researchers identify three basic dimensions of the condition: inattention, impulsivity, and hyperactivity. As with many mental and behavioral conditions, the underlying causes of ADHD remain elusive, and there are no physical markers or neurological tests that demonstrate its presence. The disorder itself, then, is essentially synonymous with its symptoms.

Technically, the ADHD diagnosis replaced hyperkinesis in the 1980 DSM-III. However, this replacement meant broadening the diagnostic criteria, which in part made possible the dramatic expansion in the number of children eligible for diagnosis.[32] The relatively rare diagnosis of hyperkinesis was replaced with a diagnosis that, by 1997, was estimated by the American Academy of Child and Adolescent Psychiatry to be the most common category for referrals to child and adolescent psychiatric health services.[33] The expansion of the ADHD category was not only an indication of a broadened sense of an existing medical condition, but also part of a broader shift in psychiatry away from psychoanalytic, talk-based therapy and toward the identification of symptom-defined disorders, the use of pharmacological therapies, and a belief in the biological origin of psychiatric problems.

ADHD researchers see the rise in ADHD diagnoses as evidence of expanding awareness of problems that have always existed in more or less the same form and have always been observable. Thus it is often claimed that long before the ADHD diagnosis existed, researchers had documented clusters of traits in their subjects that would later be recognized as ADHD. Most discussions of the historical origins of ADHD begin with George Still. Still was a physician at King's College Hospital in London around the turn of the twentieth century who claimed to have observed a particular organic "defect of moral control," distinguishable from intellectual defects, in a group of twenty children. Russell Barkley, an ADHD researcher and a leading author on ADHD, speaks confidently of the connection of ADHD to past research, specifically citing Still when he writes, "The actual nature of the disorder has changed little, if at all, from descriptions nearly a century ago," a claim that is at best dubious.[34]

Whether or not one accepts Barkley's claim that ADHD was already recognized by the early twentieth century, the recent expansion of the diagnosis must still be explained. Which actors were involved in promoting improved recognition and what vested interests in it do they have? What barriers to recognition have they overcome? How broadly does improved recognition extend into the lay population? And finally, what constitutes "recognition"? Critics doubt there is any bona fide diagnosis to be recognized. Child psychiatrist John Rosemond, for instance, facetiously suggests that inattention, impulsivity, and hyperactivity are "not ADHD, but TIP, Toddlerhood in Perpetuity," the result of lax parenting, not brain chemistry. A milder critic like Lawrence Diller argues that ADHD is a real condition but that the enormous growth of the diagnosis is partially the consequence of "ADD-ogenic" conditions in families, schools, and the broader society. Yet such criticisms also do not explain when and why behaviors that are at least partly social in origin come to be seen as having organic causes.[35]

Identifying causes for the expansion of alleged symptoms of ADHD—for example, bad parenting or a "fast-paced" culture—also cannot fully explain why ADHD diagnoses expanded, for someone must also allege that these symptoms are symptoms, and they must somehow make the allegations stick. Schools, of course, may play this role. Indeed, they might have a particular incentive to do so. If a child who is distracted and impulsive in class is given an ADHD diagnosis, then it is likely that he or she will be given a stimulant medication like Ritalin or Adderall, treatment that will control many behavior problems without the teacher's having to do anything.

However, unlike LD and mental retardation, ADHD is a diagnosis made by a medical doctor, not a school psychologist. Thus schools may suggest that a child be evaluated for ADHD, but this evaluation and any subsequent diagnosis will normally be done by a physician provided by the child's parents. Ordinarily, before a child is given an ADHD diagnosis, then, parents must either see a potential problem themselves or be persuaded by the school that a problem exists and subsequently obtain an appointment for an evaluation with a pediatrician or child psychiatrist.

There is some evidence that privileged parents are more likely to be involved with ADHD diagnosis in these ways. A number of studies have attempted to determine differences between white and minority parents and between high-income and low-income parents in relation to the ADHD diagnosis. Bussing, Schoenberg, and Perwien find, for instance, that white and high-income parents have greater knowledge of the ADHD diagnosis than poor and minority parents. In another study, Bussing et al. interviewed parents whose children the researchers had independently found to have ADHD and examined the factors determining whether the children were already diagnosed with ADHD and being treated for it. They identified a number of "barriers" to diagnosis and treatment, finding that poor and minority children's parents were less likely to believe that being diagnosed with ADHD could have positive results, were more likely to see disability diagnosis as stigmatizing, and were less inclined to see schools as playing a helpful role in identifying and accommodating ADHD. Accordingly, poor and minority students were more likely than other students not to have been diagnosed with ADHD. Practically speaking, low-income parents are also less likely to have regular access to primary-care physicians who could establish an ADHD diagnosis or make referrals to specialists. It is not surprising, then, that low-income parents, when explaining why they did not take the steps toward ADHD diagnosis, cited financial barriers as well as greater concerns about stigma and less confidence about the possible benefits of such a diagnosis. Yet one trait more prevalent among higher-income parents *was* associated with a decreased likelihood of seeking an ADHD diagnosis: higher-income parents were more likely to believe their children did not have any special needs.[36]

While these and other studies seem to suggest that ADHD rates should be higher among white, high-income students than in the general population, there is only limited direct evidence of this. Indeed, a recent report on children aged four to seventeen released by the Centers for Disease Control and Prevention indicates a more complex picture. On the one hand, "advantaged" children were found to be diagnosed at higher rates than disadvantaged children across a number of contrasts: Hispanic children versus non-Hispanic; children in families where the primary language spoken is not English versus those in English-primary homes; boys in poverty-level families versus boys in higher-income families; and children in families without heath-care coverage versus children with coverage. On the other hand, the positive association of ADHD with social privilege was not confirmed or was even reversed in a number of ways: girls showed no significant differences across income levels; there was no significant difference between black and white students; and children in families with the highest education levels had lower ADHD rates than children in families with less education, although the rate was also lower for the least educated families.[37]

It is also not clear whether there is a true high road to ADHD diagnosis in terms of the benefits it provides to students. There are certainly reasons to believe the diagnosis might be advantageous. Stimulants like Ritalin have been shown since the late 1970s to provide a boost on tests of academic skills, both to students diagnosed with ADHD (or hyperkinesis) and to "normal" students. Behavioral changes—especially reduced hyperactivity—are also consistently produced.[38]

ADHD diagnosis alone can also be the basis for valuable educational accommodations. The U.S. Department of Education identifies three components to educational accommodations that teachers can use for students with ADHD: academic instruction (e.g., providing students with an advance overview of the lesson plan and giving ADHD students extra time on quizzes and tests); behavioral interventions (e.g., consistently praising positive behavior and selectively ignoring negative behavior); and classroom accommodations (e.g., providing a low-distraction environment for ADHD students during study time and during tests).[39]

Research suggests that such accommodations help students with disabilities like LD and ADHD and, in some cases, students without disability diagnoses. In some cases it appears that privileged parents are quite aware of the advantages that may come from even a fraudulent ADHD diagnosis, and whether or not they truly believe their children are disabled, they may draw on their social connections and personal wealth to obtain ADHD diagnoses from willing physicians. At the very least, this seems to describe parents who obtain last-minute ADHD diagnoses in order to win accommodations when their children take the Scholastic Aptitude Tests.[40]

Yet there are also reasons to question whether obtaining ADHD diagnosis and treatment is truly advantageous. Numerous concerns have been raised about possible negative side effects of children's stimulant use. Some studies suggest, for instance, that Ritalin may cause insomnia, abdominal pain, weight loss, irritability, anxiety, heart problems, and social withdrawal. Although these problems may not impair academic performance, data on long-term academic improvement among children taking stimulants have been inconsistent, and there have been claims that Ritalin limits users' creativity, although relevant findings here have also been inconsistent.[41]

In light of these concerns and the considerable costs of long-term use of prescription stimulants, some parents have felt that their own attempts to learn about and seek ADHD diagnosis have wasted money and may have harmed their children. In Texas, California, and New Jersey, class-action lawsuits have been filed by parents alleging a conspiracy to boost Ritalin sales by exaggerating the prevalence of ADHD and the effectiveness of Ritalin in treating it. The coconspirators named by the lawsuit were Novartis Pharmaceuticals Corporation, the primary supplier of Ritalin; Children and Adults with Attention Deficit/Hyperactivity Disorder (CHADD), a nonprofit organization; and the American Psychiatric Association.[42]

The naming of CHADD as a coconspirator, based on the 1995 revelation by the U.S. Drug Enforcement Agency that Novartis had donated $748,000 to CHADD from 1991 to 1994, is particularly interesting. By identifying CHADD's role in misinforming parents, these parents acknowledge their own role in identifying and accommodating disabilities and the obligation of organizations like CHADD to support parents in that role. The high road to disability, it seems, has its risks.

THE AUTISTIC SPECTRUM

Of the conditions I consider in this book, conditions in "the autistic spectrum"—including "classic" autism and Asperger's syndrome—are perhaps the most dynamic and enigmatic. Controversies abound about causes of autism, causes of recent increases in the number of autism diagnoses, and appropriate modes of treatment. In the 1960s it was widely accepted in the psychiatric community that autism was caused by upbringing. This "parent blaming" argument essentially held that parents—in particular mothers—caused their children to be autistic by emotionally rejecting them. Leo Kanner, who first identified early infantile autism as "children's *inability to relate themselves* in the ordinary way to people and situations from the beginning of life,"[43] is also credited with the notion that autism was caused by the emotionally detached parenting of "refrigerator mothers." In 1956 Kanner, with his colleague Leon Eisenberg, concluded from the record of case histories of autistic children that "these children were, in general, conceived less out of a positive desire than out of an acceptance of childbearing as part of the marital contract. Physical needs were attended to mechanically and on schedule according to the rigid precepts of naïve behaviorism applied with a vengeance. One can discern relatively few instances of warmth and affection. The usual parental attitude is cold and formal; less commonly, it is laden with great anxiety."[44] A 1960 profile of Kanner in *Time* discussed his research on autistic children, noting, "All too often this child is the off-spring of highly organized, professional parents, cold and rational—the type that Dr. Kanner describes as 'just happening to defrost enough to produce a child.'"[45] In 1967 Bruno Bettelheim's highly successful book on his work with autistic children, *The Empty Fortress*, also suggested that parents were to blame for their children's autism and compared mothers of autistic children to concentration camp guards.

In arguing that cold, impersonal parents were at least in part to blame for children's autism, Kanner's work had also repeatedly alluded to the social traits of these parents—in particular, their tendency to be highly educated professionals. Later work claimed a positive association between parents' high social class characteristics and their children's chances of being autistic, although other work did not confirm this association.[46]

While the notion that parents are to blame for their children's autism has largely been discredited, the question of allegedly higher rates of autism diagnosis among educated professionals remains. This question usually translates to whether privileged parents use their resources to obtain autism diagnoses for their children. In a 2002 study of autistic patients being served by the California Department of Developmental Services (DDS), Croen, Grether, and Selvin discovered that the likelihood of autism was significantly higher for children whose mothers had more education. Specifically, they found that women with a postgraduate education had a four times greater risk of having an autistic child than women with less than a high school education, and twice the risk after adjusting for a number of education-related factors and child characteristics. The authors primarily consider the social factors that might link autism diagnosis (not autism itself) to social class. They suggest, "Families with the advantages of more education... may be more successful in navigating the often-difficult process of intake and diagnosis that is a prerequisite to a determination of eligibility [for DDS services]."[47]

This kind of argument implies that parents' involvement in the diagnostic process is partly the cause of the recent increase in autism diagnoses. In 2002 this increase was dramatically confirmed by a report showing that the number of autistic people being served by the California Department of Developmental Services had increased by 273 percent between 1987 and 1998.[48] There is good reason to expect that at least part of the increase is due to historical changes in diagnostic criteria. Uta Frith, for instance, notes that researchers' estimates of autism's prevalence were very low when the diagnostic criteria used were those established by Leo Kanner—for instance, a 1966 study put the rate at about 4.5 per 10,000 people. The two criteria established by Kanner, with his colleague Leon Eisenberg, were social aloofness and impairment in imaginative play. Later researchers set out to determine the actual distribution of a broader set of characteristics associated with classic autism, which Frith describes as follows: "severe social impairment, defined as inability to engage in reciprocal two-way interaction, especially with peers; severe communication impairment, defined as inability to communicate by both verbal and nonverbal means; and severe impairment in the pursuit of imaginative activities with the substitution of repetitive behavior."[49] Data analysis using these broader criteria determined that the combination of aloofness and impairment of imaginative play specified by Kanner and Eisenberg's criteria was relatively rare. The former was a specific form of social impairment found mainly in individuals with low IQs, while the latter was difficult to discern until higher levels of intelligence were present. Other combinations of autistic traits were found to be more common, and with these new combinations as the basis for diagnosis, estimates for the rate of all autistic spectrum disorders are now about 60 in 10,000, or about thirteen times the rate estimated in 1966.[50]

Some researchers and many parents, however, argue that, whatever the effects of changing diagnostic criteria may be, the increase of autism diagnoses still reflects a true increase in prevalence, attributed to various environmental causes. Among the alleged causes, the best known are those related to children's vaccinations—in particular, the presence of the mercury-based vaccine preservative thimerosal. Proponents of a thimerosal-autism link claimed further support for their argument when it was recently discovered that the incidence of autism cases had stopped expanding in 2002 and even showed some signs of declining thereafter,[51] a pattern they explained by historical changes in vaccination practice. The number of vaccines mandated in the United States for children before age two, many of which contained thimerosal, doubled in the 1990s, exactly when the number of autism diagnoses was expanding.[52] By 1998 thimerosal was being phased out, and by 2002, when the number of new autism diagnoses apparently began to decline, a cohort of children who had largely avoided vaccines with thimerosal reached the ages at which they could be diagnosed with autism.[53]

However, the argument for an autism-vaccination link has been sustained against strong opposition from research claiming there is no such link. For instance, in 2002 the *Journal of Autism and Developmental Disorders* published a critical review of the research on immune factors in autism, which concluded that no carefully controlled studies had verified a link between autism and vaccination. Interestingly, the authors call for further research on the autism-vaccination link, citing "parental concern," the public health risk posed by unvaccinated children, and the consequent need to "finally settle this issue."[54]

Thus a debate currently exists between those who emphasize a genetic cause of autism and those who emphasize an environmental one.[55] Though the lines are not absolute, there is a tendency for researchers to side with the genetic argument and for parents to side with the environmental argument. Why have parents emerged as advocates of the claim that environmental factors have caused their children's autism? One possible reason is that a genetic cause of autism generally implies that the recent increase in autism diagnoses is driven by changes in diagnostic practice. These changes, in turn, can be linked not only to changed diagnostic criteria but also to parents' advocacy for diagnosis. In what might seem like an updated version of the parent-blaming thesis, then, parents are blamed not for causing their children's autism but for pushing for individual children's autism diagnoses. As with the old form of parent blame, the suspicion might be especially strong for relatively privileged parents, not only because they have the resources to advocate for disability diagnoses, but also because of the reports (albeit mixed) of higher autism rates among relatively privileged children. But why would parents actually *want* their children to be diagnosed as autistic?

For any given diagnosis of autism, other labels might have been assigned to the putatively disabled child were it not for the intervention of the child's parents. One label is "normal." When the reigning definition of autism corresponded to what is now defined as "classic" autism, that label would not have been a viable alternative for many children diagnosed as autistic. However, as diagnoses of Asperger syndrome and "high-functioning autism"—once a virtual oxymoron—become increasingly common, the idea that in different circumstances autistic children might have been seen as normal becomes increasingly plausible. A diagnosis of autism thus might be particularly valuable in drawing attention to the subtle needs of children whose linguistic and cognitive abilities may make them appear normal in many circumstances but who need to be taught, for instance, how to initiate play or communication with others, how to react appropriately in various social situations, or how to understand figurative speech.

Wendy and Dan Holden, discussed above, were strong advocates for a diagnosis of Asperger syndrome (AS) for their son Joseph. For years, Joseph's school insisted he could not have AS and performed an assessment only after Wendy demanded it, which eventually resulted in a recognized AS diagnosis. Before this diagnosis, the school recognized Joseph as having ADHD, and many of his social difficulties were blamed on Wendy and Dan, who were, in the school's view, "bad parents."

Wendy first started to push for an AS diagnosis sometime after a neurologist mentioned the possibility to her. Initially she had her doubts. Joseph did not seem like the classic picture of AS she had read about—for instance, she notes, he has never had "a particular point of interest that just consumes his life." However, the diagnosis began to make more sense after she spoke to the mother of a boy who already had an AS diagnosis. As this mother explained to Wendy, AS children have a wide range of symptoms. This sense that AS can manifest itself in a range of ways was repeatedly expressed by the mothers I interviewed, and it seemed to justify their conviction that their children had AS. As one mother put it, "When you've met one kid with AS, you've met one kid with AS."

At the time I interviewed Paula Harris, her five-year-old-son Evan had already been diagnosed with Asperger syndrome by a private clinician, but the school recognized him only as having speech and language impairment, which limited the services they would provide. She had a meeting scheduled with her son's school a few days after our interview, to discuss a change in his eligibility category, and she had arranged to bring an advocate to ensure that this happened. Although she was prepared to fight, she did not need to. As I heard later in an e-mail from Paula, the meeting went better than she had hoped: the school "went in there already knowing they would be making the change." Based on past testing, the school changed Evan's eligibility category to autism and, at the same time, planned to place him in a program for gifted students.

As these examples show, my interviews support the idea that some AS diagnoses are made, or are recognized by the school, in part because parents become involved in the process of identification. Timing is also important— with a growing consensus that early intervention helps many children with autistic spectrum disorders, the difference parents seem to make by pushing for an early diagnosis can be critical.

Whether parents help to produce diagnoses of "classic" autism, which is more severe than AS and, as such, unlikely to be confused with "normality," is less clear. Croen et al. find that a substantial portion of the increase in autism diagnosis might be due to its application to children who would formerly have been identified simply as mentally retarded.[56] There would be understandable motivation for parents to seek a diagnosis of autism over mental retardation. Whatever the stigma associated with autism, it is surely not more, and is likely less, than that of mental retardation. While mental retardation is still understood as an innate limitation of cognitive ability, autism often implies abilities (even "savant" qualities) that are obscured by the individual's specific cognitive and perceptual problems. Again, the autism diagnosis may give the student access to valuable services that would otherwise be denied. One of the most celebrated treatments for autism, applied behavior analysis (ABA), involves a system of rewards and punishments designed to produce conformity with nonautistic behavior, a system implemented in school and in the home by trained analysts, usually with considerable support from a parent. Other treatments involve such costly measures as one-on-one aides in the classroom and placement in residential schools.

Yet my interviews with parents of autistic (as opposed to AS) children do not give clear support to the idea that parents' efforts could account for a shift toward autism diagnosis and away from other "severe" diagnoses. However, timing is again critical, and it did appear that interviewees pushed for *earlier* autism diagnosis. For example, Janet Davis describes how she tried to persuade her son's pediatrician that something was wrong with him, again having to use her husband for support:

> We saw that something was going on, and I kept telling his pediatrician, who is a *fool*, that something was going on, and he kept saying to me, "Well, his older sister talks a lot. That's why he's not talking." "Well, he used to talk, but now he's stopped talking, so how do you explain that?" "Well, I don't know. It's something you're doing." ... after about three months of this I brought my husband in. And once he saw the dad, it was like, "Oh, my God, you're right. Something must be wrong."

Furthermore, all the parents of severely autistic children I interviewed had also pushed, successfully, for a particular type of service for their children, which the school provided. In three of four cases, the push was for the kind of one-on-one intensive treatments that many researchers say yield the best outcomes for autistic children. In 2001, the National Research Council found that the available research "strongly suggests that a substantial subset of children with autistic spectrum disorders are able to make marked progress during the period that they receive intensive early intervention, and nearly all children with autistic spectrum disorders appear to show some benefit."[57] The assumed value of intensive interventions for autistic children is also reflected by the numerous cases in which the federal courts have ordered schools to reimburse parents for the substantial costs they have incurred in obtaining these services.[58] (Some pointed questions have been raised, however, about the efficacy and ethics of the best-known form of intensive early intervention, ABA, which I do not discuss here owing to limitations of space.[59])

Clearly, parents still have to fight for these services. Catherine Lord, chair of the panel that produced the National Research Council's 2001 report, has estimated that fewer than 10 percent of autistic children are receiving the recommended level of therapy.[60] Many parents find that the only way they can get the school district to pay for these services is through reimbursement for services that have already proved helpful to their children. To do this, of course, they must first pay for the services themselves, an investment typically complemented by substantial amounts of their time and ability.

Steve Silberman notes, "In-home therapy alone can cost $60,000 or more a year, and requires so much dedication that parents (particularly mothers) are often forced to quit their jobs and make managing a team of specialists their new 80-hour-a-week career."

As the foregoing suggests, there are a number of reasons we might argue that there is currently a high road to autism. With respect to recognition of "high-functioning" forms, there is some evidence that diagnosis reflects the individual's social advantages and that the parents may be instrumental in producing the diagnosis. With respect to accommodations, there is strong evidence that a variety of autism therapies are advantageous, at least in some respects, and that achieving the optimal amount of these interventions depends on parents' having money, time, and ability. As with the diagnosis itself, parents' knowledge of valued therapies may be a product of their distinctive cultural capital. Recognizing the need for therapy, wealthy parents may be able to afford the cost of therapy on their own. As I argue in chapter 5, some privileged parents may also be able to leverage their knowledge of law and disabilities to pressure the schools into paying for services up front or after the fact.

SURVEYING these various disability conditions does not suggest that there is only one way disability diagnosis and accommodation are related to parents' resources and background. Rather, it suggests that the relation varies across time and across disability types. Nor is it clear whether and how any given diagnosis will translate into advantages or disadvantages for the diagnosed child. Yet within all these complex relations, I argue that it is possible to discern a general tendency for privileged parents to recognize the diagnoses and services that will be most advantageous to their children and successfully advocate for them.

———— ✳ ————

CHAPTER FOUR

Looking for Answers

The Literature on Disability

There was really nobody to tell me much, so I just read everything.
   Michelle Hayes (pseudonym), mother of a child with Asperger syndrome

Your daughter or son can improve, can learn to learn, and can grow toward becoming a normal, happy adult. That success depends on you—on your action . . . perseverance, and advocacy.
                Larry Silver, *The Misunderstood Child*

O N E reason for giving parents the right to participate in educational decision making was the idea that, as parents, they know things about their children that no one else knows. As one parent testified during the Senate hearings on the EAHCA, "Who knows the child better than those who live with him?" But in reality, by itself parents' knowledge of their own children is unlikely to have an impact on educational decisions. School professionals will all too often dismiss such knowledge as biased or anecdotal. To be effective, parents need to acquire a certain sophistication about disabilities, to learn not just about their individual children's needs, but about the general characteristics of children with given disabilities, the accepted diagnostic criteria, and the kinds of services and accommodations available.

One place they can get this knowledge is in books written for parents of disabled children. There is now a popular literature targeting parents of children diagnosed with a wide range of disabilities, including ADHD, Asperger syndrome, autism, dyslexia, learning disabilities, mental retardation, obsessive-compulsive disorder, and Tourette syndrome. Because these books are written specifically for parents, they not only give readers information but also arm them for conflicts with medical and educational professionals. (And, as I will discuss below, even books not meant specifically for parents may serve the same function.) In other words, the popular literature for parents of disabled children supplies not only knowledge about disabilities, but also moral and practical support for challenging professional authority. Crucially, it rejects the idea that parents can in any way be blamed for their children's disabilities, supplying them both with facts about the nature of the disabilities and with ways of observing and explaining their children's traits that counter attempts to blame parents. By the same means, it prepares parents for a more active role in relation to professional authority by supplying them with knowledge and perspectives that are relevant to decision making in special education.

But even if the literature offers these things, how do we know parents *receive* them? We can safely assume that *some* parents read this literature, and as indicated by the survey responses reported in chapter 2, some parents read a lot of it. The growing size of the literature and the fact that many bookstores in the United States carry not just a few books, but whole shelves of books for parents of disabled children are further testimony to the strong demand. Library circulation is another indication. In 2002, twenty of the books sampled for this chapter were available in the San Diego Public Library System, representing only a fraction of the system's books on children's disabilities. From 1984 to 2002, the total number of checkouts for these twenty books (most published well after 1984) was 1,803, including multiple copies of the same book.

Furthermore, at least some of the parents who read the literature enthusiastically report on the uses they make of it. Below is a roughly representative sample of readers' comments, posted on amazon.com, about books described in this chapter:

> On Mitzi Waltz's *Obsessive-Compulsive Disorder: Help for Children and Adolescents*: "Covers everything about OCD in kids, including dealing with it in the family and at school. The parts on therapy and medications are very thorough, but it goes way past just the medical stuff. I have read some of the books written for doctors but this is down to earth and written for PARENTS–makes it easy to understand the choices you have to help your child."

> On Kathleen Nosek's *The Dyslexic Scholar*: "This book is fantastic! If your [sic] looking for a book that explains dyslexia and how to cut through the red tape at school, this is the book. I finally found some answers to my questions about dyslexia and what I need to do to get my child help."

On Harold Koplewicz's *It's Nobody's Fault*: "Koplewicz does an outstanding job of presenting factual information and valuable tips on medical management of a child's disorder. This information can save a child's life if the child has undiagnosed, untreated major depression or bipolar disorder. I have a child with multiple disorders and have found this to be the most authoritative, truly helpful book available. It is a groundbreaker."

On Clara Claiborne Park's *The Siege*: "When I discovered that my son was autistic, I read literally everything written on the subject that I could find. When I discovered Ms. Park's book, I found the single most helpful resource for a parent dealing with a child with autism. I credit this book with giving me the tools to give my son language."

For our purposes, however, the crucial questions are *which* parents turn to this literature and which ones will be able to use what they find there. One approach to these questions might begin with parents of disabled children, asking different groups how they make use of the literature. This approach, however, would have serious limitations. First, it would fail to consider those whose children were not diagnosed as disabled precisely because they were not the kind of parents who research disabilities and advocate for diagnoses. As such, while capturing differences in use of the literature among the "relevant" target audience (parents of disabled children), this approach would inevitably fail to consider how the literature helped create that relevance—that is, by encouraging parents to pursue a disability diagnosis. Second, it would require parents to remember the books they had read and the influence these books had on them, which they may be inclined to forget or downplay—especially because, as we shall see, the literature sometimes claims to show parents what they already implicitly know.

The approach I choose, then, begins not with parents but with texts and searches for clues about the audience most likely to use them. Loosely borrowing from literary theory, we can identify two ways the relation of text to audience can be inferred from the text itself. First, the text may embody certain linguistic norms (e.g., difficult vocabulary) and assumptions about the social world—for instance, about parents' relationship to children or about children's needs—that presumably coincide with the norms and assumptions of the intended audience. Thus I argue that we can infer from the content of the texts themselves some traits of the intended audience—for instance, a relatively high level of literacy, implying that readers are more likely to be well educated and middle to upper class.

Second, as with most texts, the purpose of advice literature is not simply to reaffirm norms and assumptions but to have an effect on its readers. As such, it calls for them to become different in some sense after reading the text. At the least, parents become better informed about their children's disabilities. At most, they become more likely to reject blaming themselves for their children's disabilities, to claim a kind of understanding comparable to that of special education professionals, and to see themselves as effective advocates for their children. Insofar as readers can identify with and take on this role, this too may depend on certain social traits. As I discuss in chapter 5, it is one thing for parents to have knowledge and quite another for them to use it effectively, which may depend on their possessing certain cultural and economic resources. At the same time, however, even as the literature depends for its effective use on elite parental traits, it may also strengthen those traits by encouraging parents' advocacy and reaffirming the high expectations they hold for their children.

In making these claims about how the advice literature for parents of disabled children is connected to a particular audience, however, I am mindful that some parents likely find different meanings in the literature than the ones I suggest here. As Gunther Kress observes, "Any one text may be the expression or realization of a number of sometimes competing and contradictory discourses."[1] However, this realization does not prevent us from suggesting that certain texts favor certain audiences.

REDEFINING THE PARENT'S ROLE

By turning to the literature on children's disabilities, parents acknowledge that their children have some unusual difficulty in school or in life. This is a vulnerable position, implying personal failure or a need for professionals to explain and treat the specific condition. Some early advice literature, perhaps reflecting an older and more conservative view of the lay-professional relationship, seems to reassure parents only by emphasizing their dependence on professionals. In explaining disability to parents, these early books stress the primacy of professional authority and the danger that parents' (in particular mothers') judgments might be clouded by emotion. This danger lurks in the background of Bert Smith's description, in *Your Nonlearning Child* (1968), of how parents whose son had recently been diagnosed as aphasic reacted to his unexpectedly bad performance in school: "Mr. Johnson, a chemist, did not waste time on recriminations nor on unproductive emotional reactions. He knew how to make decisions and how to arrive at useful solutions. He urged Mrs. Johnson to learn what she could both about aphasia and about treatment programs. She complied, and they were able to find another diagnostic clinic for learning problems close by" (84). The authors of *The Other Child: The Brain-Injured Child, a Book for Parents and Laymen* (1960) warn that parents may imagine they foresaw the child's diagnosis. "As the parents look back, they believe they had seen it coming," they write, while noting that parents' actual first response is usually denial and resistance.[2]

While later advice literature gives similar warnings, their meaning is subtly but importantly different. The earlier meaning, as reflected in Lewis, Strauss, and Lehtinen's skepticism of parents who "believe they had seen it coming," suggests a divide between those who understand disabilities and accept their existence (medical professionals) and parents, who need to be guided by the professionals. In this view, parents *must* fail to "see it coming" because they are not trained and disposed to understand disability. As the literature develops in sophistication, however, it shifts from seeing parents' inability to recognize disability as constitutional to seeing it as the consequence of received ideas and social and psychological pressures. Consequently, parenting literature offers parents advice on how to remove these obstacles to understanding and thereby to assume a more active role in identifying and advocating for their children's needs.

One obstacle to this more active role is self-blame. Even the early literature consistently cautioned parents against blaming themselves for their children's difficulties. For instance, early advice on learning disabilities reassured parents that brain damage, not bad parenting, was at the root of their children's difficulties. In defining the category of "minimally brain damaged" (MBD) children, who would later be seen as having "learning disabilities," psychiatrist Alfred Strauss demarcated a group of children whose academic problems were both treatable (unlike mentally retarded children, whose academic problems were seen as inevitable) and distinguishable from ordinary academic problems (including those that could be traced to the home environment). In 1973 the authors of *Something's Wrong with My Child: A Parents' Book about Children with Learning Disabilities* declared, "One of the leading known causes of learning disabilities is insufficient oxygen supplied to the brain at birth."[3] Such claims were based on notoriously flimsy grounds. Indeed, the brain damage hypothesis was soon overtaken by a brain *dysfunction* hypothesis, with the semblance of continuity being provided by the letters "MBD," referring first to "minimally brain damaged" and later to "minimal brain dysfunction."[4]

One value of locating poorly understood problems in organic aspects of the brain (its damage or its dysfunction) was that it protected parents from blame and allowed them to advocate for their children's needs. As I will discuss below, the idea that parents can in fact be excused from blame is often predicated on their displaying socially specific traits and behaviors. However, the literature does not simply deny parent blame by pointing to organic causes; instead, it focuses on the danger of parent blame itself, increasingly implying that avoiding it will depend on, and thereby prove, parents' objectivity and superior understanding.

Advice books warn parents that they will hear everywhere the messages of parent blame—guided more by unthinking moralism than anything else. Lewis, Strauss, and Lehtinen write of "how often . . . the parents of a brain-injured child [are] told by grandparents or other relatives, 'There's not a thing wrong with that child; you're just spoiling him.'"[5] Teachers, psychologists, and physicians also appear in the literature as learning-disability skeptics who blame parents. Mitzi Waltz warns against the "most painfully destructive myth" about obsessive-compulsive disorder (OCD):

> What OCD is not is the result of poor toilet training, rigid or unloving parenting styles, or sexual or other abuse. It is not the result of some hidden conflict that needs to be explored in endless insight-oriented therapy. I don't know how many parents have written to me about how guilty they feel because their child has OCD. . . . Parents, you can let go of that guilt. This is not a problem you caused, could have predicted, or could have prevented.[6]

The advice literature also warns that American society has an underlying expectation that children should conform and thus is particularly doubtful that "invisible disabilities" exist—disabilities such as learning disability, ADHD, and autism, whose organic nature is not obvious—seeing them as illegitimate excuses for failure to conform. Parents, it is argued, are no more exempt from this perspective than anyone else, and their first instinct will be to deny that any problem exists or, if that becomes impossible, to blame themselves or their children for it. Thus, recent advice literature often begins with the warning that self-blame is as common as it is misguided. In *It's Nobody's Fault: New Hope and Help for Difficult Children*, child psychiatrist Harold Koplewicz describes a group of parents of children diagnosed with various brain disorders: "When they first brought their children to see me, virtually all of them thought, or at least suspected, that what was wrong with their children was their fault. Those worried, guilt-ridden parents couldn't be more wrong. What's troubling their children is *nobody's fault*."[7]

In addition to social pressure to accept responsibility for their children's problems, parents may also, according to the literature, feel an irrational inward desire to deny disability because of the disappointment and shame that accepting a diagnosis seems to entail. Koplewicz describes his experience with parents who want to blame themselves for their children's problems: "Some parents . . . are a little downhearted that it's *not* their fault. 'I was hoping that it was our divorce that was making our daughter so crazy,' another blunt parent said to me. 'At least that way she would get over it in time.' After all, if bad parenting is what is causing a child's disease, it stands to reason that good parenting can make it better" (14). Thus, even if biological causation seems to excuse parents from blame, a disability diagnosis might be disappointing to those who want their children to be normal, to be easy, to face no obstacles to high achievement. In *Learning Disabilities and ADHD,* Betty Osman describes the typical reaction of parents on hearing that their child has a learning difference: "The response to the news is amazement, shock, disbelief."[8] If the disability is heritable, the literature warns, disappointment or denial may reflect the parents' hope that their children would transcend the difficulties and limitations the parents themselves have had to endure. Harold Koplewicz writes, "Most brain disorders have a genetic component, so many parents' reactions are complicated by the fact that they themselves grew up with a disorder similar to that of their children." A mother with social phobia tells Koplewicz, "It was sheer torture to watch my daughter go through it. I felt sorry for her, and I hated myself for giving it to her" (40). Tony Attwood points to another possible motivation for denying disability when he remarks that parents who have undiagnosed Asperger syndrome may "refuse to acknowledge the syndrome" in their children, "as to do so means that they must accept they share the condition."[9]

According to these accounts, then, parents hardly claim their children have a biologically grounded disability at the first sign of trouble. Rather, they turn to it only after months and years of frustration show them that nonbiological explanations simply do not suffice. Though parents are encouraged to accept the biological reality of their children's disability, they do so not passively and unthinkingly but, according to the literature, critically, against their own psychological resistance and despite the skepticism of outsiders. Once they overcome these obstacles, they realize that they did indeed "see it coming." Ultimately they are able to view their children's difficulties as rooted in the biological difference of disability and to believe they have arrived at this view through critical reflection on their children's natures. Tony Attwood nicely describes how parents come to recognize the biological nature of a child's Asperger syndrome after overcoming their own self-blame and despite the ongoing blame of others: "Parents may initially think the behaviour is somehow caused by some attributes of their parenting or character. Eventually, they recognise there is something wrong with the child, not themselves. Nevertheless, friends and strangers may continue to assume it is due to bad parenting" (144).

BY REJECTING self-blame, parents may take on a more active role only in a limited sense—by seeking professional help and initiating the search for a disability. And, to be sure, the literature promotes a thoroughly medical understanding of disability, with a large number of books written by child psychologists and other specialists in the field. Nevertheless, the literature does not assume that professionals will lead in discovering children's disabilities. To arrive at the proper diagnosis, parents may need to take the lead themselves. As the author of *The Misunderstood Child*, a book on learning disabilities and ADHD, argues, "No one and no single agency—not your family physician, your child's teacher, the school, or anyone else—is as vitally concerned as you are, or as informed as you can and must be."[10] In *Obsessive-Compulsive Disorder*, Mitzi Waltz describes the mother of a three-year-old girl whose psychiatrists rejected the OCD diagnosis, believing it could not apply to such a young child. The lesson she derives from this story implies that parents should be wary of professional practitioners' biases and limited experience: "If you feel that OCD is a distinct possibility, it's best to have your child evaluated by a doctor who specializes in this disorder, and who has worked with many patients your child's age" (31). Similarly, Kathleen Nosek (*The Dyslexic Scholar: Helping Your Child Succeed in the School System*) warns parents that school professionals will drop accommodations for the dyslexic child on the mistaken assumption that dyslexia can be outgrown.[11]

ACQUIRING KNOWLEDGE / CHALLENGING KNOWLEDGE

For reasons discussed in previous chapters, we might expect that privileged parents will be ready to accept this assertive stance toward professional authority, while disadvantaged parents will be more reluctant. Describing her own research findings, Annette Lareau explains that working-class and poor parents are demanding with other adults, including landlords and local merchants, but "they do not define this approach as appropriate when dealing with school or medical professionals, perhaps in part because they lack the requisite vocabulary to effectively challenge such individuals."[12] The literature for parents of disabled children implicitly draws on and adds to privileged parents' vocabulary and other knowledge by giving them detailed technical information about the identification and accommodation of children's disabilities.

Advice books frequently print diagnostic tools relevant to the given disability. Tony Attwood's guide on Asperger syndrome ("for parents and professionals") gives extensive lists of diagnostic criteria and reprints the questionnaire for the Australian Scale for Asperger's syndrome. Many books list criteria for diagnosis from the current edition of the *Diagnostic and Statistical Manual of Mental Disorders* (DSM) produced by the American Psychiatric Association, but they sometimes discourage accepting the DSM on faith. Mitzi Waltz writes, "The DSM-IV is a guide, not holy writ" (38). Green and Chee's *Understanding ADHD* provides the DSM's diagnostic criteria for ADHD as well as for a number of comorbid conditions, explaining that professionals' mistaken belief that ADHD cannot coexist with other disabilities (owing to "professional blindness") has often led to failure to identify ADHD. Parents are therefore called on to acquire some expertise about disability diagnosis to ensure the appropriate recognition of their children's conditions.

As the literature increasingly challenges the separation of lay and professional knowledge of disabilities, it would not be surprising if the boundary between literature for parents and professional literature was also challenged. When respondents to the survey described in chapter 2 were asked how many articles they had read about their children's disabilities, more than half reported twenty or more, and it seems likely that some were in research publications. Four respondents, parents of autistic children, said that they had sought information from the Autism Research Institute, which, in addition to funding autism research, serves as a sort of clearinghouse of autism research publications. Clearly, then, at least some respondents think their role as parents of disabled children requires knowledge of scientific research as well as doing "research." One respondent, for instance, writes, "At first I did not believe that my child had ADD, but after research, reading many books, articles, internet, etc., I came to believe that indeed my child did have ADD."

Given the history of high-stakes battles over autism's cause and treatments, discussed in chapter 3, it is not surprising that the literature on autism itself has been a place where parents have challenged professional authority and where the boundary between lay and professional literatures has been difficult to define. Thus it is worthwhile to consider the literature on autism as an interesting, if extreme, example of the blurring of parent and professional literature on disabilities.

THE LITERATURE ON AUTISM

In 1944 the American psychiatrist Leo Kanner first identified what he termed "early infantile autism," a rare condition found in a group of children who were severely socially withdrawn, showed repetitious behaviors, and had great difficulty acquiring language. Later, with fellow psychiatrist Leon Eisenberg, Kanner suggested that the parents of such children, among whom allegedly were a disproportionate number of intelligent, highly educated professionals, were in some measure to blame. Kanner and Eisenberg claimed that such parents caused autism by rearing their children with high expectations and little affection, creating an environment of "emotional refrigeration."[3]

Despite his protestations to the contrary, psychoanalyst Bruno Bettelheim held even more strongly to the theory of parental misbehavior as a cause of autism, a primary claim of his book *The Empty Fortress*. After noting that the behavior of autistic children resembled that of concentration camp inmates, Bettelheim suggested that autism was a form of withdrawal produced by similar conditions. He ostensibly exonerated parents, the presumed concentration camp guards, by noting that the parents of autistic children do not actually *try* to destroy them. Rather, "the figure of the destructive mother . . . is the creation of the child's imagination, though an imagining that has its source in reality, namely the destructive intents of the mothering person."[4] Some saw little difference between saying the mother had caused her child's autism and saying her destructive intent had done so, and critics later suggested that Bettelheim's rationalizations could not hide his hostile attitude toward mothers.[15]

Bettelheim's *Empty Fortress* sold over 15,000 hardcover copies by 1969, and, judging from the backlash against it, many parents of children diagnosed as autistic likely read it. Although Bettelheim may have been hostile toward mothers, his writing was popular with a lay audience, perhaps because it was written in an accessible manner, a point he prided himself on and that distinguished him from many other psychoanalysts. His work was excerpted in *Reader's Digest* and made into television dramas, and Bettelheim himself explained it on talk shows. In this sense Bettelheim was again unlike his colleagues, who followed roughly similar theories of autism's etiology but relayed them to one another in professional journals. But if parents of autistic children read Bettleheim, they clearly did not feel obliged to agree with him. According to Richard Pollak, Bettelheim's unique public visibility made him "the lightning rod for parental anger."[16]

This anger ultimately provoked written responses by parents of autistic children. The books by these parents, however, were more than offended reactions to Bettelheim's theories. In their rejection of the then-dominant parent-blaming thesis, these books asserted parents' right to use their own knowledge to challenge reigning scientific opinion—not by questioning scientific knowledge as such but by claiming to be more rigorous and responsible than the recognized researchers. In a sense these authors set the precedent for the more confrontational attitude toward professional authority in the later parent literature on disabilities.

An early and important example is Clara Claiborne Park, whose book *The Siege* described the author's experience in raising her autistic daughter "Elly." *The Siege* originally appeared in 1967, the same year as *The Empty Fortress*, but it received far less attention. *The Siege* did, however, grow to be a classic among parents of autistic children. Although not written as an advice book, *The Siege* is praised by the authors of advice literature and by parent groups and doubtless served as a guide to many parents. Most important, however, it self-consciously models a particular type of behavior for parents that rejects ignorance and passivity toward medical authority.[17]

Soon after her daughter was diagnosed as autistic, Park began digging into psychiatric case histories of autistic children, against the advice of her child's psychiatrists. She was quite aware that her family represented precisely the ambitious, intellectual environment that Kanner and others saw as autism's cause—both she and her husband were college professors. Instead of accepting this explanation, however, she chose to take her intelligence as proof of a *genetic* link between intelligence and autism and to use her academic sophistication as a resource in understanding and treating her daughter's autism. "I was," she writes, "like my friends in putting my full resources of intelligence and intuition into the task of bringing up my children. Every mother her own Piaget" (15). After years of observation and note taking on her daughter's problems, she received her first personal affirmation from a psychologist who suggested, "I think . . . that we will be able to learn from *you*" (159, emphasis in original).

Somewhat earlier, Bernard Rimland had produced another important book on autism by combining formal professional status with a parent's perspective. Rimland had obtained a doctorate in psychology in 1953, with a focus on measurement, statistics, and experimental design. It was only five years later, when he was already working as a psychological researcher with the U.S. Navy, that his two-year-old son manifested the strange behaviors that led Rimland to an interest in autism. In 1964, after years of study, he produced *Infantile Autism*, a survey of the existing research. In this book Rimland discredited research on psychogenic causes of autism (causes within the child's psychologically significant experiences) and emphasized organic causes, arguing that the reticular formation in the brain was the major site of dysfunction in autism. *Infantile Autism* appeared just three years before *The Empty Fortress*, in which Bettelheim acknowledged and then dismissed Rimland's work. But Rimland had the last word, being recognized by many as the person who discredited the theory that parents cause their children's autism.[18]

Although formally a highly technical monograph, *Infantile Autism* ultimately became, in Richard Pollak's words, "a resistance manual for parents of autistic children" (281). The parent questionnaire appended to *Infantile Autism*, which many parents completed and returned to Rimland, made it clear that parents were part of its intended audience, although the level of its vocabulary assumed a highly literate one. Other aspects of the book suggest how Rimland, the scientist as parent, might have appealed to the parent as lay scientist. Rimland's dismissal of psychogenic theories of autism, for instance, rested on both logical and moral arguments that parents could readily invoke. One logical argument, which would recur in many books on autism and other conditions, was that unusual parental behavior might point not to psychogenic causes of autism but to a genetic cause common to parent and child. "How can one say that both the child's and the parent's behavior are not related consequences of the same genetic factors?" Rimland asks. "The high incidence of the detached, over-objective personality in the children's parents is consistent with *both* the psychogenic and the biogenic views."[19]

The choice between psychogenic and biogenic theories, however, was not morally neutral, which Rimland made clear by using terms like "guilty," "innocent," and "justice": "In a court of law it is impermissible to convict a person on evidence consistent with the hypothesis that he is guilty—the evidence must also be inconsistent with the hypothesis that he is innocent. This simple point of justice has been neglected, consistently, by those who deal with families having children afflicted with autism" (65). However, Rimland was clearly uninterested in amassing more evidence to prove parents' guilt. The questionnaire in his book did not ask about parenting, thus avoiding the moral error of earlier authors.

PERSONAL KNOWLEDGE OF A CHILD'S DISABILITY

Although parent-authors like Rimland and Park have helped to remove parents from blame and, at the same time, to create an image of parents as knowledgeable actors, some parents cannot automatically take advantage of these gains. Any child's disability diagnosis might be treated skeptically by others who regard it—in the individual case or generally—as an excuse for problems that are actually caused by bad parenting, bad schooling, or personal traits within the range of "normal" human variation. While self-confidence and knowledge of disabilities may help to overcome others' skepticism, parents might also need to tie the particular experiences of their children to particular disability claims. For this they need to provide solid, objective evidence that *their* children's problems are caused by a bona fide disability with biological causes. The literature gives parents reasons to feel confident that they have such evidence and that they can use it to persuade others; but as I will later show, the approach may be presented in such a way that it is relevant and accessible only to some parents.

One type of evidence of children's disabilities suggested by the literature is parents' personal knowledge of their children and their children's relatives. For instance, parents may have knowledge of the disability because they have the same condition themselves. If they can overcome the pain of recognizing that their children will experience the same difficulties they do, they can use that insight to gain a true understanding of their children. Larry Silver notes that, because learning disabilities are often inherited, "there is about a 40 percent possibility that one parent also will have learning disabilities. As you learn about your child, you might say, 'That's me.' This may be the first time in your life that you understand why you have had so much difficulty in school and in life. If so, learn about yourself. . . . This knowledge may be needed when help for your son or daughter is discussed."[20]

Similarly, in families that include one or more children *without* a disability, the nondisabled children demonstrate that the abnormal child's difficulties must stem from a biological condition, not from poor parenting or parents' cultural deficiencies. Brutten, Richardson, and Mangel describe the case of Maureen, a learning disabled child whose *younger* brother and sister were able to teach her "much of her lesson." Another child, Jeannie, who was later diagnosed with a "neurologic impairment . . . had always seemed different from her brother, Dan. He was a placid boy, easy to raise and care for. She fussed and fumed and was miserably unhappy just about all the time."[21] Explicitly arguing against the theory that bad parenting causes autism, Lorna Wing claims that "while it is possible for parents to have more than one autistic child, in most cases the brothers and sisters are healthy and normal."[22]

Lacking the parent's day-to-day familiarity with the disabled child, outsiders are likely to overlook biological explanations and hence to misunderstand the true connection between parenting and the child's behavior.

Green and Chee note that raising a child with ADHD is such a struggle that parents may give up discipline in despair, but that "a professional, who knows nothing of their early struggle, sees the bad behavior and blames it on the apparent lack of firmness."[23] Rimland had previously severed the causal flow from parental behavior to childhood autism by suggesting their common origin in genetics. Later, some authors suggest to parents that the flow is reversed, that is, that the difficulty and passive indifference of the autistic child strains family members, making it difficult for parents to behave rationally and affectionately toward the child. Shirley Cohen writes,

> What Kanner and other professionals did not consider was the process of re-ciprocal interaction—initiation and reinforcing response—that takes place be-tween parents and their normally developing babies, and the effect on parents of having a nonresponsive child who is also difficult to understand and manage. What professionals also did not consider was that the parental behavior they were witnessing might have been the end result of a long period of uncertainty, doubt and stress about their child's development.[24]

If professionals do not understand the true relation of parents to their children's disabilities, then the parents must. Taking the blame for problems caused by a biologically rooted disability is therefore construed as a type of irresponsibility. Edward Hallowell (*When You Worry about the Child You Love*) warns, "Too often parents (and teachers and others who deal with children) do not know about the biologic or genetic basis of their children's behavior, so they blame themselves or the child unnecessarily and fail to give the child the treatment he or she needs."[25] The wrong assessment of the condition—in this case, attributing problems to social or moral causes—leads parents, teachers, and others to misperceive behaviors as something parents or chil-dren are personally responsible for, when they are actually effects of dis-ability and must be addressed as such.

But it is one thing to say that parents should refuse to take the blame for their disabled children's difficulties and another for them to be able to persuade others that they are not to blame. In her research documenting parents' relationship with the special education system, Regina Smardon notes that educators use two discourses to explain children's difficulties: a "broken brain" discourse, which attributes academic difficulties to disability, and a "broken home" discourse, which attributes them to factors in the home environment. She finds that teachers are likely to follow the broken home discourse when children's families have a low reputation in the community, a reputation that may be reinforced by the parents' failure to attend parent-teacher meetings and to help their children with homework. Notably, Lareau attributes these latter tendencies to working-class parents, while arguing that they are due more to practical constraints and lack of cultural capital than to lack of concern for their children's academic success.[26]

By contrast, even if privileged parents sometimes face difficulties in getting schools to recognize the biological basis of their children's disabilities, there are various ways that schools may be persuaded to attribute privileged children's problems to disability, and the literature sensitizes parents to this fact. As I noted in chapter 3, white, middle- to upper-class children are more likely to have average-to-high IQ scores, which in turn has made learning disability a likely explanation of their low academic achievement. This is the "discrepancy criterion," once upheld by federal law, that based LD diagnosis on the discrepancy between children's IQs and their academic achievement.[27] Describing the way schools evaluate for learning disabilities, Barry and Francine McNamara, authors of *Keys to Parenting a Child with a Learning Disability*, write, "Members of the multidisciplinary team examine the results of tests of academic ability and school performance. If there is a discrepancy between a student's potential [*sic*], a learning disability may exist."[28]

In a more general sense, the literature for parents of disabled children shores up the assumption that disabilities are best discerned against relatively privileged backgrounds. It is implied that the failure of a child with all the assumed benefits of culturally mainstream, educated, middle-class parents cannot easily be pinned on social causes. Clara Park describes her reaction when a physician classified her daughter as "normal": "We grasped well enough that this low-grade normality was no normality at all given the environment Elly lived in. Institutionalized babies, perhaps, or children bewildered in distracted families where speech was rudimentary and noise constant, might indeed appear like Elly and still be normal, having good reasons for the simplicity of their accomplishments" (41–42). Betty Osman gives an account that is remarkable for its flexible inclusion of both psychosocial causes of learning difficulty and the possibility that middle-class as well as poor children may be "culturally deprived" and therefore struggle academically owing to social causes, not to disability. Ultimately, however, she generalizes cultural deficits to all poor children, whereas in other groups cultural deficits seem to stem only from particular circumstances: "Cultural deprivation is not confined to areas of poverty," she writes, without having explained why or when cultural deprivation exists in areas of poverty. "Just because a child is well-dressed or lives in the suburbs does not mean she is necessarily immune to neglect or cultural deprivation. Children who are left in the care of *uneducated and perhaps disinterested guardians* may suffer from a lack of experience as well as concepts."[29]

Parents who cannot normally offer the presumed benefits of a middle-class upbringing are apparently not the audience for this genre of literature. *A Parents' Guide to Learning Disabilities* makes this strikingly clear with its opening paragraph: "Each day the number of children with learning disabilities grows larger. By definition, these children are not 'slow learners' or retarded. They are not the culturally or educationally deprived. They are the children of the middle class, children from culturally enriched homes and children of average to above-average intelligence."[30]

IN A sense, the literature specifically for parents of disabled children is not unlike the general literature for parents in that it presupposes an audience that sees self-education as an important aspect of parenting. This view goes back at least as far as the "scientific motherhood" movement of the late nineteenth century, which, then as now, was most favored by white, middle- to upper-class mothers.[31] Parents who have the time and the education to inform themselves about disabilities and to implement that knowledge inside and outside the home may also be implicitly expressing their superiority to other parents, while their children enjoy whatever advantages flow from this knowledgeable involvement. In these ways privileged parents of disabled children may simply be like privileged parents of nondisabled children.

However, the literature for parents of disabled children confronts a different set of problems than are dealt with in the general parenting literature. The very claim of disability justifies treating a child's needs as more technically complex than the needs of other children. Thus this genre is responding specifically to parents' need to understand their children's disabilities, conditions that likely are foreign to many. Parents need not only tools for learning about the science of disability but also encouragement to assert their ability as laypersons to acquire, apply, and criticize scientific knowledge. Consequently, besides providing crucial scientific information, the literature encourages parents to view their own relationship with their children, entailing intimate interactions and knowledge of the child's biological kin, as a source of objective knowledge of the biological nature of their problems.

Filling in a knowledge gap is only part of the task; the literature must also contend with counterproductive attitudes. Specifically, it must persuade parents that blaming themselves is not an appropriate response to their children's disability. Whereas the general literature may point to examples of bad parenting that it expects some parents may recognize in their own behavior and work to reform, the literature for parents of disabled children provides reasons to reject such an explanation, which allegedly originates not from careful consideration of children's problems but from irrational, unscientific, moralistic, and conformist tendencies of the broader culture. Thus the literature for parents of disabled children also gives them ways of demonstrating their own rational, sophisticated, and critical awareness of their children's needs.[32]

The argument here has been that privileged parents are in a better position to use the scientific information provided by the literature, to adopt arguments presented there, and to take on the role it prescribes for parents. Insofar as we can correctly conclude that privileged parents are therefore more likely to use the literature, then we might also expect that it would support and strengthen their tendency to intervene in their children's education by drawing on their elite cultural capital. In my next chapter I address the way parents actually do intervene in the special education system and how the outcome of such interventions may depend on their economic and cultural capital.

———— ✳ ————

CHAPTER FIVE

Whose Voices Are Heard?

Due Process Hearings and Parents' Challenge to Special Education Evaluations and Placements

IN CHAPTER 1, I noted a shift that occurred between the initial justification for creating a law supporting disabled children's educational rights and the ways the law has subsequently been applied and interpreted. The initial justification was expressed as a desire for equality and social justice. As such, educational rights for disabled children appeared to be part of broader social movements that were challenging existing social hierarchies. Most obviously, the creation of specific educational rights for disabled children challenged the hierarchy that ranked their educational rights below those of nondisabled children. The new law also challenged the entrenched lay/professional hierarchy by questioning the professional and institutional judgment that had previously justified excluding disabled children from public schools. And it permitted further questioning of institutional judgment by giving parents, as lay actors, a seat at the table when decisions affecting their children's education were being made. For this reason, some even hoped that recognizing parents' specific rights to advocate for their children would weaken the racial-ethnic and social class hierarchies that special education seemed to perpetuate.

Over time, however, these concerns to promote equality and social justice through and within special education diminished. When put into practice, the new educational law seemed mainly to say that the diagnosis and placement of disabled children were not matters of social justice but individual and technical issues, and that parents had a right to participate in decision making only insofar as they contributed to a more technically adequate outcome.

This legislation apparently assumed that all parents would be able to participate effectively in decision making. But that was unrealistic. Parents' differing resources and backgrounds meant that some were far more capable of acquiring and using the technical knowledge that special education decisions require. Hence, rather than leveling the playing field, the legislation created new opportunities for children of privileged parents to enjoy a relative advantage in the public education system, further entrenching the social class and racial-ethnic hierarchies within the relationship between families and schools.

This chapter focuses on the part of parent advocacy where the stakes are highest and where parents' resources are therefore most critical: the administrative (or "due process") hearing. As a highly visible stage of the IEP (individualized education program) procedure, the due process hearing reveals how some parents are more adept than others at obtaining their desired ends. It is also a highly consequential stage because it is the last opportunity to challenge the school's decisions short of an appeal to the state or federal courts.

The IEP procedure begins when parents or guardians request or consent to an evaluation to determine if their children have disabilities that would qualify them for special education services. If an assessment, conducted by individuals specifically qualified to assess the student in all suspected areas of disability, determines that the child has a qualifying disability, an IEP meeting is convened. A new IEP must be formulated each year, and therefore an IEP meeting must be held each year that the child is eligible and enrolled in special education. Ideally, it is at this meeting, to which the child's parents or guardians must be invited, that the IEP is approved. (However, many parents do not attend the IEP meeting and participate in the approval process only through the mail.) The "IEP team" includes one or more of the student's parents or a representative of the parents (or both); at least one of the student's regular education teachers (if the child is enrolled at all in regular education); at least one of the student's special education teachers/providers; a representative of the school district (e.g., a district special education coordinator); and, whenever appropriate, the student.

If parents are not satisfied with the proposed IEP and cannot reach a satisfactory compromise with the school, a possible next step is to request a due process hearing, where an independent hearing officer (presumably independent based on being an employee of the state Department of Developmental Services, not of the school districts whose claims are being heard) will determine if the school has offered an appropriate IEP. Although most hearing requests are sent to mediation, some do reach a hearing, and beyond that some hearing decisions are challenged and are heard on appeal in the state or federal courts.

I have chosen here to look only at the life of claims in the due process hearing system and not at their posthearing life in the state and federal courts. Due process hearings provide more data for analysis because they normally result in decisions that are made publicly available, whereas court cases seldom reach a hearing and only a small proportion of these will result in published decisions. Perhaps more important, in its *Rowley* decision the Supreme Court cautioned the federal courts against "imposing their view of preferable educational methods upon the States" and cited its own previous finding that courts "lack the 'specialized knowledge and experience' necessary to resolve 'persistent and difficult questions of educational policy.'"[1] Following the *Rowley* standard, courts now review due process hearing decisions primarily to question their legal reasoning (their "findings of law"), while deferring to the hearing officer's findings of fact. That is, the courts are required to give "due weight" to the previous decision of the hearing officer when it comes to factual issues such as whether the child has a given disability and whether a given placement is appropriate. Therefore due process hearings provide better examples than court cases do of parents' challenges to the schools' technical judgments about students' disabilities and related needs, as well as a much larger volume of records.

The following discussion will focus on whose voices are heard in the due process hearing system. What does it mean to ask whose voices are heard? On the one hand, it is simply to ask which parents bring due process challenges. The answer to this question is fairly straightforward. Parents with more income and education are more likely to bring such challenges and, in this sense, to be "heard." On the other hand, it is to ask whether even those parents who bring due process challenges are truly being heard. This is an issue because special education decisions raise highly technical issues related to law and disabilities. Although the law formally requires schools to seek parents' involvement in making decisions in special education, many school professionals do not see parents as true partners in such complex decisions. In the words of one school representative, current special education law "has forced [parents] into thinking that they could really have a true partnership with the professionals. . . . But I think personally it's somewhat unusual to expect. It's like saying to you, you can have a partnership with the doctors who are going to treat you. You should have just as much say in all of your treatments. You can't really have as much say because it's so complicated."[2]

Therefore, despite their formal right to contribute to special education decisions, when parents disagree with the school's judgments they may struggle to make their voices heard, and this struggle may extend all the way to a due process hearing. In due process hearings, parents must persuade the presiding hearing officer that their claims conform to demanding legal and technical standards. What enables parents to do this?

A central argument in this chapter is that the parents who are most persuasive in their due process challenges possess elite cultural capital. In earlier chapters I discussed the particular types of knowledge, attitudes, beliefs, and practices that constitute this cultural capital. In this chapter I draw on the records from due process hearings to reveal the variety of ways parents draw on their cultural resources to effectively advocate for their children's needs—and, at the same time, the variety of ways they fail to be effective for lack of such resources.

Besides elite cultural capital, privileged parents' economic capital is a factor in getting their voices heard in due process hearings. Parents with enough money can hire professionals with relevant expertise to represent them, or they may seek outside evaluations and placements that can leverage their claims. Indeed, it might seem that money alone could often decide the outcome of disputes between parents and schools and that in such cases parents' voices are heard only in the dubious sense in which one could say that consumers' preferences are "heard" through their purchases. Yet I also argue that money alone is usually not sufficient to ensure success. Due process challenges more commonly combine the efforts of professionals paid by parents with the parents' own actions and words. Parents' contributions can have effects that *complement* those of professionals but that are independent of the effects of economic capital. Furthermore, parents' actions and words can be the *reason* professionals' contributions are effective in due process hearings. In other words, the effects of economic and cultural capital may be interdependent, so that parents' effective use of cultural capital may be the condition for their effective use of economic capital.

This idea suggests that the dominant sociological understanding of the relation between economic and cultural capital needs to be expanded. The understanding of cultural capital in the work of Bourdieu and many other sociologists holds that cultural capital's effects are independent of those of economic capital. While it is doubtless true that individuals' cultural and financial advantages operate in distinct markets, or "fields," as Bourdieu and others maintain, economic and cultural capital are not used independently.

In their usual formulation, cultural and economic capital are distinct in modern society in that there are institutions that serve to objectify specific types of individual advantages. Whereas at a premodern stage an individual's social power depends on personal interactions in which symbolic status is constantly reestablished and is implicated with one's claim to material wealth, in modern societies specific social institutions objectify one's possession of specific forms of wealth. Material wealth is translated into the objectified form of money through institutions such as banks, while cultural competence is translated into, among other things, academic credentials from government-certified institutions of education.

As a result of this objectification, different types of advantages operate in relatively autonomous fields. In the field of culture, it becomes possible to invest in purely cultural competencies, which yield specific symbolic profits, including objectified forms of cultural capital. As such, culture is tied to class relations not as an ideology that rationalizes class exploitation, as it appears in classical Marxism, but as a specific dimension of class privilege. Culture is not subordinate to the material economy but is an economy in its own right, in which the rarest types of knowledge, tastes, and abilities—rare because they are produced by the most difficult-to-attain conditions of existence of the upper classes—are given the greatest rewards and are seen by others as naturally superior to other types of knowledge, tastes, and abilities.

Despite its relative autonomy from economic capital, cultural capital does appear to serve a legitimating function vis-à-vis economic capital. By using one's economic capital to obtain access to opportunities that produce cultural capital, one may successfully convert a form of social power (economic capital) that can readily be seen to be arbitrary in its transmission—children who inherit their parents' economic wealth do not necessarily seem to merit this advantage—into a form of power (cultural capital) that is recognized as legitimate because it resides in the individual and appears to be innate. In successive generations, cultural capital transmits itself almost automatically and invisibly: children acquire high cultural capital not so much because of their parents' ability to afford an expensive private education but because, at the earliest ages, they absorb their parents' rare cultural abilities and dispositions. This mode of acquisition of cultural capital leads to social recognition for the bearer, which misrecognizes cultural capital as innate traits, so that its value reflects the individual's exceptional nature rather than the exceptional nature of the social conditions that produced those traits. The apparently disinterested nature of cultural capital corresponds to the apparently disinterested uses of cultural capital—for example, the ability to appreciate a painting has no direct economic value, but it does distinguish its bearer from the mass of individuals who lack similar appreciation.

When wealthy families can transform some share of their raw economic advantages into the education of their members, thereby producing in them elite dispositions, tastes, and modes of perceptions, their social class advantages acquire a legitimacy that wealth alone lacks. Furthermore, as this cultural capital is passed down the generations, it becomes more legitimate as its origin in economic wealth become more obscure. As Bourdieu writes, "Transmission of cultural capital is no doubt the best hidden form of hereditary transmission of capital, and it therefore receives proportionately greater weight in the system of reproduction strategies, as the direct, visible forms of transmission tend to be more strongly censored and controlled."[3] In the educational system, as family ties and wealth become increasingly illegitimate as ways to secure access to educational opportunities, the importance of personal merit is increasingly emphasized. As a result, advantages associated with class are increasingly sublimated. Parents pass on subtle cultural advantages to their children outside the classroom, but in theory their influence ends at the school door.

The idea that schools restrict parents' direct involvement in their children's education—in part to maintain the appearance that education is a meritocracy, free of the social hierarchies of the broader social world—has obvious limits. It perhaps applies well to certain times and places—for instance, France in the 1960s, the time and place of *Les héritiers* (*The Inheritors*), a work in which Bourdieu and Jean-Claude Passeron presented many of the original arguments about the relation between cultural capital and academic success. However, the same idea clearly does not describe the contemporary American public education system. As Annette Lareau noted in her research conducted in the early 1980s, in the American school system parents are strongly encouraged to be actively involved in their children's education and to attend parent-teacher conferences.

However, this encouragement of parents' involvement does not mean that schools readily recognize and accept the fact that, through such involvement, privileged parents use their social advantages to influence their children's educational fate. Rather, according to Lareau, school representatives typically "misrecognize" (Bourdieu's term, borrowed by Lareau) the greater involvement of privileged parents as the outcome of their superior values as parents. Because their involvement is undergirded by subtle forms of class-specific cultural capital, such as their familiarity with the practices and terminology of the educational context or their confidence in challenging the authority of teachers, upper-middle-class parents' interventions in the educational system may not be perceived as grounded in social class advantages. Thus, while teachers praise parents for their involvement, they seldom recognize the social conditions of that involvement.

The same implicit belief that parents' involvement is socially neutral exists in special education. Thus it is essential that when parents advocate for their disabled children, they do so in ways that appear to be socially neutral. That is, they must appear to participate not as privileged parents who leverage their advantages to support a particular view of their children's needs and abilities, but as concerned parents with valuable insights into their children's distinctive needs and abilities. That privileged parents may actually help to produce a more accurate understanding of their child's underlying needs and abilities only obscures the fact that an equally accurate and advantageous representation may not be possible for disadvantaged children because their parents lack the necessary cultural capital. By the same token, if parents appear ill-informed about children's disabilities and too obviously try to use their economic capital simply to seek whatever diagnoses and accommodations seem to give their children a leg up in school, then they threaten to undermine the legitimacy of their own participation. This is precisely the threat that appears when privileged parents enlist professional support for their special education claims for their children. That sense of violation is expressed in the headline of a story in the *New York Times* on the greater tendency of high-income students to receive accommodations for disability when taking the SATs: "Paying for a Disability Diagnosis to Gain Time for College Boards" (September 26, 2002).

However, what is obvious in the aggregate—that privileged parents are more likely to be able to take advantage of their disabled children's educational rights—may be obscured at the individual level if privileged parents are sensitive to the institutional requirements for objectivity. In advocating for their children, privileged parents can reveal their knowledge and understanding of disabilities and educational rights to institutional authorities, who can feel satisfied that, by securing parental participation, they are deciding individual cases based on a fair assessment of the individual child's rights and needs. In short, that the system is not disinterested and that economic capital can be a factor when parents advocate for their children's rights can be obscured by effective use of their cultural capital. One purpose of this chapter is to demonstrate how this happens.

WHAT DOES A DUE PROCESS HEARING REPRESENT?

In theory, when parents and schools in California cannot reach an agreement about a student in special education (or a student one party believes is eligible for special education), either party can submit a request to the California Special Education Hearing Office for a due process hearing. In practice, it is usually parents who bring an initial claim. In some cases parents' claims lead schools to bring defensive counterclaims.[4] Occasionally the school may request a hearing independently, but even then the request may be a defensive gesture designed to quell complaints and possible future challenges from parents. For instance, in case 589-98, the Calaveras Unified District requested a due process hearing to determine whether it had offered an appropriate placement for an autistic child, a question that centered particularly on whether an aide assigned to the student was adequately qualified. As it emerged in a subsequent hearing, however, the parents had previously made and withdrawn their own request for a hearing, presumably on the same issue. Furthermore, the district later withdrew its request after the hearing officer denied its motion for summary judgment (a prehearing motion that, if granted, would have resolved various issues in the district's favor before they reached a hearing). After the district withdrew its request, the parents renewed theirs, which finally resulted in a hearing. Thus, although the district did make an independent hearing request, it was clearly a response to the parents' past actions and likely future actions.

It is not surprising that most due process hearing requests come directly or indirectly from parents' complaints. Schools can provide services and placements, while parents can only request them. If parents are denied the services and placements they request, they may turn to a due process hearing to force the school to provide them. Alternatively, parents may obtain private services or placements for their children and later try to prove, in a due process hearing, that because the school failed to provide appropriate accommodations it should reimburse them for their costs.

Schools have more limited reasons for making hearing requests. In some exceptional cases, they do so to override the "stay put" requirement, which ordinarily requires parents' consent before a change is made in a disabled student's placement or services. However, schools usually support rather than challenge this requirement, because it limits changes and puts the burden of proof on parents when they think their children's needs are not being adequately met. In other cases the school may request an administrative hearing to override the parental consent requirement if parents refuse to allow their children to be evaluated. For instance, a school may wish to remove a student deemed a behavior problem from the regular classroom by having him or her designated "severely emotionally disturbed" and may use a hearing to override parents who refuse evaluation to avoid the stigmatizing label of "disturbed" or the associated placement. However, conflicts that begin with a school's hearing request are rare.

Before I proceed with the analysis of hearing requests, it is worth noting that, just as there are reasons we might expect more privileged parents to bring due process hearing challenges against their children's schools, there are also reasons we might expect disadvantaged parents to do so. Disadvantaged parents have much they could complain about: high rates of stigmatizing disability diagnoses among their children; more placements in special education contexts that segregate their children from mainstream students; and inferior special education services. However, the findings presented below suggest that privileged parents are far more likely to make hearing requests and also to appear at hearings.

DISTRIBUTION OF HEARING REQUESTS

To analyze hearing requests and hearings within different school districts, I have categorized California school districts into three types: "wealthy white" districts, "middle-class" districts, and "poor minority" districts. These types are based on characteristics of parents of public school children within a given district—family income, education, and race—although "middle-class" districts are defined only with respect to family income and education. Each characteristic is estimated through data from the 2000 U.S. Census and represents data for all families within the district that had children in public school in the 1998–99 school year. "Income" represents median family annual income in 1999. "Education" is the percentage of parents with a bachelor's degree or higher. "Race" is calculated as the percentage of parents self-identifying as "black or African American" or "Hispanic or Latino."[5] (These racial categories were selected to capture the contrast between disadvantaged minority groups and nondisadvantaged groups, including whites and Asian Americans, since the latter generally experience relatively high levels of academic and economic success.) As with "income" and "education," "race" is an aggregate measure—that is, it tells us nothing definite about the specific parents who make hearing requests or appear at hearings. Therefore the local proportion of "Black or African American" or "Hispanic or Latino" is used here as a way of capturing the types of socioeconomic disadvantages that are more common among all families that live in areas with high proportions of those groups as much as to capture the disadvantages that are more prevalent *within* those groups.

Two district classifications, "wealthy white" and "poor minority," are based on income, education, and race. Wealthy white districts are districts with income higher than $60,000, "education" higher than 30 percent, and "race" lower than 15 percent. Of 913 total districts, 102 were classifiable as wealthy white. Poor minority districts have income lower than $35,000, "education" lower than 10 percent, and "race" higher than 50 percent: 114 districts were classifiable as poor minority. Middle-class districts are defined only with respect to income (between $35,000 and $60,000) and "education" (between 10 percent and 30 percent). The distribution of the proportion of minority parents in this middle range of income and education was too wide to justify using race as a criterion. It is worth pointing out, though, that "middle-class" districts might not actually be middle-class, but could include a combination of wealthy and poor individuals that might be stratified across racial lines. There are 319 districts classifiable as middle-class. A fourth, residual category ("unclassified") comprises all districts that do not fit into any of the first three categories—for instance, Mount Pleasant Elementary School District, which has a relatively high percentage of minority parents (61.3 percent), an average level of education (17.9 percent of parents with a BA or higher), and a rather high median family income ($75,320).[6] Clearly, the labels I have chosen should not be taken too literally. For instance, it would be more accurate, though cumbersome, to refer here to "wealthy white districts" as "predominantly upper-middle-class to upper-class, low Hispanic or black districts."

When data on hearing requests for the 2001–2 academic year are broken down by districts fitting into these categories, a clear pattern emerges, as the data in table 5.1 show. Wealthy white districts have the largest percentage with one or more requests (64.7 percent) and the highest rate of requests per 1,000 parents (0.75); poor minority districts have far smaller values; middle-class districts (as well as unclassified districts) fall between the extremes in both categories. At only 0.75 requests per 1,000 parents, the "high" rate of requests in wealthy white districts might still seem quite low. It should be remembered, however, that this is the proportion among all parents (not just parents with children in special education), and that it represents only a single year of any given student's career. (It should also be remembered that requests per 1,000 parents is not the same as requests per 1,000 children and that the relation of the former to the latter will depend on the (unknown) parent-child ratio within each district.) Furthermore, while a hearing re-

TABLE 5.1 Number of Due Process Hearing Requests by District Type, California School Districts, 2001–2

District type	Total districts	Percentage of districts with at least one hearing request	Total requests for hearings	Number of requests per 1,000 parents
Wealthy white	102	64.7	332	0.75
Middle-class	319	41.1	657	0.33
Poor minority	114	14.9	86	0.19
Unclassified	378	42.6	1,787*	0.59*

Note: Data sources: California Special Education Hearing Office and National Center for Education Statistics.
* Of the 1,787 requests, 968 (over half) are from Los Angeles Unified School District. If these requests and the corresponding 665,255 parents were removed from the sample, the rate of requests per 1,000 parents for unclassified districts would only be 0.35.

quest might seem like a minor event from the outside, for parents it can be the culmination of months or years of conflict with the child's school. In this sense hearing requests and due process hearings can perhaps be taken as a proxy for much more common everyday conflicts between parents and schools. Finally, however unlikely it may be that any given parent in a wealthy white district will request a hearing in a given year, parents in poor minority districts are clearly even less likely to do so, making requests at roughly one-fourth the rate of wealthy white districts (0.19 in poor minority districts as opposed to 0.75 in wealthy white districts).[7]

Note also that, while hearing requests are rare, actual hearings are even rarer. Data from the Hearing Office show that of 2,831 requests made in the 2001–2 school year, the Hearing Office first sent 2,785 to mediation, where the underlying dispute could be resolved by the parties' negotiating an agreement.[8] In the same year, 2,280 cases reached a resolution, were withdrawn, or were dismissed before or after mediation, while only 123 ended in a hearing decision.[9]

LOS ANGELES UNIFIED

While the distribution of hearing requests reveals a clear contrast between privileged and disadvantaged districts, it does not, to be sure, explain all of the variation in rates of hearing requests. In part this is because districts that are matched on a few summary statistics may differ greatly in the variety of groups within their borders and their internal dynamics.

One district that stands out is the vast and troubled Los Angeles Unified School District (LAUSD). The hearing request rate in LAUSD is very high—about 1.5 requests per 1,000 parents. Demographics alone would not suggest such a high rate. Indeed, although it is an unclassified district, it is on the cusp of being a poor minority district. It fits into the latter category by its median family income ($31,280) and by its percentage of minority parents (66 percent) but is disqualified by the percentage of parents with bachelor's degrees—12 percent, just slightly above the 10 percent threshold. If we consider that LAUSD very nearly qualifies as a poor minority district, then its high rate of hearing requests seems to make it an exception to the rule of low hearing request rates in poor minority districts. It is worthwhile, therefore, to examine the case of LAUSD to illustrate the complex factors that sometimes enter into the relation between privilege and place.

Los Angeles itself is, of course, a land of extremes—in particular, extreme privilege and extreme disadvantage—and it is difficult to imagine a single demographic classification that would make any sense of it. When such extremes are close together yet segregated, as they are in Los Angeles and many other American cities, summary statistics obscure not only the underlying diversity of a city, but also the social dynamics that go with it: vast institutional inequality (e.g., in the quality of schools by neighborhood); interracial hostility and violence; and as a result of these, large differences in the norms, knowledge, and experience of different groups. When the Los Angeles riots broke out in April 1992 (looting, arson, and murder in response to the acquittal of four police officers who had been videotaped beating Rodney King, an African American man, in the Lake View Terrace neighborhood of the city), it was claimed that the real cause of the riots was not the acquittal but the social conditions of south-central Los Angeles: racial segregation, decaying infrastructure, high unemployment, high crime rates, and a long history of police discrimination. Charles Whitaker, writing in *Ebony*, claimed that inferior education was to blame too, citing urban experts who argue that "making universal improvements in the educational system is a critical component in any effort to address the myriad social ills that led to the riots in Los Angeles." [10]

In November 1993, about a year and a half after the Los Angeles riots, another collective protest against social injustice in south-central Los Angeles got under way, this time with less violence and publicity, but perhaps with just as much long-term impact. Eliza Thompson, the mother of Chanda Smith, an African American student enrolled in Manual Arts High School in Los Angeles, filed a legal complaint against LAUSD. For two years Ms. Thompson had repeatedly requested that Chanda be tested for learning disabilities, but the district had not complied. Chanda, who had received special education services in middle school, was now seventeen years old but read at the second-grade level and did mathematics at the third-grade level. When Chanda failed the tenth grade for a second time without having had an evaluation, her mother sought legal representation. Her complaint eventually became a class-action lawsuit with legal representation from the American Civil Liberties Union (ACLU).[11]

Like Rodney King, Chanda Smith represented much more than an isolated case of injustice; she represented the situation of thousands of students in Los Angeles. The class-action lawsuit that continued to carry Chanda Smith's name was made on behalf of the entire class of children with special needs in LAUSD.[12] With about 640,000 students and 65,000 special education students in LAUSD, the plaintiff class was large, and the ACLU alleged that many members of the class had had experiences similar to Chanda's.[13] According to the original complaint, thousands of currently enrolled LAUSD students had experienced long delays in evaluation and in obtaining appropriate placements.

Court-appointed investigators soon determined that this claim was true. They also found that the overwhelming majority of special education students were segregated from regular education students for at least part of the school day. Of LAUSD's 65,000 special education students, the investigators found that only 170 had "full inclusion" placements, that is, they received all of their education in a regular classroom. Delays in evaluation and placement and extreme segregation of special education students put LAUSD in clear violation of the federal regulations implementing the Individuals with Disabilities Education Act, and the district admitted as much.[14]

To date the Chanda Smith case is still unresolved, in spite of a settlement reached in 1996 (subsequently known as the Chanda Smith Consent Decree) after a long process of negotiation and public hearings. The decree required LAUSD to appoint an assistant superintendent for special education; to make improvements in mainstreaming special education students; to make prompt disability evaluations and special education placements; to create a computer system to track all 640,000 of the district's students; to provide special education training for regular education teachers; and to improve its recruitment of well-trained special education teachers.[15] To implement these reforms, the district was also required to work with both parent committees and expert committees.

By 2001 the district was growing increasingly critical of the decree's numerous provisions, and it submitted a petition in court to dismantle many of them.[16] Although the court rejected this request, the parties were subsequently sent to mediation, and, in May 2003 they reached another agreement, termed the Modified Consent Decree. The Modified Consent Decree sought many of the same goals as the previous decree but gave the district more flexibility in achieving them, simply specifying benchmarks in eighteen outcome areas that needed to be reached within a specified time.[17]

When Carl Cohn, a court-appointed monitor, reported in July 2005 on the district's progress in reaching its first set of benchmarks, which were supposed to be met by the following summer, he was profoundly skeptical. He wrote, "If the Consent Decree were a three mile race, at this point in time, the District should have completed the second mile and be aiming for the finish line. Instead, the District has gone a little more than one third of the distance in two thirds of the time with the steepest part of the race still ahead."[18] Among the eighteen outcomes sought by the Modified Consent Decree, Cohn rated the district's performance "high" on only five, "mixed" on three, and "low" on six, while performance on the remaining four outcomes could not be determined.

A number of the low performance outcomes are notable for their direct or indirect impact on disadvantaged students. Cohn gave a poor rating to the district's progress in completing, in a timely manner, translations of students' IEPs for non-English-speaking parents, finding that requests for translations were met within the thirty-day outcome goal only 11 percent of the time. Cohn also claimed that the district was making "abysmal" progress in reducing the "severe" disproportionality in the number of African American students identified as emotionally disturbed, and he found that the overwhelming majority of students classified as emotionally disturbed, regardless of race, did not meet diagnostic criteria the district was legally bound to apply. (Special education researchers claim that schools implicitly use special education placements and diagnoses like "emotionally disturbed" as part of a continuum of disciplinary practices, including suspension, that are disproportionately applied to minority students.[19]) Although he does not report on race-specific or disability-specific rates of disciplinary actions, Cohn does find that the rate of disciplinary suspensions in special education was unacceptably high in the preceding year; 14.12 percent of special education students were suspended in the 2004–5 school year, making them more than twice as likely to be suspended as students in general education. Finally, Cohn notes in his report that, ironically, the district was making poor progress in addressing the issue that was at the root of Chanda Smith's complaint, the timely completion of evaluations; in the 2004-5 academic year, 38 percent of evaluations were not completed in the required fifty days from the parents' request. Thus, although Chanda Smith was the primary plaintiff in a case that led to significant changes in the special education system—including, according to some critics, a steady increase in the percentage of LAUSD students placed in special education and a corresponding increase in the special education budget[20]—it is not clear that students like Chanda benefited. If anything, the district's poor progress in producing the desired outcomes—in particular, in areas that affect disadvantaged students the most—testified to the district's ongoing inability or unwillingness to improve the situation of disadvantaged students in special education.

Given the conditions in LAUSD described above, what are the possible explanations for the district's high rate of due process hearing requests? Does the lack of progress in reforming special education explain the high rate of requests in 2002? Might the state's most disadvantaged parents be impelled to atypically high levels of legal activism by the sheer severity of problems in the LAUSD special education system? Although definitive answers to these questions may not be possible, there are reasons to think that in both cases the answer is no. It is neither the poor performance of LAUSD's special education system nor an unusually high level of requests coming from disadvantaged parents that explains the district's overall high rate of requests.

Two general observations indicate why those are unlikely explanations and suggest once again that the high rate of requests is largely attributable to privileged parents. First, in the years following the Chanda Smith Consent Decree, parents of individual students seemed more likely to protest the changes called for by the decree than to protest the failure to produce those changes. In particular, many parents objected to the decree's strong calls for integrating special education students into regular education. One reason was that the services provided to special education students in regular education were often greatly inferior to those that could be obtained in the district's special education schools or in private placements that the district often funded.[21]

Second, it seems that the parents making most of the hearing requests in LAUSD were among the district's most privileged, and their requests may have been due precisely to their resisting integration, believing their children were better off with the status quo, in which they had already found a relatively advantageous niche. In 1995 the district was sending an estimated 3,500 LAUSD special education students to private schools, which cost $60 million annually and made LAUSD's rate of private special education placements three times the statewide average.[22] By 2002 the district was spending about $145 million annually on outside contractors and private schools to provide special education services.[23] Shortly after he was named the new district superintendent in 2000, Roy Romer began to push for such students to be transferred into LAUSD public schools, but his efforts met strong resistance from many parents who wanted to keep their children in their current placements and out of regular education. David Pierson, writing in the *Los Angeles Times,* therefore credits the district's changed attitude toward private placements with a doubling in the annual number of due process hearing requests in LAUSD after 1999.[24] Admittedly, this theory is the one advanced by Superintendent Romer, for whom it was suspiciously convenient to argue that a rise in hearing requests was due to this single factor rather than acknowledging the wide range of criticisms he faced from parents with children in special education.

Whether or not parents are requesting due process hearings out of a desire to keep their children in private placements, it seems that it is the most privileged parents who are making the requests. Pierson notes, "More than half of the requests in L.A. Unified come from the more affluent areas of West L.A. and the West Valley. The three subdistricts covering those areas . . . account for 23% of L.A. Unified's special education population, but accounted for 62% of the district's 934 hearing requests in the 2000–01 school year." He claims that, unlike many of the district's poor parents, these parents are well informed about their rights, are willing to fight, and can afford legal representation. These parents can command the district's attention, and in reimbursed legal fees alone they claim substantial amounts of the district's money; for the 2001–2 school year, the amount was $1.2 million. Notably, two of the five areas in which Carl Cohn determined the district's performance was "high" concerned its response to individual complaints from parents.

What the case of LAUSD shows us perhaps is what happens when relatively privileged students are combined into a large and extremely troubled district. While the problems these students experience may be serious compared with what their privileged counterparts experience in other districts— which explains the extremely high rate of hearing requests—they are surely less than the problems of disadvantaged students in the same district. Privileged students and parents are less likely to experience the passive neglect of schools—for example, the long delays in producing evaluations, placements, or translations that the court-appointed LAUSD investigators found—and they are less vulnerable to the school's discriminatory uses of disability diagnoses and discipline. At the same time, privileged parents in disadvantaged districts likely retain many of the traits that make them advocates for their children elsewhere. They may be more likely to see their children's difficulties as individual problems that can and should be solved through technical interventions. And they still have the resources to advocate individually for their children. As such, they do not need to concern themselves with the entire district's ills or to join forces with other parents to fight those ills. At the same time, the district's treatment of privileged parents is probably shaped indirectly by the parents' resources, which give them the ability to advocate for their children's rights and make it less likely that the district will simply fail to evaluate and place their children in a timely manner.

On the one hand, this is to say that privileged parents in poor urban districts have much in common with privileged parents in wealthy white districts. On the other hand, their behavior may be particularly distinctive in poor urban districts. In such areas, parents need to be particularly aggressive if they want to avoid being assimilated into the district, thereby taking on all of its problems with bureaucratic delays and inadequate services. However, if they do choose an aggressive approach, they may find that their relatively uncommon ability to advocate for their children's rights (uncommon within the broader population of parents in poor, urban districts) gives them leverage on an enormous budget—in 2002, the estimated annual special education budget in LAUSD was $1.3 billion[25]—and therefore access to high-quality services. In this sense the high proportion of students receiving private education through public funding in LAUSD may be seen not only as flowing from parents' demands for something better than the dismal services available to most students; it also further encourages privileged parents to expect that good things can come from a poor, urban district and that when they do not come freely, they should be fought for.

DUE PROCESS HEARINGS

To this point, I have considered parents' due process hearing challenges only at a distance, by looking at their distribution across different types of districts or subdistricts. In general, this distribution shows that hearing requests are more prevalent in more privileged districts, but this does not prove that individual privilege is, in fact, an important precondition to parents' involvement in due process hearings. Nor does it tell us about the substance of their challenges (why they make hearing requests) or the consequences (whether and why they get what they want). In the rest of this chapter, I suggest some answers by looking at individual cases up close.

Details about individual cases can be found in the official records generated whenever the Special Education Hearing Office of the California Department of Education (SEHO) issues an order or a hearing decision, which is then put in an online database available to the general public. Most of the cases I discuss below came from searches of this database, using the names of districts randomly sampled from within the demographic types discussed above. I sampled twenty districts each in the wealthy white and middle-class categories. In an attempt to compensate for the low number of due process hearing requests made in poor minority districts, I sampled fifty poor minority districts. While the analysis that follows was originally based on cases selected in this manner, cases from LAUSD were also reviewed, one of which is discussed below.

Most hearing requests, which are assigned a case number by SEHO, will be settled, dismissed, or withdrawn without leaving a record that can be publicly accessed. When a case does generate a record, it comes in one or both of two forms: orders and hearing decisions. Orders occur outside an actual hearing, usually in preparation for a hearing that may or may not take place and are made by SEHO in response to a motion of one of the parties involved in a hearing request. For instance, parents often make a request and later, before a hearing, enter a "stay put" motion alleging that the school district is violating the stay put requirement, which prohibits the school from changing a child's placement as long as a hearing request is pending. In response to a stay put motion or any other type of motion, the Hearing Office issues an order either denying the motion or granting it. Hearing *decisions* are the product of hearings that have actually taken place. At the hearings, both sides normally appear before the hearing officer, make arguments, present evidence, and question and cross-examine witnesses. Hearing decisions contain a summary of what took place before the hearing and at the hearing, the hearing officer's findings of fact and law, and orders based on those findings.

Any given case may produce one or more orders, a hearing decision only, or a hearing decision plus one or more orders. The case number assigned to each hearing request makes it possible to identify which orders and hearing decisions belong together. In the available text of orders and decisions, parents' and students' names are made anonymous, that is, parents' names become "PARENT," "MOTHER," or "FATHER," while students' names become

"STUDENT." The text leaves intact the names of schools, school districts, attorneys, school representatives (teachers, psychologists, and administrators), and private professionals.

I searched the SEHO database for cases in the randomly sampled wealthy white, middle-class, and poor minority districts. Counting both cases that reached a hearing and those that did not—those that produced a hearing decision and those that did not—there were forty-one cases in the twenty sampled wealthy white districts.[26] Only twenty-four cases came from the twenty middle-class districts. This contrast is all the more striking when one considers that there are only 68,900 parents in the twenty wealthy white districts, but 129,040 parents in the twenty middle-class districts. Even more striking is that the fifty poor minority districts sampled (representing 158,265 parents) yielded only four cases.

This distribution of cases again reveals that parents in more privileged districts are more involved in the due process hearing system. It does not by itself show us that it actually is more privileged parents who are the most involved. Nor do the contents of orders and hearing decisions allow us to prove this directly, since parents' income, education, and race-ethnicity are not ordinarily part of the record made available through orders and decisions. These individual traits could perhaps be inferred from the very fact that parents live in a particular demographic type of district. However, this inference risks committing a version of the "ecological fallacy," that is, believing that individuals' characteristics and behaviors can be inferred from aggregate characteristics and behaviors in the population they are drawn from. A potential example of the ecological fallacy was suggested above, where one might conclude from the high rate of hearing requests in LAUSD and the relatively disadvantaged position of LAUSD's families that disadvantaged families are more likely to make hearing requests than privileged parents, but more disaggregated data (and an examination of the broader pattern among school districts) forces us to question this conclusion. Here the ecological fallacy is a risk inasmuch as the general pattern—that is, for hearing requests and hearings to appear in more privileged districts—might not be due to a specific tendency for privileged parents to challenge the school's authority. It might even be due to a quite contrary tendency. For instance, poor and minority students who happen to live in wealthy white districts may experience high levels of discrimination there—as suggested in chapter 2—which in turn might cause their parents to request due process hearings at high rates.

In short, in the absence of direct information about parents' race, income, and education, one can only infer that the observed patterns are due to privileged parents' greater tendency to challenge school decisions. I support this inference here by considering the nature of parents' challenges as revealed by orders and hearing decisions. What do parents want? What actions have they taken before requesting a due process hearing? What actions and statements leading up to and during an actual hearing tend to make parents effective in their challenges? And ultimately, what resources, what individual cultural and economic capital, do all of these things imply? In answering these questions, I argue that the typical due process hearing challenge does, in fact, presuppose a fair degree of parental privilege.

If parents who make due process challenges do bring resources to their challenges that are atypical in the general population, this does not just mean that privileged parents make more due process challenges than other parents. It also means that what goes on in these challenges sustains the illusion that privileged parents' concerns are the main concerns that parents in general have with special education and that the means by which they fight for their claims are not unusual but can be implicitly assumed to belong to most parents. In the most obvious sense, this illusion is sustained by the overrepresentation of privileged parents in the due process hearing system. But perhaps more important, it is sustained by the SEHO discourse itself, as revealed in the hearings records, which treats the manifestations of privilege as normal parental behavior—remarking on privilege only when privileged parents too obviously transgress the boundary between lay knowledge and professional authority. Correspondingly, it treats disadvantaged parents' failures to act strategically as exceptions to rules established by privileged parents' behavior.

In the following, I will first consider the ways SEHO seems to define the norm of parental behavior through its reactions to the deviations from that norm—what I am calling parents' "failures" and "transgressions." Following that discussion, I turn to the ways privileged parents' cultural capital allows them to subtly conform their claims to the assumed norms for parental practice. I look first at how parents make effective claims to reimbursement (a use of economic capital that is justified through their use of their cultural capital) and, second, at how parents draw on their cultural capital in their personal testimony in due process hearings.

FAILURES AND TRANSGRESSIONS

Significantly, hearing decisions from SEHO do not reveal the social identities of the hearing's participants. Instead, participants have identities assigned to them, identities that, in general, correspond to nothing more and nothing less than a particular role in the hearing process. Thus, at the beginning of each decision's record, the hearing officer answers questions dictated by the structure of roles in the hearing process and by who is available to fill those roles: Who represents the student? Who represents the school district? Who are called as witnesses for these parties and in what capacity? In answering these questions, the hearing officer assigns participants to restricted roles—attorney, parent, teacher, psychologist, and so on—that will determine how they fit into the equally restricted structure of the rest of the decision, defined by the following headings that appear in each decision: "Issues," "Contentions of the Parties," "Background Facts," "Findings of Fact and Conclusions of Law," and "Order." The hearing decisions reveal that "parents," even if they are not successful in their claims, usually play their role properly by presenting "issues" at the right stage of the hearing process, producing relevant "facts" (supported, where necessary, by witnesses with professional qualifications), and presenting legally relevant arguments. Their exemplary behavior is perhaps testimony to what it takes to arrive at a hearing in the first place, that is, a favorable combination of economic and cultural capital. That the expectations implicitly held for parents and the parents' actual behavior generally coincide can make it difficult to see how less privileged parents might not meet these expectations, since they are drastically underrepresented in the hearing system. Again, this makes unusual privilege appear to be normal.

Some parents who appear in hearing decisions or orders, however, do not fit neatly into the process, and their deviations draw attention to the assumed norm. Some, because of their disadvantages, may fail to live up to the expectations of their role as parents. Others may too obviously draw on their advantages and assume too much authority for themselves and thereby transgress the expected role for parents. In various ways, the content of these cases draws attention to parents' failure to conform to the institutionalized notion of "parents" and also provides evidence of how such parents do not match the demographic norm (white, wealthy, and well-educated) undergirding that notion. Or if parents do correspond to the demographic norm, the hearing officer's reaction to their failures and transgressions may tell us what is normally assumed about how parents are expected to influence decision making.

For instance, in rare cases a parent's or a student's race-ethnicity becomes evident—inevitably because they are not white or culturally mainstream. A case in the middle-class Moreno Valley Unified School District (case 885-95), which results in four orders but no hearing or hearing decision, seems to illustrate a common pattern in which minority-group membership comes up precisely in cases where parents struggle to meet the expectations of the due process hearing system. In this case the student's race is never mentioned directly, but it appears likely that he is African American, since at one point he expected to have legal representation from the NAACP. This expectation, combined with the fact that one of the stated issues for the hearing is the student's expulsion from school, strongly suggests that a claim of racial discrimination might be involved. Although these facts emerge only incidentally in the series of orders, they fit into an overall picture of a student and a family whose relationship with the school system is characterized by difficulty and disadvantage.

The first order is issued in April 1996, about six months after the October 1995 date of the originally scheduled hearing. In the intervening period, the parties had agreed to continuances (postponements of scheduled hearings) on four occasions, but this time the school district objects to the mother's request for a continuance, requiring the hearing office to issue an order. In requesting the continuance, the mother says her son is scheduled to appear in juvenile court on the same day. The Hearing Office grants her request, noting that the student wants to be present to assist in his representation, and the hearing "includes serious issues such as a proposed expulsion." It is in this same order that the student claims to have replaced his previous attorney with a representative of the NAACP. In the second order, issued in September 1996, it emerges that a hearing was not held on the date scheduled under the previous order but was continued two more times by agreement of the parties, and yet another continuance was requested by the district but opposed by the mother, leading to the present order. The Hearing Office grants a continuance, noting that the district has had to find new legal representation just two weeks before the scheduled hearing. At the next scheduled hearing on October 1, 1996, both parties finally appear— the district with new legal representation, the student with none. However, before the taking of evidence, the mother requests a one-day continuance, citing fatigue and emotional distress because an intruder entered her home the previous evening. The hearing officer grants a ninth and final continuance to the following day, but the mother never arrives, at which point the hearing officer dismisses the case in the third order. In a fourth and final order, the hearing officer rejects the mother's request to vacate the dismissal. In a letter to the Hearing Office, the mother tries to show good cause for her failure to appear. In her letter, she explains that she needed to take her sick granddaughter to the emergency room on the day before the rescheduled hearing, a claim she supports with a hospital invoice. For a number of reasons, the hearing officer finds this explanation inadequate and refuses to vacate the dismissal. Multiple features in this case suggest that this student's unsuccessful interaction with the special education system is founded on social disadvantage: the implication of racial discrimination; the student's legal and disciplinary issues; and the mother's apparent inability to secure legal representation, to attend scheduled hearings, and to manage the various crises of her life.

Race also appears in case 240-1994 in LAUSD. Again, it appears only incidentally—in this case, because it is mentioned, as background, that the student spent two weeks out of school after allegedly being the target of a racial slur by his bus driver. We can probably assume that the student is a member of a racial-ethnic minority group, not only because of the slur, but also because of the racial makeup of his high school. In 1999, just four years after his first enrollment at Narbonne Senior High School, only 5 percent of the students at the school were white, with most being African American, Hispanic, or Filipino. In the same year, 52 percent of the students at Narbonne were socioeconomically disadvantaged (defined as all students participating in the free or reduced price lunch program or indicating that neither parent graduated from high school).[27] The demographics of the high school thus further suggest that this student is likely to be relatively disadvantaged.

The main concern of the student's mother seems to be her eighteen-year-old son's designation as "trainable mentally retarded" (TMR). He was first given this diagnosis after his first assessment by the district in 1990, an assessment made at the mother's request. That diagnosis was reaffirmed in his last assessment at age fifteen. Yet the mother first raises her objection to this designation at the hearing, when, as the hearing officer notes in her decision, it is too late. When the hearing concluded in February 1996, the student was eighteen years old and had academic skills in the kindergarten to first-grade range.

The mother apparently spent the intervening years running from the diagnosis. Based on its initial TMR diagnosis, the district offered the student a placement, but the mother rejected it. For the next two years it is unclear how much education the student received. The mother said at the hearing that she sent her son to a private school for "several months" in 1990-91, but, in the words of the hearing officer, she "had no recollection" of whether her son attended school during 1991-92 (perhaps because she feared the consequences if she said he had not). In the fall of 1992 the student began attending a special day class at Carnegie Junior High School, at which point the mother requested another assessment. Again, the evaluating psychologist determined that the student was TMR and the mother, disagreeing with the diagnosis, refused to sign the resulting IEP. In April 1994, after the mother had requested a hearing and the parties were in mediation, the district offered to conduct another assessment of her son. This time the mother refused because she felt that, in the words of the hearing officer, "STUDENT needed to 'learn something' before he could be accurately assessed." Later, when the case reached a hearing, the district claimed it had the right and the obligation to conduct a new assessment. (Under federal law, a new assessment must ordinarily be conducted for special education students every three years.) However, the mother opposed a reassessment at the hearing. Again in the words of the hearing officer, "She contended that an assessment of STUDENT at this time would reflect STUDENT's absence from school rather than his actual abilities. Therefore, she requested that STUDENT's assessment be delayed until he had the opportunity to 'catch up' academically in a tutoring program."

Although the mother obviously objects to the TMR diagnosis, she does not approach that problem through the hearing process. First of all, the original basis of her hearing request centered not on assessment and diagnosis, but on her son's social problems in school. In his time in school, her son was clearly unhappy. He was frequently teased by other students, and he often engaged in conflict with students and school personnel. After another student hit him in the face and broke his glasses, his mother requested a due process hearing to address the broken glasses. By the time a hearing was reached the mother's goals had changed, but they still did not directly address the TMR diagnosis. Instead, she wanted the district to be prevented from reassessing her son; her son to be given home tutoring for the rest of the school year; her son to be enrolled the following year at the Kelter Center; and her son to be given perceptual training or vision therapy.

Based on the record of the hearing decision, the mother seems not to grasp the reasoning of the special education system in a number of ways, and although the hearing officer finds that the student's short-term emotional issues justify his being tutored at home for the rest of the school year, she rejects all of the mother's other requests. The mother apparently believes her son needs the opportunity to learn without the encumbrance of the TMR diagnosis so that his true ability will be apparent and his true disability-related needs can then be assessed. This approach, which perhaps rests on the understandable notion that her son's current TMR diagnosis stigmatizes him and limits his opportunities to learn, is completely untenable within the context of the due process hearing. As the hearing officer notes, the mother did not question the TMR diagnosis until the hearing had already been convened. Perhaps more important, the logic of her requests does not match the scientific logic of special education, which calls, first, for assessments to determine needs and, second, for placements that follow from the assessments. The mother's request for a new special education placement to reveal her son's abilities rests on her belief that she knows his true abilities, even though they have not been determined through assessment and, in her view, cannot be determined this way. Yet it is routinely assumed in special education that it is possible and necessary to determine children's abilities apart from the impact of their education. This is not to say that performance in educational placements is never used as a basis for reevaluating a child's disabilities. However, the mother's implicit argument that this possibility alone can justify a placement makes no attempt to work with the observations or the tools of the school's representatives. Indeed, it asks them to trust the mother's judgment without any justification. As the hearing officer notes, the mother has not even supplied information on the Kelter Center program. Notably, the hearing officer not only rejects the logic of the mother's argument but, by placing phrases such as "learn something" and "catch up" in quotation marks, seems to call attention to the lack of sophistication in the mother's language and its dissonance within the hearing context.

Cases like this one are striking because they are so uncommon. In the hearing process, it is not common for parents to display social disadvantage in such obvious ways; on the contrary, it is typical, and therefore not treated as remarkable, for them to invest in legal representation, professional evaluations, and reimbursable services that would be beyond the means of many parents, if not most. It is also typical, and therefore unremarkable, for parents to represent their demands in ways that seamlessly connect with existing legal provisions. And it is typical, and therefore unremarkable, for parents to present personal testimony on their children's needs that is compatible with professional interpretations of disabled children's needs. As a result, parents who are unable to meet these expectations—often lower-class and minority parents—are often excluded from the hearing process, which keeps their needs and concerns hidden. Their exclusion, in turn, makes possible the illusion that the issues privileged parents raise in due process hearings and the way they raise them are common to all parents.

The social basis of some parents' difficulties at hearings would perhaps be more obvious if it boiled down to legal representation. However, parents who bring due process hearing challenges in more privileged districts sometimes do so without professional support but nevertheless do not seem to have the same difficulties as disadvantaged parents. Such parents seem to reveal through their unassisted advocacy the gap between themselves and more disadvantaged parents that is due to cultural capital alone.

For instance, in case 927-97, the parents of a twelve-year-old learning disabled boy in the wealthy white Ross Valley School District represent their son at a hearing without a lawyer. The issue for the hearing is whether the district is obliged to reimburse the parents for tuition at the Sterne School, where they placed their son after rejecting the district's offered placement in a special day class (SDC) at White Hill Middle School. Before his enrollment at the Sterne School, the student had attended Marin Horizons, a private school based on the Montessori philosophy, without any accommodations for disability. During the course of the hearing, the parents present a number of witnesses to support their contention that their son is highly distractible and therefore requires a more structured setting than the White Hill SDC. They also testify in support of their own claims. The hearing officer summarizes the parents' testimony, which is based on their observations at White Hill: "[The student's parents] observed the class for approximately one hour and were concerned by what they characterized at the hearing as a distracting environment. Their observations included multiple level tasks, multiple instructions on the board, different students doing different tasks, and some students walking around. It is their concern that the environment is too distracting for STUDENT to function well."

They also testify that their son requires a highly structured educational placement. The hearing officer again paraphrases the parents' testimony at length: "MOTHER and FATHER testified that it is hard to keep STUDENT on track. FATHER stated that STUDENT starts a lot of things but has difficulty finishing the task. MOTHER stated that he has trouble making the transition from one task to another."

Although the hearing officer denies the parents' request for reimbursement, this does not mean they were entirely unsuccessful. As I discuss in more detail below, a successful claim to reimbursement for a private special education placement depends on demonstrating two things: first, that the district has not offered an appropriate placement; second, that the private placement for which the parents seek reimbursement is appropriate. Because the parents in this case do not provide adequate evidence about the Sterne School, they fail to meet the second condition, and the hearing officer rejects their request for reimbursement. However, the parents do persuade the hearing officer that the district's offered placement was not appropriate because, among other things, it was not structured enough to meet their son's needs. Therefore the hearing officer orders the school district to convene an IEP meeting to offer a placement with "a small structured class, teachers knowledgeable in educating students with learning disabilities, and counseling."

Although the fact that these parents have sufficient income to send their child to an expensive private school[28] suggests they can afford a lawyer, they choose to mount their challenge without assistance, and they do quite well. Their ability to advocate for their child in an appropriate manner without a lawyer makes them part of the parental norm that current law and policy implicitly assume. When parents fail to conform to this norm of advocacy, it is treated as an exception to normally legitimate institutional expectations. For example, a father of a child enrolled in a school in the middle-class Moreno Valley District asks to have a denied motion reconsidered based on evidence submitted after the fact, claiming that the lateness of the submission "is no reason to not honor a piece of vital evidence that disproves the allegations made by the District." The hearing officer writes, "While lack of attorney representation by itself does not necessarily constitute an explanation for failure to previously provide information, in the present case the lack of representation and Petitioner's lack of familiarity with Hearing Office procedures constitute a sufficient explanation for Petitioner's failure to previously provide or mention the IEP (individualized education plan)" (case 134-99). Contrary to the father's sense of everyday justice, failure to present evidence at the right time ordinarily *is* a reason to reject its use, but his own remarkable ignorance—remarkable for the same reason that exceptional knowledge is taken to be unremarkable—and his lack of legal representation are the basis for an exception.

This tendency for hearing decisions to ignore the advantages implied in some parents' ability to acquire legal representation and to understand their legal rights reinforces an unacknowledged norm. This can be seen again in a case in the Ross Valley District. In this case (case 257-97), which appears through three orders and does not reach a hearing, the school district, seeking to address the mother's withdrawal of her son from special education and her refusal to sign an IEP, is the original petitioner. In response, the mother raises two issues for hearing: the IEP process and the district's failure to address her son's needs. In preparation for the hearing, the mother makes a number of requests to the Hearing Office. Two are particularly notable. First, she requests that the school district be required to pay her attorney's fees. (At the time of this request, she does not have legal representation.) Second, she requests that the district be prohibited from using an attorney if it is not required to pay attorney fees for her.

These requests seem to illustrate the mother's simultaneous and interrelated lack of economic capital and lack of cultural capital. On the one hand, she clearly cannot afford her own legal representation, and, unlike many parents who appear in due process challenges, she does not follow up her rejection of the school's placement by placing her son in a private setting. On the other hand, not only can she not afford a lawyer, but she obviously needs one, which can be seen, ironically, in the very ways she seeks to address her lack. First, it is revealing that, unlike some parents, she is clearly not comfortable with representing herself. Second, her request that the district be compelled to pay her attorney fees reveals a fundamental ignorance of the relevant laws, which, as the hearing officer notes, require the district to pay her fees only if she is awarded them by a court *after* she has prevailed at a hearing. He explains, "There is no legal authority for requiring a school district to pay a parent's legal fees during the pendency of the due process proceedings." Finally, and most strikingly, her request that the district be prohibited from using an attorney invokes a colloquial sense of law as power, where a lawyer's expertise does not contribute to a more legally appropriate outcome so much as it tips the balance in favor of the party that has it. This notion reveals the mother's lack of cultural capital—her failure to understand the most basic features of legal ideology—and is apparently so completely at odds with that ideology that the hearing officer does not address it at all. Whether quotation marks are placed around parents' words or their arguments are simply ignored, parents who do not have high cultural capital become symbolic exceptions to norms established by the behavior of those who do have it, whose norms are ratified by the seamless integration of their statements into the discourse of hearing orders and decisions.

Errors by parents may also provoke evaluative comments. For instance, in another case in the Ross Valley District, the hearing officer makes the following comment in a decision regarding a girl with a language impairment: "It is . . . *troubling* that Petitioner believes she is entitled to reimbursement for these expenses because they were incurred by Petitioner 'in order to present' her case. Based on section 56329, Petitioner is only entitled to reimbursement for independent assessments upon a showing that the District's assessments were inappropriate" (case 503-98, emphasis mine).

In some rare cases, the hearing officer may imply that parents' ignorance of the law is a normal circumstance that should be taken into consideration. For instance, the hearing officer lets the mother of a student in the wealthy white Arcadia Unified School District raise an issue that was technically resolved in a previous settlement "with prejudice," that is, in an agreement that stipulated the issue could not be raised again:

> While STUDENT and his mother were represented by advocates during the negotiation of the settlement agreement, those advocates were not attorneys and their conduct prior to and during the first day of hearing cast great doubt upon their competence to represent STUDENT's interests. The District was represented by an attorney, as were the County Office of Education and the SELPA [Special Education Local Plan Area]. While the terms [sic] "dismissal with prejudice" may have a clear meaning to those attorneys, it is unlikely that STUDENT, his mother or their advocates understood that meaning. STUDENT's mother stated that she did not understand the meaning of "dismissal with prejudice." It is fair to say that some degree of special expertise would be needed to understand the intended meaning of those terms (case 176-03).

This degree of acceptance of parents' ignorance is rare. More common are criticisms of their failures, undergirded by the assumption that parents can normally meet higher expectations. What is perhaps even more revealing of this assumption are the cases (albeit rare) where the hearing officer criticizes parents when they betray the exceptional nature of their knowledge and opinions. For instance, the parents of a child enrolled in the wealthy white Palos Verdes Peninsula Unified School District argue that the district has wrongly rejected the finding that their son had ADHD, a finding made by an evaluator the parents had hired. The hearing officer notes, "This conclusion [that their son had ADHD] was supported by the results of a number of assessments instruments that were completed by STUDENT and his parents. . . . STUDENT's parents stated during the hearing that they had another child who had been diagnosed as having ADHD and they believed STUDENT also had ADHD. It is likely that this perception had an effect on their answers on the various tests" (case 1856-99).

Apparently the hearing officer is concerned that opinionated parents who are experienced with disabilities could compromise the professional objectivity of diagnosis. Although this concern is in itself understandable, citing it as a particular objection to the parents' claim that their son has ADHD presupposes that diagnoses are not normally shaped by parents' foreknowledge. As I have argued in the preceding chapters, upper-middle-class parents are probably more inclined than other parents to educate themselves about disability diagnosis and to use what they learn as a basis for advocacy. They often educate themselves about specific disabilities before a diagnosis is given. Thus it would not be surprising if most parents who challenged their children's schools over their disability diagnoses were as opinionated and as well informed as these allegedly are. The hearing officer implies, on the contrary, that this challenging attitude is unusual and that parents normally act as passive and ignorant clients of professional expertise.

The two deviations from the parental norm of behavior discussed in this section, failure and transgression, demonstrate the tension within that norm. On the one hand, parents fail when they lack the advantages presupposed by that norm, even though in the general population these advantages are hardly normal. On the other hand, parents may need unusual advantages to be successful, yet if they act as if they know as much as or more than doctors and special education professionals about the technical aspects of their children's needs, they may be chastised for transgressing their proper role. As David Engel shows, education professionals are prone to see parents' attempts at advocating for their children as a threat to their professional authority.[29]

However, in the exceptional environment of the due process hearing—an exceptionality that, as the data presented above show, has much to do with the socioeconomic circumstances of parents—parents' failures and transgressions are not the norm. Although parents who make due process challenges are certainly not always successful, they usually support their claims with strong legal arguments and arguments grounded in technical understanding of disability, while appearing to do so in a way that fits with their role as parents.

WHAT PRIVILEGED PARENTS DO

That privileged parents are the assumed norm in the hearing process means their distinctive voices are in some ways more difficult to hear. Effective due process claims are not idiosyncratic; they overlap institutional understandings of legal rights and disabilities. For this reason they may even seem not to come truly from parents so much as from the paid professionals who serve privileged parents. I have argued, however, that parents' own voices play an important role in supporting successful claims. There are a number of ways parents' knowledge, attitudes, and judgments (their cultural capital) may be crucial to their case even when they have the support of paid professionals. First, it is parents who decide when and for what reasons to seek legal representation, outside evaluations, and outside placements. Although it is their money that makes these decisions possible, it is their own sense of parental rights and obligations that, in the end, motivates them to make them. Second, whether these decisions will result in successful challenges to a school's decisions depends in part on whether they are "good" decisions. That is, before making a due process challenge and in the course of that challenge, parents must act on an understanding of their own rights and of their children's rights and needs that roughly conforms to the understanding of a hearing officer. Similarly, parents' claims will be stronger if the *results* of their decisions (e.g., to provide particular services to a child that have been denied by the school) appear to the hearing officer to justify the decisions themselves. Third, regardless of the actual value of parents' decisions, their ability to express their sense of judgment, that is, to justify their decisions, may also depend on a particular understanding of how to present evidence and arguments in an institutional environment. Finally, in many cases it is important that parents be able to justify their actions and claims in their own words. While these justifications may reflect parents' class-bound cultural capital, their greatest significance perhaps lies in the fact that, unlike other conditions of parents' advocacy, they do not directly depend on material privileges.

In the following sections I discuss two opportunities for parents to advocate for their children's needs that are affected by elite cultural capital. First, I examine parents' opportunity to claim reimbursement from the school district. Second, I examine their opportunity to testify at a hearing. These two opportunities illustrate different ways parents use their economic and cultural capital in advocating for their children. When parents claim reimbursement for services they have obtained for their children, they first must have the economic capital to pay for these services. However, to be successful in that claim, they need to make appropriate decisions and to justify them at a hearing, both of which may depend on possessing elite cultural capital. If parents can testify effectively and in a way that seems to reflect a natural awareness of their rights and of their children's needs, then they may make the most effective step in legitimating both their claims and the system that supports their advocacy, however much that advocacy may actually depend on economic and cultural privilege.

REIMBURSEMENT

Few parents request due process hearings, and even fewer pursue their claims all the way to a hearing. The cost of mounting such a challenge, the intensity of the conflict involved, and the time it takes to reach a hearing generally make it much more reasonable either to address problems through other avenues or to "lump it." Only strong incentives can motivate parents to confront the obstacles to realizing their goals through a due process hearing. Similarly, in the absence of strong incentives, most school districts will seek to resolve a dispute before it reaches a hearing.

When parents have already invested money in outside services on the assumption that reimbursement might be possible, strong incentives to persist in conflict exist on both sides. If parents who have spent thousands or tens of thousands of dollars in services for their child see even a chance of recovering these costs in a hearing, they may be willing to try whatever they can to get their money back. Similarly, if a district feels it has even a chance of avoiding that cost, it may wish to pursue that chance. It is not surprising, then, that of all the cases that reached a hearing in the random sample of districts, 60 percent (sixteen of thirty) involved reimbursement claims.

Under the Individuals with Disabilities Education Act, parents are entitled to reimbursement for money spent on services for a child if the public schools failed to offer or provide a "free, appropriate public education" to a child eligible for special education and if the parents provided such an education at their own expense. Similarly, if, in determining the child's disabilities and needs, the school did not provide an appropriate evaluation and the parents paid for an outside evaluation that compensated for the school's failure, then the school district may again be required to reimburse the parents. Although some parents obtain reimbursements from school districts without ever reaching a hearing, school districts presumably provide them because they anticipate that a hearing officer could later force them to do so.

Reimbursement claims run from the small to the large. The smallest reimbursement claim in the sample used here was for $1,350 for an assessment conducted by a private educational psychologist,[30] obtained by the guardians of a girl in the wealthy white Pleasanton Unified School District (case 226-00). The guardians sought the assessment because they disagreed with the district's finding, based on its own assessments, that the girl, who was currently repeating the first grade, did not have a disability that would qualify her for special education services. The decision to spend money on an outside assessment was a gamble, though not as large as many in the due process system. In this case the gamble did not pay off. The private psychologist, like the school district, found that the girl did not have a disability that would qualify her for special education. Although the psychologist did diagnose her with a "nonspecific learning disability," she did not find a "specific learning disability," which would have qualified her for special education services.[31] Had the outside assessment overturned the district's past finding that the girl was not eligible for special education services, then she might have received the services her guardians sought, and the cost of the assessment could have been reimbursed. Since it did not, the guardians did not get what they sought, and they lost $1,350.

Most claims with cited dollar amounts are much higher. The largest claim in the sample, over $54,000, is for a boy in the wealthy white San Carlos Elementary School District (case 2006-02). He was first referred for special education evaluation by his school when he was in the fourth grade, when he was found to have numerous emotional and behavioral problems. At the time of his evaluation, he had multiple psychological diagnoses and was taking multiple psychotropic medications. Shortly after his evaluation by the district, his medications were changed, and he had a series of episodes of aggressive and self-injurious behavior, including taking an overdose of Adderall (a stimulant used to treat ADHD) and threatening to jump out a second-story window. His parents took him to the California Specialty Hospital, where he remained for twenty-three days. By the time he was discharged, he had been diagnosed with mood disorder NOS (not otherwise specified), obsessive compulsive disorder, intermittent explosive disorder, and conduct disorder of childhood. The parents and the school were able to agree on IEPs for the student from the fourth grade through the beginning of fifth grade. For a time, he was enrolled in a combination of general education and special education classes and had a mental health treatment plan that was designed by his mother and a licensed clinical social worker. In the fall of his fifth-grade year, however, the student's problems seemed to worsen. Following a referral by the district to San Mateo County Mental Health, he was recommended for psychiatric hospitalization and subsequently spent nine days in Mount Diablo Hospital, where he was labeled with a new list of psychiatric disorders, which differed considerably from the previous list. In the second half of the school year the student's behavior worsened. The parents began using private educational consultants and private evaluators, which led to a recommendation that their son be placed in a residential facility. Following this recommendation, the father personally submitted notice to the district of the parents' intention to unilaterally place their son in a private residential facility.

In response to this notice, the district convened an IEP meeting in May 2002, one of many meetings held between February and July of that year. At the meeting, the district agreed to assess the student to determine his eligibility for a residential placement. After this assessment, the district convened an IEP meeting. The evaluator for the district recommended that the student be placed in a residential facility to allow for careful observation, with the goal of arriving at "a more definitive diagnosis and a more effective treatment plan." To that end, the district offered an IEP, which provided that another meeting would be convened after a placement had been determined and that the parents would be contacted within a week with possible placements. The father refused to sign the IEP on the grounds that he needed more detail about placements that would be offered. Over the summer, the parents, with the assistance of educational consultants, and the district simultaneously undertook searches for a residential placement. The parents rejected a number of facilities suggested by the district. In early September 2002 the parents requested a due process hearing and shortly thereafter placed their son at Laurel Ridge, a residential psychiatric hospital in San Antonio, Texas. Although the district continued to make some effort to contact the parents to reach an agreement about a placement within California, a written offer describing a placement and its suitability for the student did not come until December 2002, and the district did not try to schedule another IEP meeting until January 2003. No IEP meeting was ever held in January, but in late January a due process hearing was held. In it, the parents requested reimbursement for the cost of travel to Texas and for Laurel Ridge's charges, estimated at $9,000 to $10,000 a month. At the time of the hearing, the student had been a resident of Laurel Ridge for six months, so the minimum the parents were requesting in reimbursement was $54,000.

The first question in determining the parents' entitlement to reimbursement is whether the district offered the student an appropriate placement. The hearing officer, in apparent agreement with the student's father, finds that the district did not do so because it failed to offer a placement specifically tailored to his needs as it was required to do. Indeed, the district did not even make a placement offer in writing until December 2002, when it proposed Families First in Davis, California, a placement simply described by the district as "an appropriate placement that can meet Student's therapeutic and educational needs and is much closer to his home and family than Laurel Ridge in Texas."

The second question is whether the parents placed the student in an appropriate alternative. The hearing officer notes that testimony from the student's treating psychiatrist at Laurel Ridge established that the staff were experienced with a variety of psychiatric disorders in children around the student's age and that therefore his primary need for careful observation of his moods, behaviors, and medications was met. Furthermore, this observation led to changes in the student's medication, a resulting stabilizing of his moods and improvement in behavior, and an alteration of his diagnoses—to Asperger "disorder" and bipolar disorder, without OCD or ADHD. The hearing officer also finds that the placement met the student's educational needs, especially because the program was designed to help him with his social skills, which are the main difficulty in Asperger syndrome.

As a result of these findings, the hearing officer determines that the student's parents are eligible for reimbursement. However, she grants only 60 percent of what they requested on the grounds that they did not make sufficient efforts to reach an agreement with the district. Of course, greater efforts might have required the parents to accept a placement of the district's choosing, which might have been less desirable (and less costly) than the Laurel Ridge facility. "Appropriate" placements do not have to be ideal placements, and the student's parents may have selected Laurel Ridge for reasons not strictly related to its appropriateness under the law. Indeed, a witness for the district gives uncontradicted testimony that when she informed the father that the district could not afford for-profit facilities (such as Laurel Ridge), he told her he had heard there were "ways around this." Alternatively, the district's own failure to provide adequate evidence of the appropriateness of its proposed placements may indicate either that it had not seriously considered the student's specific needs in making recommendations or, worse, that it knew the placements it was willing to recommend were not technically appropriate.

Whether because of the parents' high expectations or the district's inability to offer an adequate placement, the student got a placement, later subsidized by the district, that the parents found better and that perhaps *was* better, than anything the district had offered. If the student's parents had lacked the disposable income to make such a placement in the first place, he would have had to accept what the district had to offer or to struggle in his current placement. As the father testified at hearing, he had been told over the years that a student must fail at each placement level before being moved to a higher, more restrictive, level of service. At the very least, then, it is clear that economic capital can leverage certain benefits from the public school system. But to what extent does cultural capital also play a role here?

The parents' heavy reliance on professional expertise to support their challenge to the school district—including an attorney, multiple outside evaluators, multiple educational consultants, and professional staff from a private facility (as witnesses)—is unusual even for due process hearings in wealthy white districts. It might seem, therefore, that the parents are not speaking so much as they are being spoken for. One might argue that if they are successful in their challenge, it is because they have been able to pay top dollar for professional services. Perhaps they have only done what any parents with an equally troubled child would do if they had the same material advantages.

This is, of course, possible. But the idea that parents' advocacy depends solely on their ability to buy professional services ignores a number of things. First, parents may not be universally disposed to challenge the school district's authority when their children are struggling. Earlier research and the arguments here suggest that the disposition to challenge the school's authority regarding the identification and accommodation of children's disabilities is a particular characteristic of privileged parents, a characteristic that is encouraged by the cultural and social conditions of their existence as well as the economic conditions.

Second, obtaining and using professional services effectively, on an ongoing basis, may depend on parents' cultural capital. Parents base a challenge to a school district on their beliefs about children's needs, the possible ways of meeting those needs, and how and when they can get the district to meet them. These beliefs undergird the decisions to hire a lawyer, an advocate, or a consultant; to seek an outside evaluation; or to place a child in a private facility. Having decided to obtain professional services, parents must know enough to avoid people who would not ultimately help their cause. Even after they secure help, parents can support professionals by contributing their own perspectives on their children and their children's schools. Thus, although professionals clearly help parents make their case at a due process hearing, parents, in addition to making independent contributions to their own case, indirectly support the contributions of paid professionals.

During the hearing, it is the parents' actions, not those of paid professionals, on which the hearing officer bases his or her decision. It is parents who make the decisions that the hearing officer judges to be appropriate or inappropriate. These are often difficult decisions about whether and how to challenge the district's authority. From the hearing officer's perspective, determining the appropriateness of such decisions is not just a question of examining the case record to decide if parents had a legitimate reason to believe their children's rights were being denied. It also involves, in some cases, determining whether parents can *prove* the appropriateness of their decisions through their results.

Such proof is particularly important in cases involving reimbursement, since parents may have to prove, through the very results of the placements they have chosen for their children, that they have made correct decisions. This is part of what decides a case in the wealthy white Palos Verdes Peninsula Unified School District in which the parents of a boy diagnosed with a learning disability and post-traumatic stress disorder (PTSD) seek reimbursement for a private school placement (case 658-00). The student, seventeen years old at the time of the hearing, was apparently diagnosed as learning disabled in the fourth grade and began receiving special education services. In 1999 he enrolled in the ninth grade at Palos Verdes Peninsula High School (a school that is, like the district, clearly "wealthy and white").[32] Early in the year he was robbed by a fellow student, who threatened to kill him and his family if he reported it. He reported the incident to the school and was subsequently attacked, threatened, and harassed by the student who had robbed him and by other students. At the principal's recommendation, the student withdrew from school and began home tutoring. Although he returned to school in December 1999, he had significant psychological problems while in school and eventually returned to homeschooling in March 2000.

In the following months, the parents and the district tried unsuccessfully to reach an agreement about the student's needs. As an alternative to Palos Verdes High, the district recommended the Westview School, a nonpublic school forty-five minutes from Palos Verdes, which the student and his parents visited. The parents rejected Westview as a placement and decided to enroll him at Rolling Hills Preparatory, on Palos Verdes Peninsula. The school then contacted the parents' attorney to arrange for an IEP meeting and contracted with a psychologist to assess the student. The psychologist found, in agreement with the student's treating psychologists, that he suffered from PTSD. He also found that the student had above-average intelligence, but that this intelligence, as well as his academic ability, was being masked by emotional problems. He recommended that the student be placed in a high school with "normal" adolescent role models and a college preparatory curriculum, accommodations for his learning disability, and psychiatric services. When the IEP team met, it recommended placement in a school that conformed to these recommendations and sent a written copy of this recommendation to the students' parents, who were unable to attend the meeting. By the time the recommendation was sent, the student had already begun classes at Rolling Hills Prep. At a subsequent IEP meeting, with the parents present, the district made essentially the same offer it had made before. The parents arrived at the meeting with a counselor from Rolling Hills Prep, who reported on the school's program. The parents again rejected the offered IEP.

Again, the hearing officer's decision to reimburse the parents for their costs in making a private placement (this time in full) depends on his finding that the district's proposed placement was inappropriate and that the parents' placement was appropriate. In this case, the first finding is made because the district's only proposed placement, the Westview School, did not meet one of the district's own stated criteria, that the placement should be with "normal peers." The Westview School is designed for students with a range of abnormal conditions—such as learning disabilities, ADHD, and mild emotional problems—and, as such, would not have provided the student with the sense of security and the role models that the district's own evaluator said he needed. The second finding depends on a less stringent requirement. While parents are not required to make an "exact proper placement," they must choose a placement that meets the student's needs and that provides educational benefit. Meeting the student's needs simply depends on making a placement that addresses each of the individual needs described in the IEP, which the placement at Rolling Hills Prep clearly did, based on testimony of the student's counselor there. In theory, it should have been possible to determine before making the placement that this condition could be met. The question of educational benefit, however, depends on what actually happened in the placement. The hearing officer summarizes these results based on the testimony of Shelia Zaft, the student's counselor, and his father:

> Has STUDENT received educational benefit? Ms. Zaft [a school counselor in STUDENT's private placement] testified that STUDENT did average to above average work in all of his classes during the 2000–2001 school year (B's and C's), and is doing better this year.... Ms. Zaft also testified that STUDENT has friends at school, is socially active, is playing football and plans to play basketball, and generally seems happy. FATHER also testified that STUDENT is happy and thriving at [Rolling Hills Preparatory School].

In another case in the Palos Verdes District (case 1073-02), the effect of the parents' placement decision not only demonstrates its appropriateness but also puts the district's diagnosis of the student into question. The specific controversy centers on the parents' claim that their seven-and-a-half-year-old daughter, diagnosed with autism at age two, was experiencing difficulties in producing speech owing to verbal apraxia, "a speech production disorder" in which "persons afflicted are unable to produce combinations of syllables and words" and the brain "is unable to signal correctly to speech production centers."[33] The district, claiming that the girl's speech production difficulties are due to dysarthria, a weakness in the tongue and jaw muscles similar to multiple sclerosis, denies that she has apraxia and therefore denies her related "extended school year" (ESY) services, which are provided over the summer to prevent regression in skills. The parents provided these services at their own expense and claimed a right to reimbursement at a due process hearing. The hearing officer grants reimbursement, noting that the district's own testimony unwittingly demonstrated the effectiveness of the services:

> The Hearing Officer notes that District speech pathologist Susan Weber testi-fied with respect to ESY 2001, "I do not think that services beyond the regular summer program were necessary." In support of that conclusion, she testified that she observed "impressive" improvement in STUDENT's skills when she was reassigned as STUDENT's therapist in September 2002. Since Ms. Weber was not Petitioner's therapist during the entire period from June 2001 until September 2002, she did not know until the hearing that a significant part of STUDENT's speech and language treatment during that period was the supple-mental treatment privately provided by Janice DeMore for apraxia. It follows, therefore, that Ms. Weber's approval of STUDENT's improved skill levels is an unknowing endorsement of the apraxia therapy as an integral component of STUDENT's eleven week summer treatment plan, the service provided by Ms. DeMore during the summer recess.

From this and other testimony, the hearing officer concludes that the student does in fact have apraxia. Therefore, not only are the services the parents provided reimbursable, but, precisely because they worked as the parents believed they would, they also helped to demonstrate a need that might not otherwise have been recognized. These services would not have been provided, and the need would not have been recognized, if the parents had lacked either the economic capital to hire outside evaluators and to purchase private treatment services or the beliefs and knowledge (which may be seen as reflecting cultural capital) that led them to question the school's authority and to seek outside help in the first place. Just as the use of economic capital may be conditioned on parents' cultural capital, the exercise of cultural capital may be most valuable when it supports and is supported by economic capital. If, for instance, the parents had believed their daughter had apraxia—a belief that was itself the product of an outside evaluation—but had not been able to pay for private services over the summer, then they might still have been able to claim a right to compensatory services, especially if their daughter had significantly regressed in her verbal ability over the summer. However, if she had not received services and had merely made no progress over the summer, then her apraxia might have gone unrecognized. Thus, when a child's needs have been neglected they may be more difficult to recognize than when they are already being effectively accommodated.

A case in the middle-class Calaveras Unified School District (case 867-98) shows what can happen when children's educational needs are not met because their parents cannot pay for reimbursable services and must seek compensatory education. The parents of a nine-year-old boy, diagnosed as autistic at age three, requested educational services to compensate for their son's lack of public education services for five months, during which the parents and the school were unable to reach an agreement about an appropriate public school placement. The hearing officer denies the claim to compensatory education, finding that "Petitioner has not demonstrated that he suffered any significant harm as a result of the loss of about five months of classroom time." Notably, while in this same case the mother taught her son at home with the help of an instructional aide, her son did not show significant improvement in most areas of academic achievement. Ironically, this lack of improvement, which was not taken as a sign that the student required educational compensation, *was* taken as a sign that the mother's services did not qualify as reimbursable. While it is possible that this would have been the result even if her son had been receiving professional services, it is also quite conceivable that the boy, who is autistic, did in fact require the help of trained professionals and that he would have benefited had they been provided. That is, if he had received such services and they had provided benefit, then *these* services would presumably have been found to be necessary and therefore reimbursable. As in the preceding example, he would have shown by experience that denying such services was inappropriate.

The point, ultimately, is that the advantage that economic capital gives parents in demanding resources from the public schools works in tandem with cultural capital, inasmuch as the judgment and knowledge that embody cultural capital make it possible for parents to question school placements and to choose private placements in ways that seem to be justified later. However, this later justification is only partly a question of making the "right" choice—that is, of the actual consequences of the decisions. Parents also need to be able to justify their decisions, and in this sense they encounter a need that applies more broadly to all relevant decisions parents make about their disabled children's education (not just decisions about reimbursable placements). In justifying these decisions in a hearing, parents can rely on professional testimony, but it will help if they can draw on their own distinctive observational and communicative skills to persuade the hearing officer through their personal testimony.

The ability to testify effectively distances parents even further from the obvious class privilege involved with paying for private services. It seems to embody universal qualities of "good" parents, that is, parents who are assertive on their children's behalf and who know their needs through direct experience. However, as previous chapters have suggested, there are rare dispositions underlying such assertiveness, and parents with more cultural capital are more likely than other parents to acquire institutionally relevant knowledge of disabilities and disability-related needs and rights. As I discuss next, there are also distinctive abilities involved in *applying* that knowledge, as parents do when they testify at a hearing.

PARENTS' TESTIMONY

Parents' testimony at a due process hearing reveals their distinctive knowledge and perspectives and their skills in applying them. It can show that their claims for their children's rights are justified by an understanding of their condition that comes from personal observation. It can also show that parents' demands come from a direct understanding of how their children are being educated and how well this education addresses their disability-related needs. In displaying such knowledge, parents can also show that they know something about scientific opinion on how disabilities should be evaluated and treated. Although no group of parents has exclusive possession of these forms of knowledge, they are more likely for privileged parents, who are also more likely to be able to use them effectively in an institutional context. As Annette Lareau shows, upper-middle-class American parents are more familiar with the technical and legal terminology used in educational decision making and, given their own class position, may see it as part of their parental role to intervene in that decision making. Diane Reay observes similar tendencies within the British educational system. Sharon Hays, Julia Grant, and Jacquelyn Litt document, in different ways, a greater tendency for white, middle-class mothers to see parenting as a scientifically grounded activity involving mothers' self-education and their intensive observation of children's individual needs. Beth Harry has analyzed the opposite tendency among parents from racial-ethnic minority groups. She argues that such parents are often not as disposed as culturally mainstream parents to challenge professional authority or to engage in conflicts that depend on impersonal, decontextualized discourse. Thus, insofar as effective parental testimony is grounded in parents' observations and their ability to challenge professional authority using abstract, technical arguments, it may presuppose the cultural capital of privileged parents and be just as exclusive as the private services and placements that privileged parents can afford.[34]

The most distinctive testimony that parents can give is based on their personal knowledge of the child. In a case I have already described (case 927-97), the parents of a twelve-year-old learning disabled boy successfully challenged their school's offered placement on the grounds that it was too unstructured to meet their son's needs. The challenge was based in part on the parents' observation of the deficiencies of the offered placement, in part on their personal knowledge of their son. The hearing officer, who agrees with the parents, cites among the relevant evidence the parents' own testimony: "MOTHER and FATHER testified that it is hard to keep STUDENT on track. FATHER stated that STUDENT starts a lot of things but has difficulty finishing the task. MOTHER stated that he has trouble making the transition from one task to another."

Similarly, in a case in the wealthy white Ross Valley District (case 503-98), the father of a thirteen-year-old girl diagnosed with a language impairment testifies in support of his claim that she needs the support of a one-on-one aide in class, which is affirmed by the hearing officer. The father's testimony is summarized by the hearing officer in the following way:

> STUDENT's father . . . testified that STUDENT has a hard time taking in information and that she tends to withdraw due to her difficulties. Mr. PARENT also testified that STUDENT is hesitant to do new things because she does not trust her ability to get the information she needs to accomplish the new activity. It is only after many repetitions that STUDENT becomes familiar and comfortable with an activity.
>
> . . . Mr. PARENT testified . . . that without a 1:1 [one-on-one] aide, STUDENT would probably not understand what is expected of her.

In a case in the wealthy white Arcadia Unified School District (case 1359-01), the parents of a nine-year-old boy, diagnosed with autism at age three, claim that the school district denied their son services that were necessary for an appropriate placement. In particular, they argue that their son required the services of a one-on-one aide not only in school, as the school argued, but also at home, where he could learn social and communicative skills that could be generalized to the school environment. In her decision, the hearing officer agrees that the boy requires a one-on-one aide in the home. As a condition of this finding, she first concludes that the child has needs that are not currently being met, a conclusion she reaches based in part on the parents' own testimony: "[The parents] testified that he was unable to ask appropriate questions, was rigid and fell apart if things did not go his way, touched people inappropriately, was unable to respond to simple topics, obsessed on television shows, had problems with verbal sequencing, and did not understand if he was being teased." The mother

> described STUDENT as "looking perfect" because he has language, no self-stimulating behaviors, and "savant" skills, such as knowing days of the week by the date, memorizing all the items on maps, and performing fifty subtraction problems correctly in sixty seconds. However, according to his mother, many people do not know that STUDENT has a problem because his needs are subtle.

Contrasting the parents' views with the views of several of the student's teachers, the hearing officer prefers the former because they know him better than some other witnesses do:

> The Hearing Officer gives greater weight to those persons who know STUDENT best, including his parents, Mr. Maier, and Ms. Blasdell. As these witnesses testified, STUDENT has the ability to look good to someone who does not know him well, and has the ability to look as though he is participating appropriately in class and in social interactions when, in fact, he merely "looks good" because he is not disruptive.

Aside from their personal knowledge of the child, parents may also use their observations of their children's educational setting and services in their testimony. In a case in the middle-class Antelope Valley Elementary School District (case 2841-02), the adoptive mother of an emotionally disturbed eleven-year-old does exactly this. Her son's biological parents both had diagnosed psychological disorders and substance abuse problems. After his adoption at age three, he was diagnosed with post-traumatic stress disorder and began receiving psychiatric treatment. He originally qualified for special education services in the third grade based on his need for speech/language services; at the end of the fourth grade he was identified as emotionally disturbed, and in the fall of the fifth grade he began attending school in a separate classroom with other children with learning and behavior problems. He was given a "behavioral support plan"—a plan that describes interventions for teachers to use to prevent and manage a student's negative behaviors. The Tehama County Health Services Agency (TCHSA) provided relevant training to the student's teachers and a one-on-one behavioral aide to help him in the classroom. As part of his IEP, the student was also given the chance to determine when he needed time away from the classroom in order to calm down, and he was given a "time away place" for this purpose. In the summer before the sixth grade, the student assaulted his mother and so was briefly hospitalized for monitoring and adjustment of his medications. When he returned to school in the sixth grade, TCHSA stopped providing him with a one-on-one aide, claiming it was not obliged under law to provide long-term services. The student's behavioral problems increased, and he was frequently suspended for various offenses, including physically and verbally assaulting classmates and school employees.

The student's mother challenges the district's decisions on a number of counts. Two of her claims are particularly notable. First, she testifies that her son's increased behavioral problems are a direct consequence of the district's failure to provide a behavioral aide to replace the one provided by TCHSA during the previous year. The hearing officer summarizes her testimony in the following passage:

> STUDENT's mother, PARENT, testified that STUDENT performed better academically and behaviorally during the 2001–2002 school year when he was assisted in the Community Day School by a one-to-one therapeutic behavioral aide (TBA) provided by TCHSA. PARENT stated that without a behavioral aide, STUDENT has been suspended, up to the time of hearing, a total of twenty days during the 2002–2003 school year, and that STUDENT had only been suspended for eleven days during the 2001–2002 school year when he was assisted by the TBA.

This testimony is not relevant to the final decision because the hearing officer determines that, in light of the student's hospitalization before the beginning of the school year, the district should have begun the year with a new behavioral support plan, which it failed to do. In the argument of the hearing officer, the student's behavioral problems might have been addressed by an appropriate plan, so it is not possible to determine if the student also required a one-on-one aide. Although the mother's specific argument is not the deciding factor here, the hearing officer generally agrees that the district is to blame for the student's increased behavioral problems and hence requires the district to provide tutoring to compensate for the student's loss of education during his frequent suspensions.

The mother's testimony on a second issue appears to be more decisive. This concerns the student's "time away place," which she criticizes for its lack of privacy. Primarily based on the undisputed testimony of the student's mother, the hearing officer orders the district to provide a better time away place. He summarizes her testimony in the following passage:

> Petitioner's mother testified that, at first, STUDENT's time away place was on the porch at the Community Day School and that other students would taunt

STUDENT when he was engaged in time away in order to calm down. However, the time away place was changed to an office setting in a structure across from the Community Day School. PARENT stated that students and STUDENT can still see each other through the office window and that they taunt each other during STUDENT's time away.

Some parents bring considerably more than the fairly basic awareness of the student's placement suggested in the foregoing example. For instance, in the earlier case in which the student's parents objected to the "distracting environment" in a proposed placement, they testified about their personal observations of "multiple level tasks, multiple instructions on the board, different students doing different tasks, and some students walking around."

Parents' testimony is generally most effective when it also has a close relation to technical interpretations of proper diagnosis and accommodation. Sometimes parents' claims to possess knowledge on a par with experts in the field are particularly striking. For instance, in the middle-class Moreno Valley Unified School District, the mother of a boy who is deaf and mentally retarded claims that her son requires sign language, not the "picture exchange communication system" (PECS) used by the school. The hearing officer, who ultimately accepts the mother's claim, summarizes her testimony:

> MOTHER testified that signing is more universal and allows for greater range of communication than PECS. She also testified that when STUDENT understands, he is more cooperative and compliant. MOTHER related a recent incident to illustrate her point. She stated that one morning, STUDENT had one of his socks on backwards. He refused to allow her to change it until she signed that she was going to turn it around. He apparently did not understand what was going on and may have assumed that by her wanting to take off the sock, he would not be going out. MOTHER testified that a PECS would not have allowed for this type of communication. MOTHER testified that the ultimate goal for STUDENT is to be as independent as possible, given his disabilities. She stated that the ability to communicate in sign language promotes this goal. MOTHER additionally testified that if STUDENT is not spoken to, he will "tune out" (case 1382-97).

This mother's claims are upheld by the hearing officer, partially because of her effective testimony. On close examination, the testimony is remarkable. The mother uses a personal observation to support her claim about the "universal" nature of sign language and about its ability to produce compliance and cooperation in her son. Having generalized her observations to the educational context by mentioning concerns familiar to professional educators (compliance, cooperation, independence, "tuning out"), she places the burden of proof on the school.

Parents who lack this sophistication may be less successful in their testimony. For instance, the mother of a girl diagnosed with a learning disability in the wealthy white Oak Park Unified School District is unsuccessful in her claim that the school should have assessed her daughter for a "disability in the area of memory" (case 1599-00). The hearing officer dismisses the mother's testimony in support of this claim, noting that "the anecdotal testimony of Petitioner's mother, who testified that STUDENT did not remember certain lessons she had been taught in class after returning home from school" is best explained by the district's claim that "STUDENT's medication for ADHD, which is designed to remain effective during the school day to control hyperactivity, no longer controlled hyperactivity by the time STUDENT was home from school." In direct contrast to the previous case, the district here makes a general observation that extends to the home context and explains the child's behavior there, while the mother's isolated observation of the child at home is dismissed as "anecdotal."

Although, as we have seen, parents sometimes successfully assert their authority through their own testimony, they do not easily stand on an equal footing with formally trained professionals. Compared with teachers and evaluators, parents may have the advantage of a wealth of experience with the child, but they must find a way to raise this experience above the level of the merely "anecdotal." The mother who claims her child has memory problems is discredited because she does not account for the difference between the child's behavior in the home and at school. On the other hand, the mother who communicates to her child exclusively in sign language offers not only personal experience but a theory, supported by that experience, of how failure to communicate in sign language may lead her son to be non-compliant and to "tune out" in school. In effect, she combines observation of her child with an understanding of the educational environment to make an effective challenge to the professional authority embodied in the school's decisions.

The forms of parental advocacy observed in due process hearings can be assumed to extend to lower levels. From IEP meetings to parent-teacher conferences and all the way down to informal interactions between parents and teachers, privileged parents' economic capital and cultural capital are likely to give them advantages similar to those they have in due process hearings, although the need for economic and cultural capital may be greatest in hearings. The unusual advantages that parents who appear in due process hearings have are obvious when, for instance, they spend tens of thousands of dollars out of pocket and later seek to be reimbursed. Similarly, the effect of economic privilege is obvious when parents can draw on the support of a lawyer or an educational advocate, as most parents in due process hearings do. Although parents themselves may weigh the benefits of private services against their own ability to pay, they justify their claims not in economic terms, but in terms of their children's objective needs and rights. What parents are able to claim therefore depends not only on what they can afford, but also on an ability to make arguments often supported by their exclusive cultural capital. At lower levels, where parents may be involved not so much in conflict as in persuading schools to make specific adjustments in their approach to a child, money may be less important than cultural capital. For this reason it may be all the more likely at these levels that the effects of parents' privileges will not be recognized—or that they will be, in Bourdieu's terminology, "misrecognized" as the consequence of a "better" (more concerned, conscientious, and intelligent) approach to parenting.

This is not to say that privileged children always get the best of everything in special education. While privileged parents are more able to affect their children's special education, this greater influence does not mean that every challenge they make ends in their favor. Indeed, even after parents have spent considerable time and money in a challenge, failure in due process hearings is common, and this likely extends to lower-level conflicts as well. To the extent that privileged parents are competing for limited resources, the school district's ability to meet any given parent's demands is limited, and in districts where parents are especially demanding, this ability may be particularly limited.

Nor does privileged parents' greater effectiveness necessarily mean their children are better served than they would otherwise be. In a case in the wealthy white Palos Verdes Peninsula Unified School District, the hearing officer finds that the student, a fifteen-year-old girl diagnosed with developmental delays in speech and language, motor skills, and other adaptive behaviors, was denied a free, appropriate public education (FAPE). The hearing officer draws this conclusion because the girl failed to make satisfactory academic progress for two years and because the district had placed her in regular education 83 percent of the day, with resource specialist program support the rest of the day. This placement, however, was made even though the IEP team had recommended that the student not be enrolled in regular education for more than half of the school day and that she spend the rest in a separate "special day class." According to the hearing officer, the school's failure to provide a FAPE depended *not* on the opinions of school professionals, which did not support such a placement, but on the school's giving *too much* deference to the parents, who demanded that their daughter spend more time in regular education. The hearing officer claims that the child's academic progress would clearly have been better had she spent more time in a separate special education classroom, and that the school ultimately harmed her interests by giving in to the parents' misguided demands.

While it is difficult to say to what extent privileged children benefit from their parents' involvement in special education decision making, the more significant point is that, in spite of its image as a dumping ground for disadvantaged students, special education can also be seen as a field in which privileged parents can push the public schools to pay for costly services that they believe will benefit their children. This may explain why, even though privileged children are underrepresented relative to disadvantaged children in special education, they receive a disproportionate share of high-cost services there.[35] Given existing definitions of children's disabilities and corresponding needs and the prevailing understanding of how to identify these disabilities and needs, it is understandable that privileged parents are more involved in advocating for their disabled children and that their children therefore derive more advantages from special education. It seems that the growth of special education as a way of identifying and meeting needs has come to be another source of privilege for already privileged children. Significantly, it is a source that may be shielded from criticism by the assumption that disabilities and disability-related needs are purely technical problems that can be met in an objective and socially neutral manner.

———— ✳ ————

CHAPTER SIX

Reflections on Disability
and Social Reproduction

IN THIS book I have begun to explore the connections between disability and parental privilege. If my findings are accepted, they lead to the conclusions that the existing special education system is fundamentally inequitable and that privileged parents implicitly contribute to that inequity when they draw on their resources to advocate for their children. These conclusions inevitably raise questions about how to judge the current system.

My intention is not to criticize parents' impulse to advocate for their children or to ignore the fact that some parents, privileged or not, are committed advocates not only for their own children but also for other people's. Even when they are most narrowly focused on the well-being of their own families, privileged parents are, after all, trying to help not themselves, but their children, and they are dealing with laws and institutional practices that limit what can be done.

Nor is my intention to claim that the principle of parents' involvement in special education should be overturned. While this principle is in many ways the precondition to the inequalities I have described, the state of special education was surely not more equitable before the passage of the EAHCA, when parents' right to be involved in decision making was first established at the federal level. It should be remembered that denial of educational services to disabled children was once relatively common, and minority students often got the worst of that exclusion.

The goal, it seems to me, should be to take some of the burden of advocacy from parents while preserving their involvement and working to include disadvantaged parents in decision making more meaningfully. However, the latter task is not simple, since the present inequalities depend in part on differences in parents' dispositions. While one might hope to train and hire special education professionals to provide services in a more egalitarian or culturally sensitive way, one cannot expect to retrain parents. How parents do the work of parenting is rooted in their differing cultural traditions, educational histories, work schedules, amounts of disposable income, and forms of racial and class consciousness, none of which can be much altered by a change in education policy. Nor would I suggest that it would be better to make them all like upper-middle-class parents.

Rather than playing the role of critic or reformer, then, I conclude by reflecting on the implications of my research for the future study of disability and social reproduction. It is apparent now that over the past few decades, special education has steadily grown as a way of addressing children's educational needs. Given the historical role of education in mediating (or rationalizing) group-based social inequalities, this expansion raises important questions about the evolution of social inequality in education. At the same time, it raises important questions about the nature of disability as a social phenomenon. The connection of these questions to special education has barely been addressed by researchers. I want to consider some of the conceptual challenges that these questions seem to pose for the current study of disability and social reproduction.

DISABILITY STUDIES

In the foregoing chapters, I have had almost nothing to say about the growing field of disability studies. Although this field has much to offer, its theoretical premises seem to provide few connections to the research presented here. I want to briefly describe here what kind of theoretical shifts might make these connections possible.

Authors in disability studies typically distinguish their understanding of disability from what is termed the "medical model."[1] The medical model of disability focuses on how physical impairments limit the disabled person and the ways medical interventions—including therapies to alter physical or mental performance, prosthetic devices to replace missing body parts, and genetic screening to prevent the birth of individuals with inherited conditions such as Down syndrome—can minimize or eliminate disabilities at the individual level. The medical model is also said to be implied in dominant institutional and cultural views of disabled people as defective individuals who need to be segregated, "cured," or rehabilitated to suit the interests of the "nondisabled." In this sense, the medical model may be said to dominate not only medical practice, but other domains as well—in particular, educational institutions, insofar as these view disability as being about individual impairment and the needs that flow from impairments.

Starting with this critical view of the medical model, many authors adopt in its place a "social model" of disability, which focuses on the social conditions that currently oppress people with physical impairments.[2] A strong distinction is therefore drawn between *impairment*—the biological condition that produces specific limitations in physical or mental functioning—and *disability*—the limitation of opportunities available to physically impaired people by social or environmental barriers. Based on this distinction, proponents of the social model insist that disability should be seen, first and foremost, as a product of social conditions and not of individual impairments. With this focus in mind, the main solutions to disabled people's problems appear to be not medical "cures" but broad social changes, such as building wheelchair ramps, that address their needs and minimize barriers to their participation in the mainstream of social life.

While few authors in disability studies would question that the social model of disability has been the source of valuable insights and that it has led to useful social reforms, some have begun to ask whether it too has "outlived its usefulness."[3] These critics argue that a rigid application of the social model has led to a suppression of the diverse and complex experiences of disabled people. Perhaps most important, while some proponents of the social model claim that disabled people's specific impairments do not fundamentally affect the experience of disability, which is ostensibly common to all disabled people,[4] critics have noted that people may have different experiences as a result of the specific nature of their impairments—for example, whether the impairment is "visible" or "invisible," congenital or acquired, cognitive or physical. Jill Humphrey further argues that the social model itself implicitly favors certain categories of disability—"physical, immutable, tangible, and 'severe'" disabilities—because these are the conditions for which "social" solutions are most relevant.[5]

It is important to consider in this regard that, as Humphrey observes, it is people with these same physical, immutable, tangible, and severe disabilities who have led the disability rights movement. Their basic assumption that disabled people are like other historically disadvantaged groups—that is, that they are arbitrarily prevented by discriminatory attitudes and practices from fully participating in public life—reflects the condition of people with these kinds of disabilities, where straightforward changes to the social environment can make clear and dramatic improvements in what they can and cannot do. A wheelchair ramp can make a great difference to people with a range of mobility impairments, but it is not clear what would be the social equivalent of a wheelchair ramp for a person with obsessive-compulsive disorder.

Here I pose a question that, so far, seems to be missing from disability studies. If representing disability in light of a social model serves the interests of one set of disabled actors more than another set, might it not also be true that, in some cases, representing disability in terms of a medical model best serves another group of disabled actors? The question, of course, is somewhat rhetorical, since one implication of my arguments is that, by making individualized and technical disability claims on their children's behalf, privileged parents draw on a medicalized construction of their children's difficulties. That is, they argue that they are proof of biological differences (assuming, in the manner of the medical model, that a disabled person's difficulties are the consequence of impairment, not social conditions). They also follow a medical model insofar as they claim that their children require individualized and technically defined services and accommodations rather than criticizing the educational practices that divide disabled and nondisabled students and put the former at a disadvantage. (This is not to say they are wrong to do so, or that some would not prefer a more "social" approach to their children's needs.)

The real question, then, is *why* disability studies has failed to recognize that the medical model of disability, whether it is "true" or "false," sometimes serves the interests of disabled people themselves. There are, it seems to me, at least two obstacles to this recognition. First, there are political considerations. To the extent that disability studies has been created, and is still dominated, by people with "physical, immutable, tangible, and 'severe'" disabilities, it is not surprising that they continue to regard the social model alone as reflecting disabled people's authentic interests and experience, since a social model of disability has seemed to offer them much more than a medical model. Furthermore, the idea that the medical model of disability might appeal to some disabled people challenges the idea, implied or stated in disability studies and disability activism, that disabled people are a politically unified group. It threatens to fracture disabled people along the lines of impairments, lines that are, furthermore, defined in terms of medically defined causes of disability and medically defined approaches to "treating" (or educating) disabled people.

Second, acknowledging that some disabled people may be best served by a medical model of disability draws attention to the fact that undergirding the claim to disability rights is the claim of disability itself, which, for the least obvious disability conditions, must be supported by medical (or quasi-medical) "proof." Yet theorists, in dividing disability from impairment, are forced to accept the objective reality of impairment as the basis on which certain actors can be said to be disadvantaged by *external* circumstances. To acknowledge that impairment is, in fact, contingent on a claim of impairment being made and being supported by certain observations (medical or otherwise) puts that objectivity into question. It raises the possibility that the claim to disability rights might, for some individuals, begin with a self-interested claim to disability itself. From this it follows that the socially constructed boundary around the group of people identified as disabled may simultaneously depend on individual biology, which puts the individual at a disadvantage within a society that is structured to favor nondisabled people, *and* on individual resources, which puts the individual at an *advantage* relative to those who have the same difficulties but are unable to claim impairment and the rights that may flow from that claim. However, the notion that disability could, even in a limited sense, be understood as a kind of social advantage runs counter to virtually all of the thinking that can currently be found in disability studies.

The failure to recognize the importance of the identification of disability is a significant limitation. Insofar as it is bound up with a focus on people with severe, physical disabilities, it prevents disability studies from recognizing the large and growing number of disabled people who have mild mental and behavioral disabilities; indeed, if one looks at children, these make up the overwhelming bulk of all disabilities. At the same time, it prevents disability studies from recognizing that the course of disability rights, especially as they are exercised in the public schools, may be taking a detour from a "social model" understanding of disability rights (as reflected in some of the early arguments in support of the EAHCA) toward a "medical model," precisely because this medical model matches the interests of some disabled children more than others.

SOCIAL REPRODUCTION

I have just suggested that disability studies is limited by its neglect of how social advantages influence the identification of disability. I would similarly argue that the study of how social advantages are transmitted across generations—that is, the study of the social reproduction of class and racial inequality—has been limited by a neglect of how social advantages interact with variations in students' ability. Looking in particular at research on how cultural capital contributes to social reproduction, there is a tendency, observed by Lareau and Weininger, to treat ability as a separate, confounding variable. However, there is an increasingly nuanced understanding of ability that appreciates its integral relation to social reproduction.

A popular understanding of public education holds that it is the great equalizer, a meritocracy in which hardworking, intelligent children are able to transcend lower-class origins. Sociologists are generally less optimistic, based especially on the strong effects of parents' educational achievement on children's educational achievement. In Bourdieu's view, this cross-generational reproduction of educational achievement can be explained by the fact that the educational system favors the distinctive traits of the dominant classes—their cultural capital and the abilities associated with it. Bourdieu explains that "dominants always tend to impose the skills they have mastered as necessary and legitimate and to include in their definition of excellence the practices at which they excel."[6]

While dominant groups collectively affect the standards students are judged by, it is critical to Bourdieu's conception of the reproduction of social class advantages that the school system applies these standards to students in a neutral fashion, without regard to their background—a meritocracy in form but not substance. In such a setting, a privileged child will ordinarily be relatively successful in school, having acquired the benefits of an elite cultural capital in the home, while a disadvantaged child, lacking the same benefits, will be likely to have lower educational achievements. Yet it is possible for the privileged child to fail in school, and it is possible for the hardworking, intelligent child of the working class (like Bourdieu himself) to be a high academic achiever. Such exceptions are also crucial, since they uphold the apparent meritocracy of the educational system. Another important component of this system is the exclusion of parents from direct involvement in their children's education, ostensibly allowing the children to be assessed on their own merits.

Lareau goes beyond Bourdieu by claiming that educational standards are shaped by class interests not simply at a collective level, but also at an individual level. That is, contrary to Bourdieu's belief, privileged parents do not simply pass on cultural capital to their children and passively wait while their abilities are recognized in school. Rather, they intervene in their children's education, bringing a range of economic, cultural, and social resources to bear on how their children are educated. Lareau sees these interventions as potentially critical to students' success, affecting the expectations teachers hold for them and how they assess their ability. Yet in making these interventions, privileged parents do not disrupt the appearance of social neutrality, because they do so by conforming to the expectations that the school holds for *all* parents.

However, as Lareau points out, not all privileged parents are equally involved in their children's education. In *Home Advantage* she finds that, whereas working-class parents were most likely to be involved when their children were succeeding in school, upper-middle-class parents were most involved when their children were doing poorly. Thus it seems that privileged parents do not attempt so much to maximize the success of their high-achieving children as to minimize the failure of the ones who struggle: they maintain a "floor," Lareau suggests, below which their children do not fall.

Lareau's observation suggests that this book's focus on involvement in special education by privileged parents of low-achieving students, who show the highest levels of involvement, may be key to understanding parents' involvement in their children's education more generally. Indeed, the simultaneous expansion of special education enrollments and expenditures, on the one hand, and parents' involvement on the other seems to support the idea that in some respects they reflect each other.

Most obviously, then, this implies the need to consider how parents' involvement, within special education and outside it, varies in response to their children's abilities and needs. This entails a complex view of the ways student ability and student outcomes are related. Typically, research on the achievement gap between privileged and disadvantaged children has taken one of two views: it has treated variation in student ability as something that can simply be ignored, perhaps seeing it as a measure that varies among privileged and disadvantaged children alike and that therefore "comes out in the wash"; or it has recognized that social advantages precede and shape a variety of abilities and hence has treated ability as a partial measure of the influence of social background on students' traits and thus on their academic achievement.[7]

The foregoing, however, raises the possibility of substantially different relations among parental involvement, ability, and student outcomes. Most significantly, it may be necessary to acknowledge that parents' involvement depends both on their resources *and* on their children's specific needs and abilities. This implies a reordering of causal relations and a shift in their expected associations. Whereas it is most common to see ability either as unrelated to social background or as an outcome of both social background and parents' involvement, this alternative view implies that in some respects ability and need stand before involvement and mediate the effects of social background. In this scenario, parents do not create the abilities in their children that lead to success; instead, they recognize their children's needs and pressure schools to adapt to them. This further implies a more complicated path to academic success (however qualified that success might be) than is often supposed. We can assume that a privileged social background generally leads to higher ability, which in turn improves student outcomes. Yet if privileged parents' involvement is also highest for the lowest-ability students (or students who have the greatest needs), then the high parental involvement that seems to represent one of the greatest benefits of a privileged background may also be associated to some degree with low ability and poor academic success. As such, it may be easy to underestimate the positive effects of parents' involvement, inasmuch as its association with low ability may mask the ways it enhances ability and seeks accommodations for its lack.

Recognizing these complicated relations suggests we need research that concerns the individual-level processes shaping the identification of children's abilities and needs without claiming to have a neutral view of those processes or to have objective measures of all the student and parental traits involved. In particular, student traits such as ability, disability, motivation, and needs will often be inherently difficult to measure and to separate from parents' involvement in individual instances. Indeed, parents' designated role in the special education system is, in a sense, to identify the kinds of need and potential not identified by teachers or by standardized tests. As such, research on that role cannot rely simply on objective measures of students' abilities and needs but must also document the ways parents make claims *about* abilities and needs.

In attempting this kind of research, then, I have tried to show not only that parents play an important role in identifying their children's disabilities and related needs, but also that this role presupposes a set of perceptions and beliefs about how parents can and should contribute—perceptions and beliefs that favor the involvement of particular groups of parents. As such, claims that are explicitly about children's needs are also, implicitly, about parents' right and capacity to make claims about them. By making explicit what is usually implicit—and by being implicit allows the special education system to appear more equitable than it is—I hope to have encouraged others to create a more equitable way of educating children with disabilities.

APPENDIX

———— ✳ ————

Parent Survey

IN LATE April 2003, a survey (reproduced below) was mailed to one thousand families with children in special education in a large urban school district in California. The total number comprised five groups of two hundred families, based on five disability categories into which their children were classified by the district: specific learning disability, speech or language impairment, mental retardation, autism, and other health impairment (including attention deficit disorder). To increase the likelihood that recipients would understand the survey well and to increase the response rate, only families with English as the first language in the home were selected.

Item response rates were very high on all closed-choice items. Slightly over half of the 157 parents who responded wrote a response to the last, open-choice item on the survey, describing conflicts they had had with their disabled children's schools over evaluation, placement, and discipline. Rates for responses on relation to the child, race, income, and education ranged from 93% (income) to 100% (relation to child). Responses for the specific race categories were as follows: 68.5% white; 13.4% African American; 6.7% Hispanic/Latino(a); and 6.0% Asian, with only 2.0% indicating multiple race. Responses for specific income categories, based on those in the 2000 U.S. Census, were as follows: 6.8% less than $17,500; 10.3% from $17,500 to $24,999; 8.9% from $25,000 to $34,999; 8.9% from $35,000 to $44,999; 9.6% from $45,000 to $54,999; 17.1% from $55,000 to $74,999; 13.7% from $75,000 to $99,999; and 24.7% at or above $100,000.

Comparing these data with district-level data from the 2000 U.S. Census available at the Web site of the National Center for Education Statistics (http://nces.ed.gov/), we can say that respondents were "whiter," wealthier, and more educated than parents in the general population of the district and, in all likelihood, than parents of special education students in the district. This bias in the response was not unexpected. Earlier research indicates that survey response rates are often lower for minorities and people with less education and income, especially when there is no incentive to respond (such as monetary compensation).[1] That a disproportionately small number of Hispanic parents responded was also predictable given the decision to exclude from the sample households where the first language was not English. While these biases would have been particularly distressing for a study focused on the experiences of *disadvantaged* parents in the special education system, here they mean that, despite a low overall response rate (157 out of 1,000), there are a good number of responses from the type of parents that is of greatest interest here—parents who are relatively privileged by their backgrounds and their resources.

PLEASE <u>DO NOT</u> PLACE YOUR NAME ON THIS SURVEY.

If you have more than one child with a disability condition, answer all questions only about the child diagnosed first.

1) I am the ☐ mother ☐ father ☐ other _____ (describe relation)
   of a child with a disability. (Please check one box.)

2) Please identify the disability (or disabilities) with which your child has been diagnosed.

☐ specific learning disability ☐ speech or language impairment ☐ mental retardation

☐ autism ☐ attention deficit disorder

☐ other _____

3) How old was your child when first diagnosed? (If diagnosed with more than one disability,
   answer for the first condition diagnosed.) _____

4) Who first said that your child had this disability? (Please check one box.)
☐ a school evaluation team
☐ a personal physician or psychiatrist
☐ other (Please explain: _____)

5) What type of placement does your child have?
☐ full inclusion in a regular classroom without an assistant
☐ full inclusion in a regular classroom with an assistant
☐ a separate special day class
☐ part-time placement in a resource room

6) About how much of the time at school does your child spend in a resource room or separate
   special day class? (Please check one box.)
☐ none of the time
☐ one or two hours per day
☐ around half of the time
☐ all but one or two hours per day
☐ all of the time

Please indicate how much you agree or disagree with the following statements by checking one box:

7) In matters involving my child's disability, I have a positive relationship with my child's
   school.
☐ strongly agree ☐ agree ☐ disagree ☐ strongly disagree

8) The school has been able to help me understand my child's disability.
☐ strongly agree ☐ agree ☐ disagree ☐ strongly disagree

9) I have been able to help the school understand my child's disability.
☐ strongly agree ☐ agree ☐ disagree ☐ strongly disagree

10) Have you ever had any doubts about whether your child is correctly diagnosed? (Please check one box.)

☐ No

☐ Yes (Please explain briefly:_____

_____

_____

_____)

The following questions concern the amount of time you have spent **learning** about your child's disability, not including your direct experiences with your child. This could include reading books and articles (print or online) for a general audience, speaking with medical or other professionals, or attending conferences or lectures.

11) **Before** your child was diagnosed, how much time did you spend learning about your child's condition?
   - ☐ no time at all
   - ☐ 1-2 hours
   - ☐ 3-10 hours
   - ☐ more than 10 hours

12) **In the first month** after your child was diagnosed, how much time did you spend learning about your child's condition? (Skip this question if your child was diagnosed less than a month ago.)
   - ☐ no time at all
   - ☐ 1-2 hours
   - ☐ 3-10 hours
   - ☐ more than 10 hours

13) **Currently**, how often do you spend time learning about your child's condition? (Skip this question if your child was diagnosed within the past month.)
   - ☐ no time at all/less than once a month
   - ☐ at least once a month
   - ☐ at least once a week

14) Please estimate:

the number of support group meetings (relating to your child's disability) you have ever attended:
____

the number of articles (print or online) you have read that concern your child's condition:_____

the number of books you have read that concern your child's condition:_____

the number of conferences you have attended concerning your child's condition:_____

15) Please name any books or articles that have been especially helpful for you in dealing with your child's condition.

Title:_____ Author (if known):_____

Title:_____ Author (if known):_____

16) Please name any nonprofit organizations that you have been involved with or sought information from as a result of your child's disability.

organization name:_____

organization name:_____

17) Please check one box to indicate your total household income for last year:

☐ $17,499 or less   ☐ $45,000 to $54,999
☐ $17,500 to $24,999   ☐ $55,000 to $74,999
☐ $25,000 to $34,999   ☐ $75,000 to $99,999
☐ $35,000 to $44,999   ☐ $100,000 or more

18) Please check one box to indicate the highest level of formal education you have completed.
☐ less than high school graduation or equivalent
☐ high school graduate or equivalent
☐ some college, no diploma
☐ A.A./B.A./B.S. (circle one) (major field:_____)
☐ other graduate or professional degree

    (Please indicate degree and field):_____)

19) Please identify your occupation: _____

20) What is your race/ethnicity? (Please check one or more boxes.)

☐ White   ☐ African-American   ☐ Asian   ☐ American Indian   ☐ Hispanic/Latino/a

☐ other:_____

21) If you have experienced a particular conflict with your child's school involving his/her disability and wish to describe it, please do so here. (Continue responses on the back of this sheet if necessary.)

Thank you very much for taking the time to complete this survey.

Notes

INTRODUCTION

1. 458 U.S. 176.

2. At the same time, the title (its content and its duality) is an allusion to Pierre Bourdieu's use of the term "distinction" (most famously, in a book with that title). The dual sense of "distinguishing" (or of "distinction") can be found in Bourdieu's work and was in many ways an early inspiration for the research presented here.

3. Extensive explanations and elaborations of the concept of cultural capital can be found in chapters 3 and 5 of this book.

4. The names of the subjects in this book have all been changed to pseudonyms. Substitute first names and last names have roughly the same ethnic-linguistic origins, and first names have roughly the same popularity around the estimated time of a subject's birth.

5. Sharon has one older son, but she had Dylan when she was thirty-six. Using the years 1999-2004 of the General Social Survey, I found a 0.80 correlation between the age of respondents at the birth of a first child and respondents' average socioeconomic status for each reported age-at-birth (including ages fourteen to forty-three).

CHAPTER ONE

1. Public Law 94-142.

2. For consistency, "disabilities" and "disabled" are used here and elsewhere even where "handicaps" and "handicapped" might have been the terms used at the (earlier) time.

3. Given the then-current definitions of disability, this figure was perhaps an exaggeration. Nevertheless, the actual number probably was in the hundreds of thousands and would have been higher in 1970, before many state and federal initiatives to provide education to disabled children had gotten under way. Clune and Van Pelt, "A Political Method of Evaluating the Education for All Handicapped Children Act."

4. Kirp and Kirp, "Legalization of the School Psychologist's World"; Mercer, *Labeling the Mentally Retarded;* Neal and Kirp, "Allure of Legalization Reconsidered."

5. Public Law 93-112.

6. Hessler, "Letter." John Hessler, a prominent disability activist of the time, claims that he and other disability activists/advocates helped draft parts of the Rehabilitation Act, including Section 504.

7. Scotch, "Politics and Policy in the History of the Disability Rights Movement"; Shapiro, *No Pity*; Skrentny, *Minority Rights Revolution*.

8. This is to refer only to the Rehabilitation Act's Section 504, the one paragraph in the act that actually addressed the rights of people with disabilities.

9. 343 F. Supp. 279 (E.D. Pa. 1972).

10. 348 F. Supp. 866 (D.C. D.C. 1972).

11. Ironically, the Department of Welfare was required by the same laws to "arrange for the care, *training* and supervision of such child" (343 F. Supp. at 281, citing 24 Purd. Stat. Sec. 13-1375, emphasis mine).

12. *EHA*, 46.

13. In response to the Mills agreement, the District of Columbia Board of Education had already passed a resolution stating its intention to "establish procedures to implement the finding that all children can benefit from education and ... have a right to it" (348 F. Supp at 872).

14. This decision was produced by the court after the District of Columbia Board of Education failed to abide by the agreement it had struck with the plaintiffs. While the board tried to justify this failure, the court found this justification unacceptable and subsequently affirmed the plaintiffs' original claims.

15. In addition to the specific rights for children and parents, the EAHCA contained provisions for training of special education teachers, requirements for state-level special education plans, funding formulas, and many other items that are not of particular interest here.

16. Melnick, *Between the Lines*, 149.

17. See reference list under Education for the Handicapped Act (EHA) and Education for All Handicapped Children Act (EAHCA).

18. *EAHCA 1*, 26.

19. *EAHCA 1*, 21.

20. Public Law 94-142, Section 612 (5)(B).

21. Public Law 94-142, Section 618 (d)(2)(A), emphasis mine.

22. *EAHCA 2*, 660.

23. *EAHCA 1*, 25.

24. *EHA*, 247.

25. PL 94-142, Section 612 (5)(C), emphasis mine.

26. *EAHCA 2*, 658.

27. President's Committee on Mental Retardation, "The Six-Hour Retarded Child," 724.

28. *EAHCA 1*, 29.

29. *EAHCA 1*, 46.

30. Clune and Van Pelt, "Political Method of Evaluating the Education for All Handicapped Children Act," 13.

31. Kirp, Buss, and Kuriloff, "Legal Reform of Special Education."

32. A more current term is "inclusion," although this often refers not just to being placed in the regular classroom, but also to how far students' services meaningfully allow them to participate equally in the regular classroom's curriculum.

33. Lipsky and Gartner, "Capable of Achievement and Worthy of Respect"; Saina, "Advocating for Full Inclusion: Mothers' Narratives"; Skrtic, Sailor, and Gee, "Voice, Collaboration, and Inclusion"; Stainback, Stainback, and Forest, *Educating All Students in the Mainstream;* Wang and Walberg, "Four Fallacies of Segregationism."

34. McLeskey, Hoppey, Williamson, and Rentz, "Is Inclusion an Illusion?" Williamson, McLeskey, Hoppey, and Rentz, "Educating Students with Mental Retardation in General Education Classrooms."

35. Coutinho and Repp, "Enhancing the Meaningful Inclusion of Students with Disabilities"; Danielson and Bellamy, "State Variation in Placement of Children with Handicaps in Segregated Environments"; Singer et al., "Variation in Special Education Classification across School Dis-

tricts." Other patterns have been found, too, although they do not seem to suggest a broad trend toward greater mainstreaming.

36. Fierros and Conroy, "Double Jeopardy."

37. Meier, Stewart, and England, *Race, Class, and Education*. Their sample included only school districts with a 1976 enrollment of 15,000 or more.

38. There is a consistent tendency for African American students to be overrepresented in specific disability categories (especially stigmatizing ones). There is uneven evidence of such a tendency for other minority groups. Some studies in the 1980s suggested that Hispanic students continued to be overrepresented among mentally retarded students, but this tendency seems to have disappeared or even reversed in recent years (Parrish, "Racial Disparities in the Identification, Funding, and Provision of Special Education"; Wright and Santa Cruz, "Ethnic Composition of Special Education Classrooms in California"). Recent studies also indicate that black students and American Indian students are overrepresented in the categories of mental retardation and severe emotional disturbance (Parrish; Wright and Santa Cruz; Oswald and Coutinho, "Trends in Disproportionate Representation"; Oswald et al., "Ethnic Representation in Special Education"). In general, Asian American students are underrepresented relative to white students in special education (see, e.g., Office of Special Education Programs, *Twenty-second Annual Report*).

39. Singer and Butler, "The Education for All Handicapped Children Act: Schools as Agents of Social Reform." On parents' low attendance and participation at IEP meetings, see also Clune and Van Pelt, "Political Method of Evaluating the Education for All Handicapped Children Act."

40. "SEELS Info and Reports: Wave 1 Wave 2 Overview" (http://www.seels.net/seels_textonly/info_reports/w1w2_overview.htm), accessed January 20, 2008.

41. Engel, "Origin Myths"; Mehan, Hertweck, and Meihls, *Handicapping the Handicapped*.

42. Harry, "Ethnographic Study of Cross-Cultural Communication with Puerto Rican–American Families in the Special Education System," 472.

43. On the different threshold for disability in minority families, see Harry, "Trends and Issues in Serving Culturally Diverse Families of Children with Disabilities." Harry's research on Puerto Rican families appears in "Ethnographic Study of Cross-Cultural Communication."

44. 458 U.S. 176.

45. 483 F. Supp. 528, 532 (SDNY 1980).

46. On the general downturn in class-action suits, see Douglas Martin, "The Rise and Fall of the Class-Action Lawsuit," *New York Times*, January 8, 1988.

47. 476 F. Supp 583 (E.D. Pa. 1979).

48. The original plaintiffs were five children who were either in the category "severely and profoundly impaired" (IQ below 30) or "severely emotionally disturbed" and were certified as representing the class of "all handicapped school aged persons in the Commonwealth of Pennsylvania who require or who may require a program of special education and related services in excess of 180 days per year and the parents or guardians of such persons" (476 F. Supp. at 586 [E.D. Pa. 1979]).

49. 967 F.2d 1298 (9th Cir. 1992).

50. 34 C.F.R. Section 300.550.

51. Thomas and Rapport, "Least Restrictive Environment."

52. Clune and Van Pelt, "Political Method of Evaluating the Education for All Handicapped Children Act."

CHAPTER TWO

1. Bourdieu and Passeron, *Inheritors*; Bourdieu, "Cultural Reproduction and Social Reproduction," 73.

2. Lamont and Lareau, "Cultural Capital," 156.

3. Lareau and Shumar, "Problem of Individualism in Family-School Policies."

4. Brown, "'Third Wave'"; Reay, *Class Work.*

5. Lareau, *Home Advantage,* 170.

6. Reid and Valle, "Discursive Practice of Learning Disability," 475.

7. In reporting the number of articles they had read, some parents used terms such as "a lot" or "tons." I have placed such responses in the "above fifty" range.

8. In the case of multiple diagnoses, it was not possible to determine which was given at the reported age. Therefore median age estimates for specific diagnoses refer here only to isolated cases—only, that is, to cases where the given condition is not indicated alongside another condition.

9. As in most cases of multiple diagnosis, it is not clear which was given at the reported age of diagnosis, or if diagnoses were given simultaneously.

10. Child Find programs, which are set up to locate and identify young children with disabilities who might be in need of early intervention programs, are a requirement for states to receive funding under the Individuals with Disabilities Education Act, the successor to the EAHCA.

11. Respondents were instructed to answer all questions about the first child diagnosed if they had more than one child with disabilities.

CHAPTER THREE

1. Estimates are based on the number of students aged six to seventeen enrolled in U.S. public schools. The data come from tables given in the 1997 and 2004 Annual Reports to Congress of the U.S. Department of Education Office of Special Education Programs and from an electronic data file distributed by the Office for Civil Rights (OCR) in the U.S. Department of Education (Elementary & Secondary School Civil Rights Compliance Report Time Series Data, 1968-1998).

2. Estimates are based on the number of students aged six to seventeen enrolled in U.S. public schools. The data come from tables given in the 2004 Annual Report to Congress of the U.S. Department of Education Office of Special Education Programs and from an electronic data file distributed from the Office for Civil Rights in the U.S. Department of Education (Elementary & Secondary School Civil Rights Compliance Report Time Series Data, 1968-1998).

3. Parsons, *Social System.*

4. Epstein, *Impure Science: AIDS, Activism, and the Politics of Knowledge.* See also Arksey, "Expert and Lay Participation in the Construction of Medical Knowledge," and Brown, "Popular Epidemiology and Toxic Waste Contamination."

5. Epstein, *Impure Science,* 263.

6. Dunn, "Special Education for the Mildly Retarded—Is Much of It Justifiable?"; U.S. Department of Education, Office of Special Education Programs, Twenty-second Annual Report; Oswald and Coutinho, "Identification and Placement of Students with Serious Emotional Disturbance"; "Trends in Disproportionate Representation"; Oswald, Coutinho, and Best, "Community and School Predictors of Minority Children in Special Education"; Parrish, "Racial Disparities."

7. MacMillan and Reschly, "Overrepresentation of Minority Students."

8. See, e.g., Argulewicz, "Effects of Ethnic Membership, Socioeconomic Status, and Home Language on LD, EMR, and EH Placements"; Coles, *Learning Mystique: A Critical Look at "Learning Disabilities"*; Smith, *How Educators Decide Who Is Learning Disabled.*

9. On early claims of LD's being a white, middle-class condition, see Coles, *Learning Mystique;* Gelb and Mizokawa, "Special Education and Social Structure"; McLaughlin and Owings, "Relationships among States' Fiscal and Demographic Data and the Implementation of P.L. 94-112"; and *Smith, How Educators Decide Who Is Learning Disabled.* On the reverse claim, see, e.g., Artiles et al., "English-Language Learner Representation in Special Education in California Urban School Districts," and Coutinho, Oswald, and Best, "Influence of Sociodemographics and

Gender on the Disproportionate Identification of Minority Students as Having Learning Disabilities."

10. Crawford, "History of LDA."

11. Carrier, *Learning Disability;* Gearheart and Gearheart, *Learning Disabilities.*

12. Carrier, *Learning Disability,* 100.

13. Such collective pressure is evidenced by two notable class-action suits: *Larry P. v. Wilson Riles* (343 F. Supp. 1306 [N.D. Cal. 1972]) and *Diana v. California State Board of Education* (C-70-37 [RFP] [N.D. Cal. 1970]). In *Larry P.* the plaintiffs, black schoolchildren in California, alleged that racially discriminatory IQ testing was leading to an undue number of black children being identified as mentally retarded. In *Diana,* which ended in a consent decree before reaching a hearing, the plaintiffs alleged that Mexican American students were being incorrectly identified as mentally retarded because IQ tests were not administered in Spanish. Both cases resulted in agreements favorable to the plaintiffs.

14. Mehan, Mercer and Rueda, "Special Education."

15. Agbenyega and Jiggets, "Minority Children and Their Over-representation in Special Education"; Eitle, "Special Education or Racial Segregation?" On high-stakes testing and special education placements, see Allington and McGill-Franzen, "Unintended Effects of Educational Reform in New York."

16. On low spending for minority students, see Chambers, Kidron, and Spain, *Characteristics of High-Expenditure Students with Disabilities, 1999-2000;* Parrish, "Racial Disparities." On discriminatory segregation of minority students in special education, see Eitle, "Special Education or Racial Segregation?" and Fierros and Conroy, "Double Jeopardy." On advocacy of mainstreaming, see McLeskey, Henry, and Axelrod, "Inclusion of Students with Learning Disabilities," and Skrtic, Sailor, and Gee, "Voice, Collaboration, and Inclusion."

17. The following discussion is based on a more rigorous statistical analysis I conducted. Some of the results have been published elsewhere (Ong-Dean, "High Roads and Low Roads: Learning Disabilities in California, 1976-1998"). This article gives findings for the years 1976, 1986, 1998. A later (unpublished) analysis I conducted, using the same method and models, included data for 2002. Data for all these analyses are taken from Elementary and Secondary School Compliance Reports to the Office for Civil Rights in the U.S. Department of Education. In the present analysis it was necessary to eliminate cases where, within a given district, a small sample of students of a certain race might by chance contain a very high or very low percentage of students with LD, exerting undue influence on estimated group rates of LD. Therefore all districts with fewer than thirty students in any of the racial categories (Hispanic, black, or white) have been eliminated from the analysis below. Districts with LD rates higher than 20 percent were also eliminated.

18. For instance, when district-level minority percentage of California school districts in the year 2000 is matched with district-level median family income in 2000, there is a strong, though hardly perfect, negative correlation of -0.403. The correlation between the percentage of school-age children (five to seventeen years old) below the poverty line and minority percentage is 0.471. These figures are based on data obtained from the National Center for Education Statistics Common Core of Data (http://nces.ed.gov/ccd). In an earlier analysis, other district-level demographic variables were incorporated into the models, including the proportion of householders with a bachelor's degree or higher, median household income, and the proportion of households within various ranges of the statewide income distribution. However, this approach limited selection of years to those closest to census years, and variables were not reported consistently across years. Furthermore, district matches of OCR and Census data may not have been perfect. In general, "minority proportion" showed stronger effects than these demographic variables. Given the problems of year and district mismatches, it is possible that "minority proportion" is actually a better measure (albeit a proxy one) of districts' socioeconomic

status, and it also has the advantage of covering dimensions of disadvantage these other variables might miss. For all these reasons, the other demographic variables were dropped from the models.

19. See Ong-Dean, "High Roads and Low Roads: Learning Disabilities in California, 1976–1998." While this analysis does not include data for 2002, my own unpublished findings indicate a continuation of the trend in 2002.

20. Note that in the data underlying this and the following three figures, all districts with thirty or fewer students in the given racial group were eliminated when computing averages in order to avoid undue influence of misleadingly high or low LD rates that are possible among very small samples. In 1998 and 2002, districts were also eliminated if they had LD rates above 40 percent and obviously served a special function. Although each such case had a distinct district code, they were labeled "Office of Education" for a given district.

21. For consistency, I do not use the terms "developmentally delayed" or "developmentally disabled," which are now often preferred to "mentally retarded." The former terms have the disadvantage of including conditions that are clearly different from what is recognized as mental retardation and of conveying the possibly false impression that individuals will ultimately "develop" past their impairments. The justification that "mental retardation" should be replaced because it is stigmatizing brings to mind Robin Lakoff's observation that when a new term is created to refer to a stigmatized group, the stigma is not removed; instead, the new term acquires the existing stigma.

22. Daily, Ardinger, and Holmes, "Identification and Evaluation of Mental Retardation"; Leung et al., "Mental Retardation."

23. Jones, "Education for Children with Mental Retardation."

24. Castles, "'Nice, Average Americans,'" 354.

25. Friedman, *Identity's Architect*. According to Friedman, Erikson reached the decision and signed the requisite papers while his wife, Joan, lay unconscious in the hospital, not yet informed that her newborn son had Down syndrome.

26. Hughes and Seneca, "Housing Bubble or Shelter-Safe Haven?"

27. 343 F. Supp at 287.

28. Castles, "'Nice, Average Americans'" Jones, "Education for Children with Mental Retardation."

29. Davila, Williams, and MacDonald, "Memorandum to Chief State School Officers."

30. The corresponding figures for searches on "attention deficit/hyperactivity disorder" are lower but show the same trend.

31. Lakoff, "Adaptive Will."

32. American Academy of Child and Adolescent Psychiatry, "Practice Parameters for the Assessment and Treatment of Children, Adolescents, and Adults with Attention-Deficit/Hyperactivity Disorder."

33. Popper, "Disorders Usually First Evident in Infancy, Childhood, or Adolescence." It is commonly claimed, without attributing it to original research, that one-third to one-half of all referrals to child mental services are for children with ADHD, a claim that goes back as far as 1988 (Barkley, "Attention-Deficit/Hyperactivity Disorder"; Wells et al., "Psychosocial Treatment Strategies in the MTA Study").

34. Barkley, "Attention-Deficit/Hyperactivity Disorder," 75. It is true that Still's concern with lack of moral control, also described as a defect of "inhibitory volition," seems to suggest the alleged impulsiveness of the ADHD child. Also consistent with the later ADHD diagnosis is Still's remark that "a quite abnormal incapacity for sustained attention" is "a notable feature in many of these cases of moral defect without general impairment of intellect" (Still, "Some Abnormal Psychical Conditions in Children," 1009, 1081). Yet these similarities to the later ADHD diagnosis are difficult to discern in the broader pattern of behavior Still identifies in this group

of children, a pattern characterized by "(1) passionateness; (2) spitefulness-cruelty; (3) jealousy; (4) lawlessness; (5) dishonesty; (6) wanton mischievousness-destructiveness; (7) shamelessness-immodesty; (8) sexual immorality; and (9) viciousness" (1009). Clearly these are not the defining characteristics of the current disorder.

35. Rosemond, "ADHD? Sure, But It's Not Organic," *San Diego Union-Tribune*, May 17, 2003, E-9; Diller, *Running on Ritalin*. See also Armstrong, *Myth of the A.D.D. Child*, and Breggin, *Talking Back to Ritalin*.

36. Bussing, Schoenberg, and Perwien, "Knowledge and Information About ADHD"; Bussing et al., "Barriers to Detection, Help-Seeking, and Service Use."

37. Centers for Disease Control and Prevention, "Mental Health in the United States." The specific measure of family education is the most highly educated adult in the child's family, with the lowest level being "less than high school," the next level being "high school graduate," and the highest being "more than high school."

38. A study led by Judith Rapoport, "Dextroamphetamine-Cognitive and Behavioral Effects in Normal Prepubertal Boys," is commonly cited as the original proof that the effects of stimulants on "normal" children were similar to their effects on "hyperkinetic" or "MBD" children. Later studies have claimed there are nevertheless differences in the degree of stimulants' effects depending on whether or not the subjects are ADHD and on the severity of their symptoms (DuPaul, Rapport, and Vyse, "ADHD and Methylphenidate Responders"; Teicher et al., "Rate Dependency Revisited"). That stimulants can reduce ADHD symptoms—in particular, hyperactivity—has been supported by many studies, but long-term improvements in academic achievement have often not appeared (MTA Cooperative Group, "A 14-Month Randomized Clinical Trial"; Schachter et al., "How Efficacious and Safe Is Short-Acting Methylphenidate?").

39. U.S. Department of Education, *Teaching Children with Attention Deficit Hyperactivity Disorder*.

40. On parents and fraudulent ADHD diagnoses, see Kenneth R. Weiss, "New Test-Taking Skill: Working the System," *Los Angeles Times*, January 9, 2000. For an overview of research on the effects of test accommodations for disabled students, see Sireci, Li, and Scarpati, *Effects of Test Accommodation on Test Performance*.

41. On the lack of long-term academic benefits of Ritalin use, see n. 38 above. For a summary of a broad range of research findings on the effects of methylphenidate (Ritalin) use, see Center for the Evaluation of Risks to Human Reproduction, *NTP-CERHR Expert Panel Report on the Reproductive and Developmental Toxicity of Methylphenidate*.

42. Lan, "Pharmaceuticals: Conspiracy to Increase Ritalin Profits Alleged."

43. Kanner, "Autistic Disturbances of Affective Contact," 242, emphasis in original.

44. Eisenberg and Kanner, "Early Infantile Autism, 1943-1955."

45. "The Child Is Father," *Time*, July 25, 1960, 78. In 1969 Kanner disavowed the parent-blaming thesis in a speech before the National Society for Autistic Children (later the Autism Society of America), saying, "I herewith especially acquit you people as parents" (Pollak, *Creation of Dr. B*). In a follow-up to his original 1943 study, he also denied responsibility for promoting the notion that parents were to blame for their children's autism (Kanner, "Follow-up Study of Eleven Autistic Children"). While it is implausible that Kanner did not promote parent blame at all, it is true that in his 1956 article with Eisenberg he had argued that deficient parenting alone could not cause autism but must be complemented by an inborn vulnerability.

46. For a description of past research claiming to confirm a positive association between social class and autism or failing to confirm it, see Croen, Grether, and Selvin, "Descriptive Epidemiology of Autism in a California Population."

47. Ibid., 221. On the discrediting of the idea that parents are to blame for their children's autism, see Dolnick, *Madness on the Couch*.

48. Thomas Maugh, "'Sobering' State Report Calls Autism an Epidemic," *Los Angeles Times*, October 18, 2002, home edition. In ProQuest (database online).

49. Frith, *Autism: Explaining the Enigma*, 61.

50. Ibid., 58–59. On the relation of changing criteria for autism diagnosis and the historical increase in the number of diagnoses, see also Croen et al., "Changing Prevalence of Autism in California."

51. Thomas Maugh, "New Autism Cases Level Off in State," *Los Angeles Times*, July 13, 2005, home edition. In ProQuest (database online).

52. Arthur Allen, "The Not-So-Crackpot Autism Theory," *New York Times*, November 10, 2002. In LexisNexis (database online); Mark Benjamin, "UPI Investigates: The Vaccine Conflict," *United Press International*, July 21, 2003. In LexisNexis (database online).

53. A 2003 report of the California Department of Developmental Services, *Autistic Spectrum Disorders: Changes in the California Caseload*, indicated that the median age at which children were being diagnosed with autism was four years. Supporters of vaccine-exposure arguments claim that vaccination may cause a regression in social and communicative ability shortly after a child is vaccinated, but diagnosis may not be immediate, ostensibly because further signs of abnormal development are required. Supporters of a genetic argument tend to describe the age at which autism is diagnosed as depending on the child's developmental stage, in part because key symptoms of autism cannot be distinguished from normal infant behavior.

54. Krause et al., "Immune Factors in Autism," 342.

55. In theory, of course, there is no reason for environmental and genetic arguments about the cause of autism to be mutually exclusive. Indeed, research findings published in 2005 suggest that autism may be caused by the coincidence of mercury exposure and a specific genetic vulnerability (Hornig, Chian, and Lipkin, "Neurotoxic Effects of Postnatal Thimerosal Are Mouse Strain Dependent"). Yet in practice there are often two warring camps, and it seems unlikely their war will end soon.

56. Croen et al., "Changing Prevalence of Autism in California."

57. National Research Council, *Educating Children with Autism*, 166.

58. A sample of such cases can be found on the autism page of Wrightslaw.com (http://www.wrightslaw.com/info/autism.index.htm). In one notable case, a state hearing officer ruled that a Colorado school district had to reimburse the parents of an autistic boy over $200,000 in costs for sending their son to an out-of-state residential school for autistic students (Karen Rouse, "Ruling Hobbles School District," *Denver Post*, July 14, 2005).

59. On questions of the effectiveness of ABA, see Gresham and MacMillan, "Autistic Recovery?" Schopler, Short, and Mesibov, "Relation of Behavioral Treatment to 'Normal Functioning'"; and Smith, "Outcome of Early Intervention for Children with Autism." On the ethics of ABA, see Dawson, "Misbehaviour of Behaviourists." Children Injured by Restraint and Aversives (CIBRA) also provides information on injuries and psychological problems related to ABA therapy at http://users.1st.net/cibra.

60. Laurie Tarkan, "Autism Therapy Effective, but Rare," *New York Times*, October 22, 2002.

CHAPTER FOUR

1. Kress, "Ideological Structures in Discourse," 27.

2. Smith, *Your Nonlearning Child*, 84; Lewis, Strauss, and Lehtinen, *Other Child*, 81.

3. Brutten, Richardson, and Mangel, *Something's Wrong with My Child*, 76.

4. Johnson, *Diagnosis of Learning Disabilities*.

5. Lewis, Strauss, and Lehtinen, *Other Child*, 88.

6. Waltz, *Obsessive-Compulsive Disorder*, xiii.

7. Koplewicz, *It's Nobody's Fault*, 4, emphasis in original.

8. Osman, *Learning Disabilities and ADHD*, 32.

9. Attwood, *Asperger's Syndrome*, 142.

10. Silver, *Misunderstood Child*, 16.

11. Nosek, *Dyslexic Scholar*.

12. Lareau, *Unequal Childhoods*, 199.

13. Eisenberg and Kanner, "Early Infantile Autism, 1943–1955"; but see chapter 3, note 45.

14. Bettelheim, *Empty Fortress*, 71.

15. Pollak, *Creation of Dr. B.*

16. Ibid., 275.

17. For other examples of narratives by parents of autistic children, see Greenfeld, *Child Called Noah*, and Kaufman, *Son-Rise*. In a more recent narrative, *Raising Blaze*, Ginsberg gives a sense of the uncertainty that can surround a diagnosis of autism. Her son Blaze has been alternatively diagnosed as autistic, mentally retarded, ADD, and PDD-NOS (pervasive developmental disorder not otherwise specified).

18. After his death in December 2006, obituaries widely credited Rimland with primary responsibility for the shift from psychogenic to biogenic explanations of autism. The *Los Angeles Times*, for instance, wrote that Rimland "demolished the generally held view that autism was the psychological byproduct of 'refrigerator mothers'" (Thomas H. Maugh, "Bernard Rimland, 78; Author Was the Father of Modern Autism Research," *Los Angeles Times*, November 26, 2006).

19. Rimland, *Infantile Autism*, 43–44.

20. Silver, *Misunderstood Child*, 38.

21. Brutten, Richardson, and Mangel, *Something's Wrong with My Child*, 21–23.

22. Wing, *Autistic Children*, 34.

23. Green and Chee, *Understanding ADHD*, 88.

24. Cohen, *Targeting Autism*, 136.

25. Hallowell, *When You Worry about the Child You Love*, 21.

26. Smardon, "Broken Brains and Broken Homes: The Meaning of Special Education in an Appalachian Community"; Lareau, *Unequal Childhoods*.

27. Notably, in recent years federal laws and regulations have discouraged the use of the discrepancy criterion. The wrightslaw.com Web site, a site on special education law and advocacy, produced an especially helpful discussion of this transition in the federal attitude in December 2005 (http://www.wrightslaw.com/idea/art/ld.rti.discrep.htm). The discussion points to a reason that even privileged parents might object to the criterion—that it might require students' achievement to fall below a certain level before they can get needed special education services.

28. McNamara and McNamara, *Keys to Parenting a Child with a Learning Disability*, 50.

29. Osman, *Learning Disabilities and ADHD*, 27, emphasis mine.

30. Fisher, *Parents' Guide to Learning Disabilities*, xi.

31. See esp. Grant, *Raising Baby by the Book*.

32. This is in no way to say that we should return to the tendency to blame parents for their children's disabilities. Rather, it is to note that the emphasis on *not* doing so may become, in this literature, a basis for claiming disability in the first place and for questioning other people's judgment about the readers' children.

CHAPTER FIVE

1. 458 U.S. at 207 and 208, citing *San Antonio Independent School Dist. v. Rodriquez*, 411 U.S. at 42.

2. Engel, "Origin Myths," 808.

3. Bourdieu, "Forms of Capital," 246.

4. Ordinarily, two such claims are consolidated by the Hearing Office into one case. Therefore, the numbers of cases in school districts discussed below are not increased by subsequent counterclaims brought by schools.

5. Currently the U.S. Census treats "Hispanic or Latino" as a category distinct from race, but it reports data that cross-classify self-identification in this category and racial self-identification. In computing "Race," I added the number of "Black or African American" parents to the number of "Hispanic or Latino" parents and subtracted the number of "Hispanic or Latino" parents who identified themselves as "Black or African American," then divided by the total number of parents.

6. Within the theoretical framework used here, it is difficult to say what such districts represent, being characterized by contradictory expectations about the relationships among race, income, and education. It does not appear, however, that unclassified districts provide many clear contrasts to the expected race-class relationships. For instance, recombining the criteria used for classifying "wealthy white" and "poor minority" districts, only 30 of the 378 unclassified districts could be described as "poor white" districts, and only 3 could be described as "wealthy minority" districts.

7. When the data were broken down across four categories of district size, the distributional pattern was the same, with the exception of the smallest size category (fewer than 481 parents), where all thirteen requests were clustered in eleven middle-class and unclassified districts. Given the small number of parents and requests in this smallest category, this pattern in smaller districts is more likely to be accidental than due to any fundamentally different tendencies in small districts.

8. That there are thirty-one more requests reported in table 5.1 presumably is because, in rare cases, more than one district is named as a respondent, so that a single request would be represented more than once in the table.

9. There is not an exact overlap between hearing requests and cases resulting in a mediation disposition because many of these 2,403 mediation dispositions would have resulted from hearings requested in the previous year, while some requested in the current year would not have ended yet.

10. Charles Whitaker, "The Rodney King Wake-up Call: Which Way America?" *Ebony* 47, no. 9 (July 1992): 116 (3). *Expanded Academic ASAP. Thomson Gale.* Accessed April 3, 2006.

11. Stephanie Chavez, "Schools Sued over Access to Special Education Classes," *Los Angeles Times*, November 23, 1993; Holly Edwards, "Catalyst of Change—10 Years Later, Smith Still Helping Special Ed Students," *Daily News of Los Angeles*, August 26, 2002.

12. Personal communication with Karen Erickson, legal assistant, ACLU of Southern California, May 12, 2006.

13. Jeanne Mariani, "Student Claims Special Education Needs Overlooked," *Daily News of Los Angeles*, November 23, 1993.

14. Amy Pyle, "L.A. on Verge of Overhauling Special Education," *Los Angeles Times*, December 10, 1995.

15. Amy Pyle, "Judge's OK Opens Door to Overhaul of Special Education," *Los Angeles Times*, April 16, 1996; Kimberly Kindy, "LAUSD Settlement Nears—District May Have to Spend Millions to Overhaul Special Education System," *Daily News of Los Angeles*, December 3, 1995.

16. Doug Smith, "Fight Erupts over Decree for Special Education," *Los Angeles Times*, August 15, 2001; Doug Smith, "Judge Rejects District Challenge to Special Ed Panels," *Los Angeles Times*, September 25, 2001.

17. Erika Hayasaki, "L.A. Unified Approves Revamp of Special Ed," *Los Angeles Times*, May 14, 2003; Cohn, *Report on the Progress and Effectiveness of the Los Angeles Unified School District's Implementation of the Modified Consent Decree during the 2004–05 School Year*.

18. Cohn, *Report*, 15.

19. See Meier, Stewart, and England, *Race, Class, and Education*; Osher, Woodruff, and Sims, "Schools Make a Difference." Notably, data for the 2002-3 school year reported to the Office for Civil Rights show that black male students in LAUSD were 2.6 times as likely to be suspended as their white male counterparts, while black female students were 4.3 times as likely to be suspended as their white female counterparts. (These statistics are based on my own analysis of data from table 07A/08A, downloaded at http://vistademo.beyond2020.com/ocr2002r/wdsdata.html, April 4, 2006.)

20. Louis Sahagun, "Surge in L.A. Special Ed Placements Questioned," *Los Angeles Times*, May 23, 1999.

21. Amy Pyle, "Parents Attack Decree on Special Education," *Los Angeles Times*, January 1, 1996; Amy Pyle, "L.A. Schools at Eye of Storm over Special Education," *Los Angeles Times*, May 13, 1995; Amy Pyle, "2 Young Pupils Show Chasm among Parents of Disabled," *Los Angeles Times*, January 28, 1996.

22. Pyle, "L.A. Schools at Eye of Storm."

23. David Pierson, "Parents Fight Changes in Special Ed," *Los Angeles Times*, September 16, 2002.

24. Ibid.

25. Ibid.

26. Note that this search was conducted in December 2003.

27. Here and elsewhere, school-level demographic data are taken from reports of the Academic Performance Index (API) run by the California Department of Special Education. In this case the data are from 1999, the first year for which the API data are available. In each case I have used API data from the year closest to the year of the student's first enrollment in the given school.

28. Tuition for kindergarten at Marin Horizon (apparently, no longer "Horizons") for the 2006-7 school year was listed as $16,620.

29. Engel, "Origin Myths."

30. This refers only to cases that reach a hearing, since it is only in a hearing decision that a dollar amount would be mentioned. In some cases, dollar amounts for reimbursement claims are not mentioned even in the decision.

31. As they were passed by Congress, both the EAHCA and its successor, the IDEA, mention only "specific learning disabilities," not learning disabilities as such, as a basis for special education services.

32. According to the school-level Academic Performance Index report for 2003 (the first year of results for Palos Verdes High), only 2 percent of students were socioeconomically disadvantaged, fewer than 5 percent of students were African American or Hispanic, and parents' average level of education was 4.43, where 4 represents college graduate and 5 represents graduate school.

33. This definition is based on the hearing officer's summary of testimony in the same case.

34. Grant, *Raising Baby by the Book*; Harry, *Cultural Diversity, Families, and the Special Education System*; Harry, "Ethnographic Study of Cross-Cultural Communication with Puerto Rican-American Families in the Special Education System"; Hays, *Cultural Contradictions of Motherhood*; Kalyanpur, Harry, and Skrtic, "Equity and Advocacy Expectations of Culturally Diverse Families' Participation in Special Education"; Lareau, *Home Advantage*; Litt, *Medicalized Motherhood*; Reay, *Class Work*.

35. Chambers, Kidron, and Spain, *Characteristics of High-Expenditure Students with Disabilities, 1999-2000*.

CHAPTER SIX

1. See, e.g., DeJong, "Defining the Independent Living Concept"; Hahn, "Toward a Politics of Disability"; Longmore, "Medical Decision Making and People with Disabilities"; Oliver,

Understanding Disability. For a discussion of the emergence of a "sociopolitical" model of disability against the background of research using a medical model, see Scotch, "Paradigms of American Social Research on Disability."

2. See, e.g., Campbell and Oliver, *Disability Politics*; Linton, *Claiming Disability*; Mulvany, "Disability, Impairment or Illness?" Zola, "Toward the Necessary Universalizing of a Disability Policy."

3. Shakespeare and Watson, "Social Model of Disability," 9. See also Hughes and Paterson, "Social Model of Disability and the Disappearing Body"; Humphrey, "Researching Disability Politics"; and Shakespeare, "'Losing the Plot'?"

4. See, e.g., Linton, *Claiming Disability*.

5. Humphrey, "Researching Disability Politics," 69.

6. Bourdieu, "Masculine Domination Revisited," 119, as cited in Lareau and Weininger, "Cultural Capital in Educational Research."

7. There are some notable exceptions here—for instance, Varenne and McDermott's *Successful Failure*. Annette Lareau's research, as noted throughout this book, also alludes to the critical role parents may play in shaping educators' view of children's abilities and the ways their resources and social background may enable that role.

APPENDIX

1. See, e.g., Goyder, Warriner, and Miller, "Evaluating SES Bias in Survey Nonresponse"; Martin, Abreu, and Winters, "Money and Motive."

References

Agbenyega, Stephen, and Joseph Jiggets. 1999. "Minority Children and Their Over-representation in Special Education." *Education* 119 (4): 619-32.

Allington, Richard, and Anne McGill-Franzen. 1992. "Unintended Effects of Educational Reform in New York." *Educational Policy* 6 (4): 397-414.

American Academy of Child and Adolescent Psychiatry. 1997. "Practice Parameters for the Assessment and Treatment of Children, Adolescents, and Adults with Attention-Deficit/Hyperactivity Disorder." *Journal of the American Academy of Child and Adolescent Psychiatry* 36 (10S): 85S-121S.

Argulewicz, Ed N. 1983. "Effects of Ethnic Membership, Socioeconomic Status, and Home Language on LD, EMR, and EH Placements." *Learning Disability Quarterly* 6 (Spring): 195-200.

Arksey, Hilary. 1994. "Expert and Lay Participation in the Construction of Medical Knowledge." *Sociology of Health and Illness* 16 (4): 448-68.

Armstrong, Thomas. 1995. *The Myth of the A.D.D. Child*. New York: Dutton.

Artiles, Alfredo J., et al. 2002. "English-Language Learner Representation in Special Education in California Urban School Districts." In *Racial Inequity in Special Education*, ed. Daniel J. Losen and Gary Orfield, 117-36. Cambridge, MA: Harvard Education Press.

Attwood, Tony. 1998. *Asperger's Syndrome: A Guide for Parents and Professionals*. Philadelphia, PA: Jessica Kingsley.

Barkley, Russell A. 1996. "Attention-Deficit/Hyperactivity Disorder." In *Child Psychopathology*, ed. Eric J. Mash and Russell A. Barkley, 75-143. New York: Guilford Press.

Bettelheim, Bruno. 1967. *The Empty Fortress: Infantile Autism and the Birth of the Self*. New York: Free Press.

Bloor, David. 1991. *Knowledge and Social Imagery*. Chicago: University of Chicago Press.

Bourdieu, Pierre. 1973. "Cultural Reproduction and Social Reproduction." In *Knowledge, Education, and Cultural Change*, ed. Richard Brown, 71-112. London: Tavistock.

———. 1986. "The Forms of Capital." In *Handbook of Theory and Research for the Sociology of Education*, ed. John Richardson, 241-58. New York: Greenwood Press.

———. 1996-97. "Masculine Domination Revisited." *Berkeley Journal of Sociology* 41: 189-203.

Bourdieu, Pierre, and Jean-Claude Passeron. 1979. *The Inheritors*. Chicago: University of Chicago Press.

Brantlinger, Ellen. 1997. "Using Ideology: Cases of Nonrecognition of the Politics of Research and Practice in Special Education." *Review of Educational Research* 67 (4): 425-59.

Breggin, Peter R. 2001. *Talking Back to Ritalin*. Cambridge, MA: Perseus.

Brown, Phil. 1992. "Popular Epidemiology and Toxic Waste Contamination: Lay and Professional Ways of Knowing." *Journal of Health and Social Behavior* 33 (3): 267-81.

Brown, Phillip. 1990. "The 'Third Wave': Education and the Ideology of Parentocracy." *British Journal of Sociology of Education* 11 (1): 65-85.

Brutten, Milton, Sylvia O. Richardson, and Charles Mangel. 1973. *Something's Wrong with My Child: A Parents' Book about Children with Learning Disabilities*. New York: Harcourt Brace Jovanovich.

Bussing, Regina, Nancy E. Schoenberg, and Amy R. Perwien. 1998. "Knowledge and Information about ADHD: Evidence of Cultural Differences among African-American and White Parents." *Social Science and Medicine* 46 (7): 919-28.

Bussing, Regina, et al. 2003. "Barriers to Detection, Help-Seeking, and Service Use for Children with ADHD Symptoms." *Journal of Behavioral Health Services and Research* 30 (2): 176-89.

California Department of Developmental Services, California Health and Human Services Agency. 2003. *Autistic Spectrum Disorders: Changes in the California Caseload. An Update*: 1999-2002. Sacramento: California Health and Human Services Agency.

Campbell, Jane, and Michael Oliver. 1996. *Disability Politics: Understanding Our Past, Changing Our Future*. New York: Routledge.

Carrier, James G. 1986. *Learning Disability: Social Class and the Construction of Inequality in American Education*. New York: Greenwood Press.

Castles, Katherine. 2004. "'Nice, Average Americans': Postwar Parents' Groups and the Defense of the Normal Family." In *Mental Retardation in America: A Historical Reader*, ed. Steven Noll and James W. Trent Jr., 351-70. New York: New York University Press.

Centers for Disease Control and Prevention. 2005. "Mental Health in the United States: Prevalence of Diagnosis and Medication Treatment for Attention-Deficit/Hyperactivity Disorder— United States, 2003." Morbidity and Mortality Weekly Report 54 (September 2): 842-47.

Chambers, Jay G., Yael Kidron, and Angeline K. Spain. 2004. *Characteristics of High-Expenditure Students with Disabilities, 1999-2000*. Report 8. Palo Alto, CA: American Institutes for Research.

Clune, William H., and Mark H. Van Pelt. 1985. "A Political Method of Evaluating the Education for All Handicapped Children Act of 1975 and the Several Gaps of Gap Analysis." *Law and Contemporary Problems* 48 (1): 7-62.

Cohen, Shirley. 1998. *Targeting Autism*. Berkeley: University of California Press.

Cohn, Carl. 2005. *Report on the Progress and Effectiveness of the Los Angeles Unified School District's Implementation of the Modified Consent Decree during the 2004-05 School Year*. Office of the Independent Monitor, Modified Consent Decree. http://www.oimla.com/pdf/imreport_2005.pdf. Accessed April 4, 2006.

Coles, Gerald. 1987. *The Learning Mystique: A Critical Look at "Learning Disabilities."* New York: Pantheon.

Coots, Jennifer. 1998. "Family Resources and Parent Participation in Schooling Activities for Their Children with Developmental Delays." *Journal of Special Education* 31 (4): 498-520.

Coutinho, Martha J., Donald P. Oswald, and Al M. Best. 2002. "The Influence of Sociodemographics and Gender on the Disproportionate Identification of Minority Students as Having Learning Disabilities." *Remedial and Special Education* 23 (1): 49-59.

Coutinho, Martha J., and Alan C. Repp. 1999. "Enhancing the Meaningful Inclusion of Students with Disabilities: Perspectives, Trends, and Implications for Research and Practice." In *Inclusion: The Integration of Students with Disabilities*, ed. Martha J. Coutinho and Alan C. Repp, 9-36. New York: Wadsworth.

Cox, A., et al. 1975. "A Comparative Study of Infantile Autism and Specific Developmental Receptive Language Disorder: 2. Parental Characteristics." *British Journal of Psychiatry* 126: 146–59.

Crawford, Dorothy. 2004. "History of LDA." *Learning Disabilities Association of America*. Retrieved April 15, 2004, from http://www.ldanatl.org/about/history.asp.

Croen, Lisa A., Judith K. Grether, and Steve Selvin. 2002. "Descriptive Epidemiology of Autism in a California Population: Who Is at Risk." *Journal of Autism and Developmental Disorders* 32 (3): 217–24.

Croen, Lisa A., et al. 2002. "The Changing Prevalence of Autism in California." *Journal of Autism and Developmental Disorders* 32 (3): 207–16.

Daily, Donna K., Holly H. Ardinger, and Grace E. Holmes. 2000. "Identification and Evaluation of Mental Retardation." *American Family Physician* 61 (4): 1059. Expanded Academic ASAP. Thomson Gale. UC San Diego (CDL).

Danielson, Louis C., and G. Thomas Bellamy. 1989. "State Variation in Placement of Children with Handicaps in Segregated Environments." *Exceptional Children* 55 (5): 448–55.

Davila, Robert R., Michael L. Williams, and John T. MacDonald. 1991. "Memorandum to Chief State School Officers: Clarification of Policy to Address the Needs of Children with Attention-Deficit Disorders within General and/or Special Education." U.S. Department of Education, Office of Special Education and Rehabilitation Services, September 16. Retrieved February 26, 2006, from http://dpi.wi.gov/sped/print/bul91–12att.html.

Dawson, Michelle. 2004. "The Misbehaviour of Behaviourists: Ethical Challenges to the Autism-ABA Industry." Michelle Dawson. Retrieved February 20, 2006, from http://www.sentex.net/~nexus23/naa_aba.html.

DeGrandpre, Richard J. 1999. *Ritalin Nation: Rapid-Fire Culture and the Transformation of Human Consciousness*. New York: W. W. Norton.

DeJong, Gerben. 1983. "Defining the Independent Living Concept." In *Independent Living for Physically Disabled People*, ed. Nancy M. Crewe and Irving K. Zola, 4–27. San Francisco: Jossey-Bass.

Diller, Lawrence. 1998. *Running on Ritalin: A Physician Reflects on Children, Society, and Performance in a Pill*. New York: Bantam Books.

Dolnick, Edward. 1998. *Madness on the Couch: Blaming the Victim in the Heyday of Psychoanalysis*. New York: Simon and Schuster.

Dunn, Lloyd M. 1968. "Special Education for the Mildly Retarded—Is Much of It Justifiable?" *Exceptional Children* 35 (1): 5–22.

DuPaul, George J., Mark D. Rapport, and Stuart A. Vyse. 1988. "ADHD and Methylphenidate Responders: Effects on Behavior Controlled by Complex Reinforcement Schedules." *International Clinical Psychopharmacology* 3 (4): 349–62.

Education for All Handicapped Children Act. 1973. Hearings on S. 896, S. 34, S. 808 before the Subcommittee on the Handicapped of the Committee on Labor and Public Welfare, U.S. Senate, 93rd Cong., 1st sess. (1973), March 20, 21, and 23, 1973.

Education for All Handicapped Children Act. 1973–74. Hearings on S. 6 before the Subcommittee on the Handicapped of the Committee on Labor and Public Welfare, U.S. Senate, 93rd Cong., 1st sess. (1973), April 9, May 7, 1973.

———. *1973–74. Hearings on S. 6 before the Subcommittee on the Handicapped of the Committee on Labor and Public Welfare, U.S. Senate*, 93rd Cong., 1st sess. (1973–74), October 19, 1973, March 18, 1974.

———. *1973–74. Hearings on S. 6 before the Subcommittee on the Handicapped of the Committee on Labor and Public Welfare, U.S. Senate*, 93rd Cong., 2d sess. (1974), June 17 and 24, 1974.

———. *1973–74. Hearings on S. 6 before the Subcommittee on the Handicapped of the Committee on Labor and Public Welfare, U.S. Senate,* 94th Cong., 1st sess. (1975), April 8, 9, and 15, 1975.

Eisenberg, Leon, and Leo Kanner. 1956. "Early Infantile Autism, 1943–1955." *American Journal of Orthopsychiatry* 26: 556–66.

Eitle, Tamela M. 2002. "Special Education or Racial Segregation: Understanding Variation in the Representation of Black Students in Educable Mentally Handicapped Programs." *Sociological Quarterly* 43 (4): 575–605.

Engel, David M. 1993. "Origin Myths: Narratives of Authority, Resistance, Disability, and Law." *Law and Society Review* 27 (4): 785–826.

Epstein, Steven. 1996. *Impure Science: AIDS, Activism, and the Politics of Knowledge.* Berkeley: University of California Press.

Equip for Equality. 2004. "EFE's Honored Event Guest, Dolly Hallstrom." Equalizer Online. 2006, February 2. http://equipforequality.org/news/equalizer/fall2004/02dolly.php. Accessed February 2, 2006.

Fierros, Edward Garcia, and James W. Conroy. 2002. "Double Jeopardy: An Exploration of Restrictiveness and Race in Special Education." In *Racial Inequity in Special Education,* ed. Daniel J. Losen and Gary Orfield, 39–70. Cambridge, MA: Harvard Education Press.

Finegan, J.-A., and Quarrington, B. 1979. "Pre-, Peri-, and Neonatal Factors and Infantile Autism." *Journal of Child Psychology and Psychiatry and Allied Disciplines* 20 (2): 119–28.

Fisher, Johanna. 1978. *A Parents' Guide to Learning Disabilities.* New York: Charles Scribner's Sons.

Friedman, Lawrence Jacob. 1999. *Identity's Architect: A Biography of Erik H. Erikson.* New York: Scribner.

Frith, Uta. 2003. *Autism: Explaining the Enigma.* Malden, MA: Blackwell.

Gearheart, Bill R., and Carol J. Gearheart. 1989. *Learning Disabilities: Educational Strategies.* Columbus, OH: Merrill.

Gelb, Steven A., and Donald T. Mizokawa. 1986. "Special Education and Social Structure: The Commonality of 'Exceptionality.'" *American Educational Research Journal* 23 (4): 543–57.

Ginsberg, Debra. 2002. *Raising Blaze: Bringing Up an Extraordinary Child in an Ordinary World.* New York: HarperCollins.

Goyder, John, G. Keith Warriner, and Susan Miller. 2002. "Evaluating SES Bias in Survey Nonresponse: A New Measure." *Journal of Official Statistics* 18 (1): 1–11.

Grant, Julia. 1998. *Raising Baby by the Book: The Education of American Mothers.* New Haven, CT: Yale University Press.

Green, Christopher, and Kit Chee. 1998. *Understanding ADHD.* New York: Fawcett Columbine.

Greenfeld, Josh. 1972. *A Child Called Noah: A Family Journey.* New York: Holt, Rinehart and Winston.

Gresham, Frank M., and Donald L. MacMillan. 1997. "Autistic Recovery? An Analysis and Critique of the Empirical Evidence on the Early Intervention Project." *Behavioral Disorders* 22 (4): 185–201.

Hahn, Harlan. 1985. "Toward a Politics of Disability: Definitions, Disciplines, and Policies." *Social Science Journal* 22 (4): 87–105.

Hallowell, Edward. 1996. *When You Worry about the Child You Love.* New York: Simon and Schuster.

Harry, Beth. 1992. *Cultural Diversity, Families, and the Special Education System.* New York: Teachers College Press.

———. 1992. "An Ethnographic Study of Cross-Cultural Communication with Puerto Rican-American Families in the Special Education System." *American Educational Research Journal* 29 (3): 471–94.

———. 1992. "Restructuring the Participation of African-American Parents in Special Educa-tion." *Exceptional Children* 59 (2): 123-31.

———. 2002. "Trends and Issues in Serving Culturally Diverse Families of Children with Dis-abilities." *Journal of Special Education* 36 (3): 131-39.

Hays, Sharon. 1996. *The Cultural Contradictions of Motherhood*. New Haven, CT: Yale University Press.

Hessler, John. 1985. "Letter." *Disability Rag*, September.

Hornig, Mady, David Chian, and W. Ian Lipkin. 2004. "Neurotoxic Effects of Postnatal Thimerosal Are Mouse Strain Dependent." *Molecular Psychiatry* 9 (9): 833-45.

Hoshino, Y., et al. 1982. "The Epidemiological Study of Autism in Fukushima-Ken." *Folia Psychi-atrica et Neurologica Japonica* 36: 115-24.

Hughes, Bill, and Kevin Paterson. 1997. "The Social Model of Disability and the Disappearing Body: Towards a Sociology of Impairment." *Disability and Society* 12 (3): 325-40.

Hughes, James W., and Joseph J. Seneca. 2003. "Housing Bubble or Shelter-Safe Haven?" In *Rutgers Regional Report*, Issue Paper number 19, 20 (Rutgers University).

Humphrey, Jill C. 2000. "Researching Disability Politics, or Some Problems with the Social Model in Practice." *Disability and Society* 15 (1): 63-86.

Johnson, Clark. 1981. *The Diagnosis of Learning Disabilities*. Boulder, CO: Pruett.

Jones, Kathleen W. 2004. "Education for Children with Mental Retardation: Parent Activism, Public Policy, and Family Ideology in the 1950s." In *Mental Retardation in America: A Histor-ical Reader*, ed. Steven Noll and James W. Trent Jr., 322-50. New York: New York University Press.

Kalyanpur, Maya, Beth Harry, and Tom Skrtic. 2000. "Equity and Advocacy Expectations of Culturally Diverse Families' Participation in Special Education." *International Journal of Disability, Development and Education* 47 (2): 119-36.

Kanner, Leo. 1943. "Autistic Disturbances of Affective Contact." *Nervous Child* 2: 217-50.

———. 1971. "Follow-up Study of Eleven Autistic Children Originally Reported in 1943." *Jour-nal of Autism and Childhood Schizophrenia* 1 (2): 119-45.

Kaufman, Barry Neil. 1976. *Son-Rise*. New York: Harper and Row.

Kirp, David, William Buss, and Peter Kuriloff. 1974. "Legal Reform of Special Education: Em-pirical Studies and Procedural Proposals." *California Law Review* 62 (1): 40-155. Reprinted in U.S. Senate, Subcommittee on the Handicapped of the Committee on Labor and Public Welfare, Education for All Handicapped Children, 1973-74: Hearings on S. 6. 93rd Cong., 1st sess., October 19, 1973; March 18, 1974, 1647-1763.

Kirp, David L., and Lauren M. Kirp. 1976. "The Legalization of the School Psychologist's World." *Journal of School Psychology* 14 (2): 83-89.

Koplewicz, Harold S. 1996. *It's Nobody's Fault: New Hope and Help for Difficult Children*. New York: Random House.

Krause, Ilan, et al. 2002. "Immune Factors in Autism: A Critical Review." *Journal of Autism and Developmental Disorders* 32 (4): 337-45.

Kress, Gunther. 1985. "Ideological Structures in Discourse." In *Handbook of Discourse Analysis*, ed. T. A. van Dijk, 27-42. London: Academic Press.

Lakoff, Andrew. 2000. "Adaptive Will: The Evolution of Attention Deficit Disorder." *Journal of the History of the Behavioral Sciences* 36 (Spring): 149-69.

Lamont, Michele, and Annette Lareau. 1988. "Cultural Capital: Allusions, Gaps and Glissandos in Recent Theoretical Developments." *Sociological Theory* 6 (Fall): 153-68.

Lan, Iris. 2001. "Pharmaceuticals: Conspiracy to Increase Ritalin Profits Alleged." *Journal of Law, Medicine and Ethics* 29 (1): 100-102.

Lareau, Annette. 2000. *Home Advantage: Social Class and Parental Intervention in Elementary Education*. New York: Rowman and Littlefield.

———. 2003. *Unequal Childhoods: Class, Race, and Family Life*. Berkeley: University of California Press.

Lareau, Annette, and Wesley Shumar. 1996. "The Problem of Individualism in Family-School Policies." *Sociology of Education* 69: 24–39.

Lareau, Annette, and Elliot B. Weininger. 2003. "Cultural Capital in Educational Research: A Critical Assessment." *Theory and Society* 32: 567–606.

Leung, Alexander K. C., et al. 1995. "Mental Retardation." *Journal of the Royal Society of Health* 115: 31–39.

Lewis, Richard S., Alfred A. Strauss, and Laura E. Lehtinen. 1960. *The Other Child: The Brain-Injured Child, a Book for Parents and Laymen*. New York: Grune and Stratton.

Linton, Simi. 1998. *Claiming Disability: Knowledge and Identity*. New York: New York University Press.

Lipsky, Dorothy K., and Alan Gartner. 1987. "Capable of Achievement and Worthy of Respect: Education for Handicapped Students As If They Were Full-Fledged Human Beings." *Exceptional Children* 54 (1): 69–74.

Litt, Jacquelyn S. 2000. *Medicalized Motherhood: Perspectives from the Lives of African-American and Jewish Women*. New Brunswick, NJ: Rutgers University Press.

Longmore, Paul K. 1995. "Medical Decision Making and People with Disabilities: A Clash of Cultures." *Journal of Law, Medicine and Ethics* 23: 82–87.

Lovaas, O. Ivar. 1987. "Behavioral Treatment and Normal Educational and Intellectual Functioning in Young Autistic Children." *Journal of Consulting and Clinical Psychology* 55 (1): 3–9.

MacMillan, Donald L., and Daniel J. Reschly. 1998. "Overrepresentation of Minority Students: The Case for Greater Specificity or Reconsideration of the Variables Examined." *Journal of Special Education* 32 (1): 15–24.

Martin, Elizabeth, Denise A. Abreu, and Franklin Winters. 2001. "Money and Motive: Effects of Incentives on Panel Attrition in the Survey of Income and Program Participation." *Journal of Official Statistics* 17: 267–84.

McCarthy, P., M. Fitzgerald, and M. Smith. 1984. "Prevalence of Childhood Autism in Ireland." *Irish Medical Journal* 77: 129–30.

McEachin, John J., Tristram Smith, and O. Ivar Lovaas. 1993. "Long-Term Outcome for Children with Autism Who Received Early Intensive Behavioral Treatment." *American Journal of Mental Retardation* 97 (4): 359–72.

McLaughlin, Margaret, and Maria F. Owings. 1993. "Relationships among States' Fiscal and Demographic Data and the Implementation of P.L. 94-112." *Exceptional Children* 59 (3): 247–61.

McLeskey, James, Daniel Henry, and Michael I. Axelrod. 1999. "Inclusion of Students with Learning Disabilities: An Examination of Data from Reports to Congress." *Exceptional Children* 66 (1): 55–66.

McLeskey, James, David Hoppey, Pamela Williamson, and Tarcha Rentz. 2004. "Is Inclusion an Illusion? An Examination of National and State Trends toward the Education of Students with Learning Disabilities in General Education Classrooms." *Learning Disabilities: Research and Practice*. 19 (2): 109–15.

McLeskey, James, and Debra Pacchiano. 1994. "Mainstreaming Students with Disabilities: Are We Making Progress?" *Exceptional Children* 60 (6): 508–17.

McNamara, Barry E., and Francine J. McNamara. 1995. *Keys to Parenting a Child with a Learning Disability*. Hauppauge, NY: Barron's.

Mehan, Hugh, Alma Hertweck, and J. Lee Meihls. 1986. *Handicapping the Handicapped: Decision Making in Students' Educational Careers*. Stanford, CA: Stanford University Press.

Mehan, Hugh, Jane Mercer, and Robert Rueda. 2002. "Special Education." In *Education and Sociology*, ed. David L. Levinson, Peter W. Cookson, and Alan R. Sadovnik, 619–24. New York: RoutledgeFalmer.

Meier, Kenneth J., Jr., Joseph Stewart, and Robert England. 1989. *Race, Class, and Education: The Politics of Second-Generation Discrimination*. Madison: University of Wisconsin Press.

Melnick, R. Shep. 1994. *Between the Lines: Interpreting Welfare Rights*. Washington, DC: Brookings Institution.

Mercer, Jane R. 1973. *Labeling the Mentally Retarded; Clinical and Social System Perspectives on Mental Retardation*. Berkeley: University of California Press.

Mesibov, Gary B., Victoria Shea, and Eric Schopler. 2005. *The TEACCH Approach to Autism Spectrum Disorders*. New York: Kluwer Academic/Plenum.

MTA Cooperative Group. 1999. "A 14-Month Randomized Clinical Trial of Treatment Strategies for Attention-Deficit/Hyperactivity Disorder." *Archives of General Psychiatry* 56 (12): 1073-86.

Mulvany, Julie. 2000. "Disability, Impairment or Illness? The Relevance of the Social Model of Disability to the Study of Mental Disorder." *Sociology of Health and Illness* 22 (5): 582-601.

National Research Council, Committee on Educational Interventions for Children with Autism, Division of Behavioral and Social Sciences and Education. 2001. *Educating Children with Autism*. Washington, DC: National Academy Press.

National Toxicology Program, Center for the Evaluation of Risks to Human Reproduction. 2005. "NTP-CERHR Expert Panel Report on the Reproductive and Developmental Toxicity of Methylphenidate." Retrieved January 15, 2007, from http://cerhr.niehs.nih.gov/chemicals/stimulants/methhylphenidate/Methylphenidate_final.pdf.

Neal, David, and David L. Kirp. 1985. "The Allure of Legalization Reconsidered: The Case of Special Education." *Law and Contemporary Problems* 48 (1): 63-87.

Nosek, Kathleen. 1995. *The Dyslexic Scholar: Helping Your Child Succeed in the School System*. Dallas, TX: Taylor.

Oliver, Michael. 1996. *Understanding Disability: From Theory to Practice*. New York: St. Martin's Press.

Ong-Dean, Colin. 2006. "High Roads and Low Roads: Learning Disabilities in California, 1976–1998." *Sociological Perspectives* 49 (1): 91-113.

Osher, David, Darren Woodruff, and Anthony E. Sims. 2002. "Schools Make a Difference: The Overrepresentation of African American Youth in Special Education and the Juvenile Justice System." In *Racial Inequity in Special Education*, ed. Daniel J. Losen and Gary Orfield, 93-116. Cambridge, MA: Harvard Education Press.

Osman, Betty B. 1997. *Learning Disabilities and ADHD: A Family Guide to Living and Learning Together*. New York: John Wiley.

Oswald, Donald P., and Martha J. Coutinho. 1995. "Identification and Placement of Students with Serious Emotional Disturbance." *Journal of Emotional and Behavioral Disorders* 3: 224-30.

———. 2001. "Trends in Disproportionate Representation: Implications for Multicultural Education." In *Special Education, Multicultural Education, and School Reform*, ed. Cheryl A. Utley and Festus E. Obiakor, 53-73. Springfield, IL: Thomas.

Oswald, Donald P., Martha J. Coutinho, and Al M. Best. 2002. "Community and School Predictors of Overrepresentation of Minority Children in Special Education." In *Racial Inequity in Special Education*, ed. Daniel J. Losen and Gary Orfield, 1-14. Cambridge, MA: Harvard Education Press.

Oswald, Donald P., et al. 1999. "Ethnic Representation in Special Education: The Influence of School-Related Economic and Demographic Variables." *Journal of Special Education* 32 (4): 194-206.

Park, Clara Claiborne. 1982. *The Siege: The First Eight Years of an Autistic Child; with an Epilogue, Fifteen Years Later*. Boston: Little, Brown.

Parrish, Thomas. 2002. "Racial Disparities in the Identification, Funding, and Provision of Special Education." In *Racial Inequity in Special Education*, ed. Daniel J. Losen and Gary Orfield, 15-37. Cambridge, MA: Harvard Education Press.

Parsons, Talcott. 1951. *The Social System*. London: Routledge.

Pollak, Richard. 1997. *The Creation of Dr. B: A Biography of Bruno Bettelheim*. New York: Simon and Schuster.

Popper, C. W. 1988. "Disorders Usually First Evident in Infancy, Childhood, or Adolescence." In *Textbook of Psychiatry*, ed. J. A. Talbott, R. E. Hales, and S. C. Yudofsky, 649–735. Washington, DC: American Psychiatric Press.

President's Committee on Mental Retardation. 1970. Bureau of Education for the Handicapped. "The Six-Hour Retarded Child: A Report on a Conference on Problems of Education of Children in the Inner City." Paper presented at Washington, DC: Government Printing Office.

Rapoport, Judith L., et al. 1978. "Dextroamphetamine—Cognitive and Behavioral Effects in Normal Prepubertal Boys." *Science* 199 (4328): 560–63.

Reay, Diane. 1998. *Class Work: Mothers' Involvement in Their Children's Primary Schooling*. Bristol, PA: University College London Press.

Reid, D. Kim, and Jan Weatherly Valle. 2004. "The Discursive Practice of Learning Disability: Implications for Instruction and Parent-School Relations." *Journal of Learning Disabilities* 37 (6): 466–81.

Rimland, Bernard. 1964. *Infantile Autism: The Syndrome and Its Implications for a Neural Theory of Behavior*. New York: Meredith.

Saina, Asha. 2001. "Advocating for Full Inclusion: Mothers' Narratives." In *Semiotics and Dis/Ability: Interrogating Categories of Difference*, ed. Linda J. Rogers and Beth Blue Swadener, 135–56. Albany: State University of New York Press.

Schachter, Howard M., et al. 2001. "How Efficacious and Safe Is Short-Acting Methylphenidate for the Treatment of Attention-Deficit Disorder in Children and Adolescents? A Meta-analysis." *Canadian Medical Association Journal* 165 (11): 1475–88.

Schopler, Eric, Andrew Short, and Gary B. Mesibov. 1989. "Relation of Behavioral Treatment to 'Normal Functioning': Comment on Lovaas." *Journal of Consulting and Clinical Psychology* 57 (1): 162–64.

Scotch, Richard K. 1989. "Politics and Policy in the History of the Disability Rights Movement." *Milbank Quarterly* 67, suppl. 2 (pt. 2): 380–400.

———. 2002. "Paradigms of American Social Research on Disability: What's New?" *Disability Studies Quarterly* 22: 2.

Shakespeare, Tom. 1999. "'Losing the Plot'? Medical and Activist Discourses of Contemporary Genetics and Disability." *Sociology of Health and Illness* 21 (5): 669–88.

Shakespeare, Tom, and Nicholas Watson. 2002. "The Social Model of Disability: An Outdated Ideology?" *Research in Social Science and Disability* 2: 9–28.

Shapiro, Joseph P. 1993. *No Pity: People with Disabilities Forging a New Civil Rights Movement*. New York: Random House.

Silberman, Steve. 2001. "The Geek Syndrome." *Wired Magazine*. Online edition. Retrieved January 30, 2002, from http://www.wired.com/wired/archive/9.12/aspergers.html.

Silver, Larry B. 1998. *The Misunderstood Child*. New York: Three Rivers Press.

Singer, Eleanor, et al. 1999. "Experiments with Incentives in Telephone Surveys." *Journal of Official Statistics* 15: 217–30.

Singer, Judith D., and John A. Butler. 1987. "The Education for All Handicapped Children Act: Schools as Agents of Social Reform." *Harvard Educational Review* 57 (2): 159–202.

Singer, Judith, et al. 1989. "Variation in Special Education Classification across School Districts: How Does Where You Live Affect What You Are Labeled." *American Educational Research Journal* 26 (2): 261–81.

Sireci, Stephen G., Shuhong Li, and Stanley Scarpati. 2003. *The Effects of Test Accommodation on Test Performance: A Review of the Literature*. Report 485. Amherst: Center for Educational Assessment, University of Massachusetts.

Skrentny, John David. 2002. *The Minority Rights Revolution.* Cambridge, MA: Belknap Press of Harvard University Press.

Skrtic, Thomas M., Wayne Sailor, and Kathleen Gee. 1996. "Voice, Collaboration, and Inclusion: Democratic Themes in Educational and Social Reform Initiatives." *Remedial and Special Education* 17: 142–57.

Smardon, Regina. 2008. "Broken Brains and Broken Homes: The Meaning of Special Education in an Appalachian Community." *Anthropology and Education Quarterly,* forthcoming.

Smith, Bert Kruger. 1968. *Your Nonlearning Child.* Boston: Beacon Press.

Smith, Mary Lee. 1982. *How Educators Decide Who Is Learning Disabled.* Springfield, IL: Charles C. Thomas.

Smith, Tristram. 1999. "Outcome of Early Intervention for Children with Autism." *Clinical Psychology: Science and Practice* 6 (1): 33–49.

Stainback, Susan, William Stainback, and Marsha Forest. 1989. *Educating All Students in the Mainstream of Regular Education.* Baltimore, MD: Brookes.

Still, George F. 1902. "Some Abnormal Psychical Conditions in Children." *Lancet,* April 12, 1008–12; April 19, 1077–82; April 26, 1163–68.

Teicher, Martin H., et al. 2003. "Rate Dependency Revisited: Understanding the Effects of Methylphenidate in Children with Attention Deficit Hyperactivity Disorder." *Journal of Child and Adolescent Psychopharmacology* 13 (1): 41–51.

Thomas, Stephen B., and Mary Jane K. Rapport. 1998. "Least Restrictive Environment: Understanding the Direction of the Courts." *Journal of Special Education* 32 (21): 66–78.

Treffert, Darold A. 1970. "Epidemiology of Infantile Autism." *Archives of General Psychiatry* 22: 431–39.

U.S. Department of Education, Office of Special Education and Rehabilitative Services, Office of Special Education Programs. 2004. *Teaching Children with Attention Deficit Hyperactivity Disorder: Instructional Strategies and Practices.* Washington, DC.

U.S. Department of Education, Office of Special Education and Rehabilitative Services, Office of Special Education Programs. 2000. *Twenty-second Annual Report to Congress on the Implementation of the Individuals with Disabilities Education Act.* Washington, DC.

Valle, Jan Weatherly, and Elsie Aponte. 2002. "IDEA and Collaboration: A Bakhtinian Perspective on Parent and Professional Discourse." *Journal of Learning Disabilities* 35 (5): 469–79.

Varenne, Hervé, and Ray McDermott, *Successful Failure: The School America Builds.* Boulder, CO: Westview Press, 1998.

Waltz, Mitzi. 2000. *Obsessive-Compulsive Disorder: Help for Children and Adolescents.* Sebastopol, CA: O'Reilly.

Wang, Margaret C., and Herbert J. Walberg. 1988. "Four Fallacies of Segregationism." *Exceptional Children* 55 (2): 128–37.

Wells, Karen C., et al. 2000. "Psychosocial Treatment Strategies in the MTA Study: Rationale, Methods, and Critical Issues in Design and Implementation." *Journal of Abnormal Child Psychology* 28 (6): 483–505.

Williamson, Pamela, James McLeskey, David Hoppey, and Tarcha Rentz. 2006. "Educating Students with Mental Retardation in General Education Classrooms." *Exceptional Children* 72 (3): 347–61.

Wing, Lorna. 1972. *Autistic Children: A Guide for Parents.* New York: Brunner/Mazel.

Wright, Pamela, and Rafaela Santa Cruz. 1983. "Ethnic Composition of Special Education Classrooms in California." *Learning Disability Quarterly* 6 (Fall): 387–94.

Zola, Irving Kenneth. 1989. "Toward the Necessary Universalizing of a Disability Policy." *Milbank Quarterly* 67, suppl. 2 (pt. 2): 401–28.

Index

Abeson, Alan, 17

Academic Performance Index (API), 185n27, 185n32

Adderall, 82, 84, 145

ADHD diagnosis, 141; benefits of, 85–86; expansion of, 82–84

administrative hearings. *See* due process hearings

advice literature, purpose of, 97–98. *See also* literature, for parents of disabled children

African American students, 69, 126, 177n38. *See also* race-ethnicity

age, of disability diagnosis, 49–50

AIDS activism, 68

amazon.com, 96–97

American Academy of Child and Adolescent Psychiatry, 83

American Civil Liberties Union (ACLU), 125

American Coalition of Citizens with Disabilities, 21

American Indian students, 69, 177n38. *See also* race-ethnicity

American Psychiatric Association, 86–87; *Diagnostic and Statistical Manual of Mental Disorders*, 82–83, 103

anonymity, in due process hearings database, 130–31

applied behavior analysis (ABA), 91–93

appropriate education, 29, 32–33. *See also* free, appropriate public education (FAPE)

appropriate placement, 146–47

apraxia diagnosis, 150–52

Arizona, 35

Armstrong v. Kline, 34–35

Asian American students, 177n38. *See also* race-ethnicity

Asperger syndrome (AS), 29–31, 49, 51, 87–93, 101–2

assessment, for special education placement, 135–37, 144–45

Association for Children with Learning Disabilities (ACLD), 71

attention deficit disorder (ADD), 82

attention deficit/hyperactivity disorder (ADHD), 82–87, 180n33–180n34. *See also* ADHD diagnosis

Attwood, Tony, 49, 101, 103

auditory neuropathy, 40–41

autism, 4–7, 40–41, 87–93, 181n45, 182n53; "high-functioning," 90, 93

autism diagnosis, 154–55; expansion of, 88–89

Autism Research Institute, 103

Autism Society of America, 181n45

autism-vaccination link, 89–90

autistic spectrum, 87–93

balancing standard, 37

Barkley, Russell, 83

Barnett, Charles, 23

behavioral support plan, 155